Social-Democracy
& Anarchism

Mastheads of journals from IWA organisations in France, Spain and Switzerland, and from German Social-Democrats

Social-Democracy & Anarchism
IN THE INTERNATIONAL WORKERS' ASSOCIATION 1864-1877

RENÉ BERTHIER

ANARRES EDITIONS

First published in English in 2015 by
Anarres Editions, an imprint of The Merlin Press
99b Wallis Road
London
E9 5LN

www.merlinpress.co.uk

First published in 2012 as *La rupture avecle bakouninisme et la fin de la AIT 'anti-autoritaire'*; Éditions du Cercle d'études libertaires Gaston Leval. An edition of this work was published in May 2015 by Editions Monde Libertaire as *La fin de la première international*.

© René Berthier, 2012

Translation, notes and appendices © A.W. Zurbrugg, 2015

ISBN. 978-0-85036-719-5

Catalogue in publication data is available from the British Library

The right of René Berthier to be identified as author of this work has been asserted in accordance with the Copyright, Designs and Patents Act 1988.

All rights reserved. No part of this publication may be reproduced, stored in a retrieval system, or transmitted, in any form or by any means, electronic, mechanical, photocopying, recording or otherwise, without the prior permission of the publisher.

Printed in the UK by Imprint Digital, Exeter

CONTENTS

Author's preface	viii
Translators' preface	x
Introductory note	1
Introduction	3
Key questions	12
The question of the conquest of power	12
The question of programme	18
Practical experiences of solidarity	25
Action and organisation	30
The Alliance	31
Organisation and the proletariat	48
Trades Sections and Central Sections	53
Bakunin's viewpoint summarised	55
After the Commune	66
The London Conference, 17-23 September 1871	67
Reactions to the London Conference	69
The Fifth Congress of the International, The Hague, September 1872	73
The Alliance for Socialist Democracy and the IWA	75
Two Congresses in Saint-Imier, September 1872	77
The reaction of the General Council of New York	81
The Collapse of the Marxist International	83
The International in Germany	85
The IWA Congress in Geneva, 1 September 1873	90
Reactions from the General Council in New York	91
The 'Anti-Authoritarian' response	93
The Congress of the Marxist secessionists in Geneva	95
The General Council had no funds	97
The dissolution of the General Council	102

The Anti-Authoritarian International and Attempted Conciliation   104
The Seventh congress of the International, Brussels,
        September 1874   104
The Eighth Congress of the International, Bern, October 1876   105
Earlier attempts at reconciliation   105
Labour candidates – a question of circumstance   106
The Congress in Olten, June 1873 – dialogue with little rancour   107
On Bakunin's tomb   109
Initiatives for reconciliation appear to gain ground   109
German Socialists oppose rapprochement   111
Debates at the Bern Congress   113
The report of the Belgian Federation   115
Questions of representation   116
The Balkans War   117
Hopes for reconciliation   118
Bakunin and parliamentary institutions   119
Julius Vahlteich   124
The Gotha Congress   126

Towards the End of the 'Anti-Authoritarian' International   131
The Ninth Congress of the International, Verviers,
        September 1877   131
Paul Brousse and Andrea Costa   134
The debate about the Ghent Universal Socialist Congress,
        September 1877   135
The Ghent Congress, 9 September 1877   140
The Congress of Fribourg, 1878. The end of the
        Jura Federation and the evaporation
        of the 'Anti-Authoritarian' International   146

The Birth of Anarchism   152
Collectivists and Communist Anarchists   152
The 'Anti-Authoritarian' concept   153

Conclusion   158

Appendices   165
1. Preamble to the Statutes of the IWA, Geneva,
        First Congress of the IWA, September 1866   165

2. Extract from the minutes of the Brussels IWA Congress,
      September 1868 — 166
3. Programme of the International Alliance for
      Socialist Democracy, October 1868 — 166
4. Resolutions at a meeting at Crèt-du-Locle, May 1869 — 167
5. Key demands of the Social Democratic Workers' Party,
      August 1869 — 168
6. The Basel Congress of the International, September 1869 — 169
7. *L'Egalité* criticises the General Council, 6 November 1869 — 173
8. Minutes of Committee Meeting, Geneva Alliance
      for Socialist Democracy Section, 14 January 1870 — 174
9. Minutes of a General Assembly Meeting, Geneva Alliance
      for Socialist Democracy Section, 2 April 1870 — 175
10. Jura Federation: Polemic against the General Council, July 1872 — 177
11. Resolutions of the Saint-Imier Congress of the IWA,
      15-16 September 1872 — 179
12. The Sixth Congress of the International, Geneva
      1-6 September 1873 — 183
13. Bakunin's last letter to Élisée Reclus, 15 February 1875 — 186
14. Current demands, the Gotha Programme of the
      German Social-Democratic Party, May 1875 — 187
15. Resolutions of the Congresses of Verviers,
      5-8 September 1877 and Ghent, 9-14 September 1877 — 188
16. 1877: The International falls apart — 191

Chronology — 195
Sources — 200
Notes — 202
Index — 220

AUTHOR'S PREFACE

It is difficult to say how satisfied I am that the present work on the International Workers' Association (IWA) has been translated into the language of the country where the IWA was founded. It is equally difficult to express my satisfaction at reading such an excellent translation.

The original text in French was entitled *The Breach with Bakuninism and the end of 'Anti-Authoritarian' IWA* (*La Rupture avec le bakouninisme et la fin de l'AIT « anti-autoritaire »*).[1] It was published in May 2015 by Editions Monde Libertaire under the shorter title *The End of the First International* (*La fin de la première international*).

It was not my initial intention to write a history of the IWA – I am not a historian and I have too much respect for that honourable body to compare myself with them. I do not pretend to have the objectivity which is expected of historians, even if a duty for objectivity is sometimes a formality, one masked behind procedures which make it a wholesale illusion. To conclude, I do not hide that I have taken sides – and I think that readers will notice this – and I intend to show that the positions adopted are based on facts and texts that cannot be refuted.

So, when I say that the individuals who controlled the apparatus of the International were bureaucrats, I cite a letter from John Hales that supports this statement. When I say there was no German [IWA] federation I cite the declaration of a German Social-Democratic paper. When I say that Marx's support for the Commune was opportunist I draw support from a letter of Marx to his friend Sorge which leaves no doubt as to my assertion.

The justice that is called bourgeois invented a procedure which I value as being wholly positive: the possibility of an accused person presenting their own defence. But when the bureaucratic clique of the General Council of the IWA decided on the expulsion of Michael Bakunin and James Guillaume, at the congress in The Hague in September 1872, the accused were not authorised to defend themselves. I wanted somehow to remedy this omission, and also to transform myself into a prosecutor.

Of course my intervention is rather late.

My experience of fifty years of activity as an anarcho-syndicalist activist in the French labour movement has made me aware that there was among libertarians a species of 'victim syndrome', which arises because winners write history. This book is an attempt to modify such things.

So, the creation of the Anti-Authoritarian IWA has been termed a 'secession'. This concept of supposed 'secession' has often even been repeated by anarchists themselves. I wished to show that it was the Marxists who were the splitters; that Marx and Engels – who were rejected by every federation of the International – expelled the totality of the organised labour movement of these times from the IWA. Such an affirmation will no doubt provoke the indignation of Marxist readers, but here too I draw support from the correspondence of Marx and Engels themselves, which leaves no doubt in the matter.

This book reflects also on the causes of the ending of the so called Anti-Authoritarian International. If I show no deference to the 'Marxists' of the International, neither do I make allowances for the 'anarchists'. Indeed, the original title suggested a 'breach with Bakuninism'. Bakunin, starting from observations that he made of the labour movement in his times, developed a certain number of principles that might have facilitated the continuity of the International Association. The first and foremost of these principles was that the International should not adopt a single programme, failing which there would be 'as many Internationals as there were programmes', the International should prioritise the organising of solidarity between all workers.

There was a 'breach' with Bakuninism on the day when activists claiming Bakunin for themselves sought to have the International adopt an 'anarchist programme'. This transformation was not the *only* cause of the dislocation of the IWA, but it was a decisive cause. I have attempted to show how this breach arose, and its consequences for the later development of the anarchist movement.

R.B.

TRANSLATOR'S PREFACE

The conflict in the International Workers' Association (First International) between Social-Democratic 'Authoritarians' and Anarchist 'Anti-Authoritarians' still resonates among socialists today. Much of the recent literature on the First International is largely deficient in one way or another: one-sided, recycling past judgements, failing to consider historical context.[2] René Berthier goes a long way to refuting such ill-considered and partial judgements.

I have added appendices documenting some of the conflict and views mentioned in the text, also a chronology, some notes, and some notes on sources (those added by me are identified by *Trans.*). The Abbreviation 'IWA' is used for the International Workers' Association. Short details on many of the persons mentioned in this text are given in endnotes. These occur usually after the first reference to an individual.

INTRODUCTORY NOTE

Like the history of the Paris Commune, the history of the International Workers' Association[3] (IWA), is full of political controversy. Various currents of thought were in contention in the history that was elaborated, all of them wishing to offer their interpretation of events. What survived was a range of schemas, partial theories and fabricated mythologies. The first purpose of this work is to throw light on these received ideas.

I seek to show that the expulsions at the Congress of The Hague provoked terrible trauma and this trauma provoked reactions which were not necessarily very helpful. In fact the most direct consequence of the expulsions at The Hague was the victory of the federalist current, a victory which was corroborated at the Congress of Saint-Imier. One of the myths fabricated around the 'Anti-Authoritarian' IWA is that the congress of Saint-Imier of 1872 was in some way, the founding act of 'anarchism'. This is completely wrong.

Saint-Imier was a victory for the federalist current. Inside that current there were, in embryonic form, two tendencies: one which would later become anarchism and another that became revolutionary syndicalism and anarcho-syndicalism. Also – something too often forgotten – some of the IWA federations which supported the Jura Federation after its expulsion did not share 'anarchist' opinions at all, and were in favour of using the ballot box to take power. They shared with the Jura Federation only the conviction that the various IWA Federations should not go along with the imposition of one compulsory, uniform strategy. It is significant that after the Congress of The Hague, these federations disappeared from circulation. What happened to them? Was their disappearance the consequence of a propensity – clearly discernible within the 'Anti-Authoritarian' IWA – that encouraged the development of an International with an obligatory 'anarchist' programme? Obviously this was one of the principal causes for the departure of the Belgian Federation.

Marx's pathetic strategic thinking was revealed in these events, as he masterminded incredibly bureaucratic manipulation to rid himself of people who obstructed him. He shot himself in the foot. Of course, such images do not sit well in a Marxist schema of thinking; and, because by and large it is the winners who end up writing history many anarchists have also come to unconsciously accept Marxist perspectives. For over a century Marxist discourse consisted of accusing federalists of being secessionists, and very often the Saint-Imier Congress was itself defined by anarchists as secession. However there was no secession at Saint-Imier! *It was the 'Marxists' who seceded.*

Incredibly, the French language Wikipedia[4] on the IWA portrays the Congress of The Hague as a secession by federalists; the secession took place at the beginning of September 1872 at the The Hague. One might ask, what were the sources for this author's text, which allowed the expulsion (however bureaucratic) of two men to be portrayed as secession? This is all that the Congress at The Hague accomplished. The bureaucratic clique around the General Council expelled just two men: Bakunin and James Guillaume. A third man was in the dock, Adhémar Schwitzguébel, but he was not excluded. Later that same bureaucratic clique expelled the Jura Federation and thereafter every other contemporary organised labour movement body was excluded from the rump 'General Council' IWA. What an extraordinary example of the infusion of the victors' perspectives.

INTRODUCTION

The problem of how the workers' movement should be organised has been set out as the 'Marx-Bakunin' debate. But there was no debate – at least not in the sense of two adversaries faithfully elaborating their positions against each other. The Marx-Bakunin 'debate' resulted with Bakunin, James Guillaume, the Jura Federation, and then almost the whole of the labour movement (as organised at that time), being excluded from the rump IWA. Bureaucratic manoeuvres that were a model of their kind were used by Marx, Engels and friends. According to George Haupt, Karl Marx's refusal to engage with Bakunin in a debate on policy

> was above all of a tactical order. Marx's every effort tended to diminish and minimalize Bakunin, to deny his rival any theoretical consistency. He refuses to recognise Bakunin's system of thought, not because he denies his consistency, as he peremptorily affirms, but rather because Marx seeks in this way to discredit him and to reduce him in dimension to the head of a sect and an old-fashioned conspirator.[5]

Sometimes it is forgotten that the confrontation within the International between Bakuninists and Marxists took an 'institutional' form reflecting divergent interpretations of IWA statutes. The former affirmed that 'the economic emancipation of the working class is the great aim to which, as a means, all political movements should be subordinated'. Such a rendition suited Bakuninists well but did not suit Marx, although it was something he had written. In the years that followed the creation of the International the Bakuninists attached themselves to a wording which Marx sought to modify. He succeeded only by recourse to terrible manipulation after having expelled from the IWA the quasi-totality of the contemporary international workers' movement.

Certainly, the *Inaugural Address*, also written by Marx, had affirmed that 'the conquest of political power has become the first duty of the working class' – but this document was never put to a vote.[6] Marxists would consider the 'conquest of power' as agreed policy and for them it came to have the force of statute, whereas activists in this era viewed the *Inaugural Address* as nothing more than the expression of one author's viewpoint.

In the 1860s a number of activists realised that an international workers' organisation was needed. The initiative to create an organisation came from two groups of workers, each involved in struggles in their own countries: a group of English trade union leaders and a group of French mutualists inspired by Proudhon. The English working class was strongly organised in the trade union field. In 1859 a great building workers strike in London had forced trade union leaders to consider solidarity with the continental workers' movement as a practical necessity to prevent the use of strike breakers. The French workers' movement suffered ferocious repression after the revolution of 1848 and with the inauguration of the Imperial regime of Napoleon III. In 1861, a Parisian typesetters' strike met a crushing defeat. A new generation of activists appeared, influenced by Proudhon's ideas supporting workers' organisation, co-operatives, and mutual credit.[7]

In 1862, on the occasion of the Universal Exhibition in London, a delegation of 340 French workers arrived in the British capital. They made contact with British trade unionists and considered recent technological and economic developments. British workers took advantage of this opportunity to propose a rapprochement with their French comrades. Ongoing relations were established on both sides of the Channel. French workers were amazed by the level of organisation of their comrades on the other side of the Channel. In 1863, English trade unionists invited French comrades over, on the occasion of a demonstration in favour of Polish independence. Large meetings were organised. About this time German workers also organised around an energetic leader, Ferdinand Lassalle. Italian workers sought unity. In 1863 Garibaldi was enthusiastically received by British trade unionists. So there was some real effervescence in Europe.

On 22 July 1864, a meeting brought together the principal London trade union leaders and six French workers. The following day the British invited the French to a closed meeting where the basis of an entente was agreed. The International Workers' Association was constituted definitively when Henri-Louis Tolain and Joseph-Etienne Perrachon, accompanied by a lace maker, Limousin, made a journey to London in September 1864. The IWA was constituted officially on 29 September 1864 at a meeting in Saint Martin's Hall. A French proposal to create European sections linked by a central committee and to be called a General Council was approved. James Guillaume, citing one of those who put their signature to the manifesto of the Sixty,[8] wrote not without reason that the International was 'a child born in the workshops of Paris and nourished in London'.[9] An Englishman,

George Odger, was nominated as president of the General Council.

The new – essentially Franco-British – organisation did however take in Italian, Polish and German émigrés. A provisional committee involving Marx, Jung and Eccarius was charged with drawing up statutes for the organisation. Contrary to the discourse of Marxist historians, the International was in no way Marx's creature. He had remained a stranger to the preparatory work which took place between 1862 and 1864. 'He joined the International at the moment when the initiative of French and English workers had brought it into being. Like the cuckoo he came to put his egg in a nest that was not his own. His design, from the first moment, was to make of the great workers' organisation an instrument for his personal views.'[10] The work in which James Guillaume expressed this perspective was published long after Marx's death. No doubt he was not without some bitterness, nor was the vigour of his perspective wholly unaffected by his expulsion [at The Hague] as a consequence of Marx's bureaucratic manoeuvres. Nonetheless, the image of a cuckoo is not false one.

The structure of the International was that of a workers' association, akin to one in a workplace or union.[11] A General Council was to establish 'relations between various workers' associations in such fashion that workers in each country should be constantly aware of developments in their class in other countries.' This was an important phrase; it was around this point that divergences would rapidly crystallize between partisans of Marx and partisans of Bakunin concerning the functioning of the General Council. The antagonism between centralisation and federalism would then make its appearance.

Local workers' sections and national federations were to be set up alongside the General Council. IWA congresses were to be sovereign and were to be held annually. On the continent sections in France, Belgium, Switzerland, Spain, Italy and the Netherlands formed very rapidly but in Britain much of the trade union movement remained aloof.

The International had provisional statutes, to be ratified by its first congress, which was scheduled to meet in Belgium in 1865 but did not take place. It was replaced by a conference in London which brought together Varlin, De Paepe, Jung, Eccarius, Dupleix, Becker, Odger, Marx and a few others. The first congress of the International was held in Geneva from 3-8 September 1866. Marx was absent;[12] Bakunin was as yet not a member. Sixty delegates attended representing sections from Britain, France, Germany and Switzerland. Hermann Jung, a clock-smith from Saint-Imier living in London, presided., according to L. Lorwin a 'neo-Christian humanist',[13] was one of the Congress secretaries. Coullery and Jules Vuilleumier represented the section of La Chaux-de-Fonds, James Guillaume the section of Le Locle, and Adhémar Schwitzguébel that of Sonvilier.

This first congress was somewhat confused, but it was notable for adopting resolutions in favour of the eight-hour day, for international legislation to protect women and children and for the abolition of night work for women. The congress pronounced itself in favour of the abolition of wage-labour. It adopted statutes written by Marx that were vague enough to permit all workers to join. There was no mention of the article on the conquest of political power that Marx would have inserted in 1872. Later, [in 1868] Bakunin would describe the Geneva congress in these terms:

> The International Workers' Association has a fundamental law to which each section and member must submit, on pain of exclusion. This law is presented in the general statutes proposed by the General Council of the association to the Geneva congress of 1866, discussed and unanimously acclaimed by this congress, and finally definitively agreed by their unanimous acceptance by sections in all countries.
>
> The '*Considering*' clauses that are to be found, prefacing the general statutes, clearly define the principals and aims of the International Association. Above all they establish: That labour's emancipation must be a work of workers themselves; That workers' efforts must tend towards the development for all of the same rights and same duties – that is to say political, economic and social equality; That the subjection of workers to capital is the source of all political, moral and material servitude; That for this reason workers' economic emancipation is the great aim, to which all political movements are to be subordinated; That workers emancipation is not a simply local or national problem – but international.[14]

In reality such thinking simply reflected the [draft] statutes of the International written in 1864 by... Marx himself and approved by the Geneva congress. Proudhon had died the previous year and indubitably it was his doctrine which had predominated at this congress, and would do so at the next one in Lausanne (2-8 September 1867).

In Geneva, and later at the Lausanne congress, little enthusiasm was inspired by the positions of the General Council, which is to say of Marx. In these first years, in a rather cordial atmosphere, various ideas coexisted and confronted each other. This second congress had a busy programme: the creation of banks to facilitate free credit for workers was advocated, mutual assurance societies were recommended, and trades societies [unions] were invited to create and fund co-operative production societies.

The perspective of this congress was one that looked to start with concrete and immediate measures, directed towards emancipating the working class. Resolutions were voted on the subject of free education, taxes, the abolition of state monopolies, the establishment of political freedoms and workshop-schools. In the discussion on private property, Pierre Coullery, a partisan of individual property, was opposed by the Belgian César De Paepe, who favoured collective property (something that that Internationalists would support at a later date). The problem would feature on the agenda of the third Congress of the International. At this congress, too, it was the ideas of Proudhon that would predominate, enraging Marx. He wrote to Engels on 11 September 1867:

> At the next Congress in Brussels I shall personally break the necks of these Proudhonist jackasses. I have managed the whole thing diplomatically and did not want to come out personally until my book (*Capital*) was published and our International had struck root. In the official report of the General Council (despite all their efforts, the Parisian babblers could not prevent our re-election to it) I will moreover give them a good hiding.

Several times in this letter Marx speaks of 'our International'. The desire of the cuckoo to take over the nest was beginning to take shape. It was at the Brussels congress, in 1868, that matters began to change. On the agenda were questions of compulsory and free education, and of women's rights and equality. The mutualists, who had opposed the examination of political problems, lost their majority. For men like Eugène Varlin and César De Paepe, the examination of political problems could not be avoided; but such problems had to be addressed within the International. Important social questions featured on the agenda of the Brussels Congress. The strike was considered as workers' main weapon. Many participants advocated the creation of *cahiers du travail* – books of labour's grievances and complaints – which were reminiscent of the *cahiers de doléances* – books of grievances of the French revolution of 1789. Delegates declared their general support for land being made the property of the collective.

There was a real turning point at the Basel Congress (6-12 September 1869). Bakunin was now a member and right-wing Proudhonists were decisively beaten by an alliance of Bakuninists, Blanquists and Marxists. This fourth congress of the International took a position on the rights of property [in land]. The Brussels Congress had certainly dealt with this question, but partisans of private property, who had then been in the minority, re-launched the debate, saying it was a complex problem and had not been resolved. The Congress, after a lively discussion, clearly expressed itself in favour of collectivism.

The question of inheritance was the second item on the agenda and produced a war of words. There was no fundamental interest in the question,[15] but for the Marxists it served as a pretext to count votes. The Marxists [aligned with the General Council] presented an amendment to the resolution, which was rejected; so amongst the congress delegates voting on this amendment and motion, the weight of the various currents appeared to be:

63 % around 'Bakuninist' collectivist texts.

31 % around 'Marxist' texts

6 % supporting Mutualist convictions.[16]

The problem of 'caisses de résistance' – strike funds – was indubitably the most important discussion in Basel. Their creation was recommended to all sections. Trustees were recommended to support federal organisations – regional, national, and international – and through these to support prolonged strikes helping workers to struggle against the bourgeoisie.[17] Federalist delegates voted through administrative resolutions which they had failed to weigh up properly, and, later they would have reason to regret their lack of attention. These resolutions gave the General Council the right to refuse admission to new associations and to suspend sections – decisions which had to be submitted to a subsequent congress. In 1872 James Guillaume wrote:

> We were all inspired by the most complete goodwill in respect of the men from London. And so blind was our confidence that we contributed more than anyone to the vote in favour of these *administrative resolutions* which gave the General Council authority, authority which they were to use so despicably. A profitable lesson and one which opened our eyes to the true principles of federalist organisation.[18]

It was at this Basel congress – with Bakunin having become a member of the International – that the two opposing currents came openly face to face. These differences were already present in Brussels, but now they became clearly delineated. On one side were those were those seen as federalists and revolutionaries: the Belgians, most of the French, the Spanish and the Jurassians; on the other side the General Council, the Germans[19] and some of the Swiss – who were centralists and Social-Democrats.

The coexistence within the International of different conceptions, such as those of statist socialists, Anti-Authoritarians and Proudhonists, and diverse tactics (political action, abstentionism, syndicalism [trade unionism], co-operation, etc.), was replaced – after the Basel Congress (September 1869) – by the aggressive action of authoritarian, statist parties, of which the principal centres were the Geneva Fabrique,[20] the German Socialist Party and the London General Council.[21]

Evidently for Marx the situation created by the Basel Congress was unacceptable. It was after this congress that systematic and most violent attacks began against Bakunin. 'This Russian, it is clear wants to become the dictator of the European workers' movement. Let him take care or he will be excommunicated' prophesied Marx in a letter to Engels dated 27 July 1869. Engels responded on the 30 July: 'Fat Bakunin is behind all this – that is evident. If this damned Russian really thinks to place himself through his intrigues at the head of the workers' movement it is high time to put him in a place where he can do no harm.' After breaking the necks of those 'Proudhonist donkeys' it was now time to excommunicate the Bakuninists.

It is true that Marx and Engels had reason to be wary. Before he joined the International Workers' Association, Bakunin had created the International Alliance for Socialist Democracy, which had requested membership of the International Workers' Association. That application was refused by the General Council for perfectly legitimate reasons, since at first the Alliance had thought of itself as an international organisation. To conform to the statutes of the International, the Alliance transformed itself into a simple IWA section. Its membership was accepted subject to this condition. Its role as an International section was not negligible since it was at its instigation that the Spanish Federation was created.

Marx and Engels developed a truly paranoid obsession with the Bakuninist 'Alliance'; they saw the worst in it and thought it was behind every initiative that, from their own perspective, erred from the proper course. The phantom of the Alliance – with Bakunin standing behind it – haunted Marx and Engels. Franz Mehring, a perfectly orthodox Marxist militant and historian, would write in his biography of Marx that there was nothing that could substantiate Marx and Engels' accusations against Bakunin – however, they were not entirely wrong.

The IWA was affected by profound changes after 1866. In Europe, artisan production – still important – declined in the face of the development of larger scale industry. The introduction of machine production successively proletarianised various branches of artisan production; new industries were developing. This restructuring of production led to price and wage movements, redundancies, unemployment and cyclical crises. A strike movement spread across Europe. The frequent use of ferocious repression served only to increase the influence of the International that had been created two years earlier. Strikes, which had hitherto been characterised as fortuitous, developed into full scale class conflicts. They provided workers with some practical experience of solidarity and support, which on occasion arrived from abroad.

The creation of the IWA was a turning point for Anarchism and Marxism. It may be useful to momentarily step back to adjust perspective and to put 'theoreticians' in their proper place. The Marxist Franz Mehring is one of the rare few who saw the situation accurately. Writing on the Bakuninist opposition, he says: it was apparent that the reason why it used Bakunin's name was that it believed that in his ideas it found solutions to those social conflicts and antagonisms, which had brought about its very existence.[22]

Strictly speaking the same might be said of Marx. So in these matters Mehring does not take an ideological approach.[23] His analysis is made in terms of class and of the contending social forces. Moreover, it is precisely here that the key to unravelling the conflict in the IWA is to be found. Bakunin and Marx invented nothing, they witnessed events and theorised about them. Let us examine the organisations which Marx thought he might rely on, organisations which could also find, in Marx, a justification for their own institutional activity:

English workers, for some years after its launch, neither showed any interest in the IWA nor formed IWA sections. Trade union leaders used the International only to help obtain electoral reform. The newly formed English Federation (constituted, note, eight years after the foundation of the IWA...) nauseated by Marx's intrigues, drew close to the positions of the Jura Federation after the congress at The Hague (1872).[24]

The German IWA never amounted to much. Franz Mehring underlines that older IWA organisations in Germany – sections that had been created by Becker – withered and declined as the Social-Democratic Party began to develop.

Four months before the congress at The Hague, which was to expel Bakunin and James Guillaume, Engels wrote an urgent letter to [Wilhelm] Liebknecht:[25] 'How many membership cards, for how many members; and where roughly have you distributed them? The 208 calculated by Fink can't amount to all of them!' As he writes there is almost a puff of panic blowing: 'Matters are becoming serious and we need to know just where we are; if not you will force us to act for ourselves, considering the Social-Democratic Workers' Party as a stranger to the International and will relate to it as an unattached body.'[26] It would be difficult to express more clearly the lack of interest that German Social-Democracy had for the International. By way of comparison, the Spanish Federation had a membership of 30,000.

As for the section in Geneva, is was composed of an aristocracy of citizen-workers in the watch- and clock-making industry bent on building electoral alliances with bourgeois radicals – 'with [its fingers] stuck in electoral compromises with bourgeois radicals', as Bakunin said.

So, when Marx decided in September 1872 to exclude federalist collectivists he was – apart from his control of the organisational apparatus – singularly lacking in trumps. Bakunin too did not have a firmer position within the International and his real 'authority' was no greater. Moreover, when the Geneva Alliance section dissolved itself,[27] its activists did not even ask Bakunin's opinion – which says a lot about the 'dictatorship' he supposedly exercised. In any case the Franco-Prussian war would put the brake on the momentum of the international labour movement, and would disperse its activists.

The intrigues of Marx and his entourage culminated in the decision to exclude Bakunin and James Guillaume, a decision made by the London conference of 1871 and made effective at the Congress of The Hague. Obviously it was no accident that at the same time article 7a was forced into the statutes of the International, declaring amongst other things that 'the conquest of political power had become the great duty of the proletariat'. Article 7a, a synthesis of the resolution adopted in 1871 at the London Conference, was included in the statutes by the decision of the Congress at The Hague, a totally rigged event, as no serious historian today denies. Doubtless, this was why it was the only one in which Marx participated.

KEY QUESTIONS

The question of the conquest of power

Marx sought over many years to have the IWA adopt the principle of the conquest of power as a prerequisite for workers' emancipation. The overwhelming influence of the Russian revolution over interpretations of Marxist theory tends to obscure the fact that Marx and Engels scarcely ever considered political activity as anything other than the conquest of power through parliament. That strategic vision was founded on the fact that the proletariat was expected to be a majority, *and* for the most part would vote for socialists. For a long time German Social-Democrats rejected the idea of electoral alliances to win power; whereas Bakunin, who was well aware of the mechanisms of the parliamentary system, believed that socialists would not get into government without some alliance with fractions of the liberal bourgeoisie. From this it inevitably followed that the socialist programme would be adulterated. There is no need to elaborate – future developments would show he was on the right track.

Bakunin's argument was that it was quite simply *impossible* for socialists to come to power through elections. The 'classes of owners, exploiters and governors,' said he, 'will never make any concession to the proletariat voluntarily, for the sake of justice or out of generosity, however urgent it may be, however feeble it may seem;' 'the proletariat should wait for nothing from the bourgeoisie: neither intelligence, nor equity, least of all their politics – be that the politics of bourgeois radicals or that of the bourgeoisie who call themselves socialist.'[28]

For some time this aspect of Marxist political strategy has been obscured by post-Leninist Marxism. Marxist revolutionaries applied in Europe not the principles that Marx had developed for industrial societies, but rather those of Lenin and/or Trotsky had, for agrarian and underdeveloped societies. Indeed, from a strictly Marxist viewpoint the politics elaborated by the French Communist Party, at least after the disappearance of the Comintern, was perfectly orthodox. It is not without some irony that the heirs of Bakunin see those of Lenin and Trotsky returning to Marxist orthodoxy – that is, to Social-Democracy.

In Germany the Social-Democratic Party created by Liebknecht and Bebel [in 1869], 'under the auspices of Mr Marx' says Bakunin, 'announced in their programme that *the conquest of political power was the prerequisite for the economic emancipation of the proletariat* and that in consequence the immediate object of the party should be the organisation of widespread legal agitation for the conquest of universal suffrage and all other political rights.'[29] (See appendix.)

The conquest of political power, as it was discussed in the debates of the International, should be considered in context. Problems as they were posed then cannot be judge in the light of subsequent developments. Marx's discourse – *whether he wished it or not* – bolstered the position of those organisations which might, or believed that they might, obtain an improvement in their lot through elections. Those who expected nothing from electoral activity swung towards Bakunin: the foreign workers of Geneva,[30] the badly paid, the despised, those without political rights, Italian youth with neither a class nor a future, the peasants of Andalusia and Italy – starved by big landlords, the miserable proletariat of Italy; workers in Catalan industry and the Belgian miners of the Borinage, two regions where there existed a concentrated and militant proletariat, where no peaceful reform could be expected, and where the smallest strikes were drowned in blood. The latter could find nothing to help or sustain them in Marx's discourse, and even where there were Marxists (we should say people who, in claiming leadership of the International, preferred activity within the law), the latter took care to destroy any movements whose demands might scare off electors, as was notably the case in Switzerland.[31]

Divergences over strategy were therefore largely based on concrete differences of living conditions amongst the European proletariat; this is a fact that cannot be passed over. These differences existed nonetheless before the foundation of the International and the latter served only as the place where they would confront each other. Indeed, over and above differences between the two principal IWA currents, the question of the necessity of the conquest of political power through elections was only one element of a wider picture:

- Should one organise in national parties to conquer through elections the power apparatus of the bourgeoisie, conserving its general form and using it in the interest of proletariat;
- Or should one conquer social power, creating new and radically different forms, in fitting with the nature of the proletariat, forms through which it would be able to go forward to social reconstruction?

In this lay the basis for the opposition between the two currents of the IWA, that would become on the one hand Marxism, and on the other Anarchism. It would be an error to see this as an opposition between Marx and Bakunin. As we have seen, these two men did not create the two contending currents. Marx had posed the problem of power in the *Communist Manifesto*, and after 1847 and down the years would revise it only in marginal fashion: 'The first step in the revolution by the working class is to raise the proletariat to the position of ruling class to win the battle of democracy.'

Such terms are not anodyne – '*the battle of democracy*' meant universal suffrage and the representation of the working class in state institutions.

> The proletariat will use its political supremacy to wrest, by degree, all capital from the bourgeoisie, to centralise all instruments of production in the hands of the State, i.e., of the proletariat organised as the ruling class; and to increase the total productive forces as rapidly as possible … Abolition of property in land and application of all rents of land to public purposes … Centralisation of credit in the hands of the state, by means of a national bank with State capital and an exclusive monopoly … Centralisation of the means of communication and transport in the hands of the State.[32]

Here again the terms are not neutral. The 'political supremacy' of the working class, evoked here, is linked to two factors: the proletariat is the most numerous class, and it comes to power through elections. The *Communist Manifesto*, a basic text and work of reference for all communists, including those revolutionary Marxist currents emerging out of the experience Russian revolution, is a manifesto only for the conquest of parliamentary democracy and workers' participation in elections. A refusal to participate in elections is perceived by Marx and Engels as a rejection of all political activity. There is only *parliamentary* political activity. Thus Engels accused the partisans of Bakunin: 'These gentlemen demand *complete abstention from all political activity*, and in particular *non-participation in all elections.*' (Letter to Louis Pio, 7 March 1872), which implied that no alternative is possible. The bitter opposition of Marx and Engels towards abstentionists arose because, without elections, communists would never come to power!

Three comments are in order: a) Electoral abstentionism was conflated with the rejection of political activity; b) This critique of abstentionism – except for very rare and brief exceptions – served to pass over and disregard the other solutions that were proposed at the time; c) Lastly as far as

Bakunin was concerned, one should note that his attitude was in fact not at all dogmatic and on many occasions he advised friends to participate in elections. One should remember that Proudhon was himself elected as a deputy in 1848. Marx understood Bakunin's project perfectly, but on this matter he expressed himself only in private correspondence, and never in a public text:

> The working class should not do *politics*. Its duty is to limit itself to organising in unions. One fine day, with the help of the International, they will supplant every existing state. (Marx even adds:)
> This donkey hasn't even understood that all class movements are as such necessarily *political* movements, and have always been so. (Letter to Lafargue, 19 April 1870.)

Despite the polemical tone, this was a perfect summary of Bakunin's thought:
a) The class structure of the International – by and large its form in unions – is a draft and sketch for the organisation of society of the future;
b) Whilst not taking part in the game of bourgeois institutions (parliament) the activity of the International is fundamentally a political activity.

This is *exactly* what Bakunin thought; he did not reject political activity as such, but denied that it was confined to parliamentary activity. As for Marx, his thought was more complex than Bakunin could know – given the writings that Bakunin could then access. If Marx did not exclude the use of extra-parliamentary activity – violence – he did so only marginally, in order to impose parliamentary forms.

While the *Manifesto* remained a basic text of Marxism, it was obvious that over many decades the founders of so-called 'scientific' socialism were able to vary their analysis a little. So, on the occasion of the twentieth anniversary of the Paris Commune, Engels, writing a preface to *The Civil War in France*, exclaimed:

> Of late, the Social-Democratic philistine has once more been filled with wholesome terror at the words: dictatorship of the proletariat. Well and good, gentlemen, do you want to know what this dictatorship looks like? Look at the Paris Commune. That was the dictatorship of the proletariat.[33]

Thus the Commune was presented as the form in which working-class power was to be exercised. This did not correspond with anything that

Marx and Engels had said before the 'Commune-alist' insurrection, or with anything that they might say afterwards. *The Civil War in France* is a work in which Marx describes the Commune from a federalist viewpoint – for his own reasons, since he hated federalism. One finds a similar process regarding the Russian revolution with Lenin's *State and Revolution*; it appears to be the acme of Marxist theory on the wasting away of the state, but the latter is only a formalistic concession used rhetorically in this text. In the same way that Marx wrote *The Civil War in France* hoping to draw towards him followers of Blanqui, Lenin wrote *State and Revolution* to try to conciliate the very active Russian libertarian movement, at a time when the Bolshevik Party did not amount to much. Franz Mehring saw *The Civil War in France* as an isolated episode of flirting with libertarians.

The expression 'dictatorship of the proletariat' encompassed completely different meanings: in 1850 it meant a Jacobin dictatorship with no popular representation – the opposite of what Engels would say in 1891. The 'dictatorship of the proletariat' was emptied of all its content – it could mean at the same time both the most authoritarian and the most libertarian of regimes! Nor was this the end of the matter. Returning to 1891, Engels criticised the Erfurt German Social-Democrat programme and affirmed the democratic republic as the specific form of the dictatorship of the proletariat: 'Our party and the working class can achieve domination only through the democratic republican form. The latter is itself the specific form of the dictatorship of the proletariat.' That same year Engels suggested as a model for the dictatorship of the proletariat a unitary Commune and democratic republic. In fact the formula 'dictatorship of the proletariat' encompassed at least three concepts:

In the *Manifesto* (1848), it meant a democratic and Jacobin republic;
In the *Eighteenth Brumaire de Louis Bonaparte* (1852) and in *Class Struggles in France* (1850), it signified a revolutionary and highly centralised dictatorship with no popular representation;
In *The Civil War in France* it signified a vaguely libertarian federation.

An attentive reader might be tempted to see some incoherence in the manner in which the founders of so-called 'scientific' socialism addressed the question of forms of power. Their conceptions on this question were in fact determined much more by circumstances of time and place, than by precise principles – although they might have a change of perspective in the same year, as Engels did in 1891. The heirs of every tendency can find something for themselves – even those who wish to create a 'libertarian Marxism': one only has to do some digging for the right text.

Most of the works mentioned – from the *Manifesto* to *The Civil War in France*, and most of the texts in which there was some historical or theoretical reflection on power and its forms, were written before the unification of Germany and the creation of the Second Reich. *After* the Franco-Prussian war German Social-Democracy constituted a model in the eyes of Marx and Engels, certainly an imperfect one, but a model nevertheless. Before the Commune and the unification of Germany under Prussian domination, the autonomy of sections of the International was not challenged by the General Council. Thus correspondence from the latter addressed to the Central Bureau of the Bakuninist Alliance declared: 'respecting our principles, we allow each section to formulate freely its own theoretical programme.'[34] The war and the unification of Germany changed things. Marx and Engels believed that the balance of forces had changed. Marx wrote a letter to Engels on 20 July 1870 in which he declared that the centralisation of the German state would be useful in centralising the German working class, assuring the dominance of the German proletariat on the 'world scene' (sic) and at the same time 'the preponderance of our theory over that of Proudhon'.[35] Allowing sections to 'formulate freely' their own theoretical programme was over. Marx and Engels reasoned now in terms of the hegemony of the German proletariat and the preponderance of 'their' theory over others. Relations within the proletariat itself had become power relations. The conquest of power was the objective, and if Marx and Engels criticised the party, going so far as to accuse its leaders of 'parliamentary cretinism', it was essentially because it was acting badly. It was this [German party] model that they attempted to impose on the International.

The idea which constituted the kernel of their doctrine was that parties represent different fractions of the bourgeoisie, that they succeeded one another in coming to power and would come to 'ruin' themselves – to use Engels' expression – before the proletariat succeeded them. Alliances between a workers' party and these parties might accelerate the process: 'And then it would be our turn.'[36]

At the Congress of The Hague (in the course of which Marx and Engels had Bakunin and James Guillaume excluded) Marx declared that the influence of institutions, customs and traditions in different countries had to be taken into account, and that it was possible that in Britain, the USA and perhaps the Netherlands workers 'may obtain their goals the peaceful means', he added, however, that 'force will act as the lever of our revolutions in most countries of the continent'. In despotic countries 'force' was the means by which the working class would accomplish political revolution to impose universal suffrage and a parliamentary regime.

The question of programme

The question of how expedient it was to conquer state power through elections was posed at the same time as the question of one single programme for the IWA. Since the Alliance for Socialist Democracy had elaborated a programme, Bakunin was not at all opposed to the principle of developing one,[37] and it was on this basis that its activists had spread propaganda to develop the IWA. Thus an Italian Bakuninist, Giuseppe Fanelli, travelled to Spain in 1868 and founded what would become the powerful Spanish Federation of the IWA. The organisational tool of the Bakuninists was the International Fraternity, which was a real organisation, in contrast with other secret societies which Bakunin had set up.[38] But for reasons of simple good sense, Bakunin opposed a definite political project being made compulsory for every national federation, because they contended with 'such different types of economic development, culture, and temperament...'[39] The heterogeneity of the International made it impossible to adopt a single programme, one applicable for all federations. Through a process of progressive development political debate should be allowed to define a collective position. One example is significant. After the English Federal Committee disavowed Marx's manoeuvres – which had resulted in the exclusion of Bakunin and of the Jura Federation – John Hales, in the name of the British Committee, wrote to the latter and in substance said they were in favour of conquering power but were not in favour of imposing such politics on all federations:

> We fully believe in the utility of political activity, and I believe that every member of our Federation is so persuaded, as we have obtained some of our best results through fear and concessions by the wealthy classes... We feel that we should take political power before we can achieve our own emancipation. We believe that you would have come to the same conclusion as us – if you found yourself in the same place – and we think that future events will prove us right. But at the same time we acknowledge your loyalty, and we are perfectly aware that there may be a similar difference of opinion as to what political direction to take, to achieve the great principles we are all fighting for. This is yet another proof that the federal principle is the only one on which our Association can be based.... With things being this way it is certain that it would be impossible to adopt one single uniform politics which might be applicable in all circumstances and countries.[40]

Bakunin considered this good sense. A text in which he most clearly developed his viewpoint was his *On the Knouto-Germanic Empire* (*Ecrit contre Marx*) of 1872. He wrote that the International should not integrate philosophical and political questions into its programme. He referred to the '*Considering*' clauses of the Geneva Congress which stipulated that the economic emancipation of the workers was the great goal to which all political movements should be subordinated'.[41] Bakunin believed that these key words 'broke the links which held the proletariat enchained to the politics of bourgeoisie'. Between the two tendencies opposed to each other on this point 'there is the same difference, the same chasm as between the proletariat and the bourgeoisie'. German Social-Democrats, setting out an electoral strategy, had 'attached the proletariat to the coat tails of the bourgeoisie', because such a political movement could only be directed by the bourgeoisie, or – even worse – by 'workers transformed by their ambition or vanity into members of the bourgeoisie'. In struggles, between different bourgeois fractions for the conquest of power, the working class would become a blind instrument. What divided Marx and Bakunin was not that the International should have politics, but the process through which it should define its programme. For the Russian revolutionary, some progressive development was needed, because between Britain and Italy or between Germany and Spain conditions were so diverse that imposing one single programme was not to be contemplated. So, such a programme should agree only a minimum and should be based on International solidarity. The single goal of the IWA is:

> ... workers' conquest of all human rights, through organised, militant, solidarity over and above differences: the diversity of trades and countries with political and national frontiers. *The supreme and one might say, single law* which each person takes on himself, when he joins this wonderful and salutary association, is voluntarily to submit themselves to the exigencies of that solidarity; and likewise thereafter: to submit all their acts, voluntarily, ardently and in full knowledge of causes; and in their own interest, as well as in the interest of their comrades of all conditions and countries.[42]

These principles are so broad, human, and at the same time so simple that one would have to be 'brutalised by bourgeois prejudices' not to understand them. So Bakunin affirms the basic principle – of the complete freedom of philosophical and political propaganda.

> The International allows no reproof, nor an official truth in the name of which reproof might be issued, because it has never yet admitted that it should present itself as a church or as a state; and it is due exactly to this abstention that it owes the incredible rapidity of its growth and development that has so astonished the world.
>
> So, freedom of debate and the absence of an official obligatory programme are conditions for the development of the IWA as a mass organisation.
>
> By eliminating from its programme all philosophical and political principles – not as objects for study and discussion but as compulsory principles it [the Geneva Congress] established the strength of our Association.'[43]

The Association should be able 'to draw into it and embrace the immense majority of the proletariat of every country of Europe and America'. So, with mass recruitment on a minimum programme Bakunin suggests a strategy for the unity of the international proletariat based on what unites workers rather than what divides them. 'Only a programme that is excessively general, i.e. vague and indeterminate, can work, because every theoretical determination corresponds fatally to some exclusion, to some practical elimination.'[44] Indeed, how could one hope that workers of every country, experiencing extremely different conditions – of culture, economic development – could submit and 'harness themselves to a uniform political programme?' If a political programme had to be introduced into the IWA, there could not be only one. If not, 'there would be as many Internationals as there are different programmes'. And so one programme would have to be imposed by force.

> Since unity in political action is recognised as necessary, if there is no hope that it should arise freely from a spontaneous understanding between the federations and sections of each country, it had to be imposed on them.[45]

It was not freedom of thought and action within the International that was to be feared – because the real unity of the proletariat was to be found not 'in the philosophical and political ideas of the day', but in the material conditions of workers' existence and in their living class solidarity. Unity arose:

[F]ully formed in the interests, needs, real aspirations, and sufferings of the proletariat throughout the world. This solidarity is not at all something to be created, it exists in reality; it is constituted by life itself, in the daily experience of the world of workers, and all that remains to be done is to make it known, and to facilitate its conscious organisation.[46]

To define one unique politics for the International would signify an imposition of 'the political programme of one country alone, either by violence, or by intrigue, or by the two together'. Whenever attempts might be made to use the International as a political power in the struggles of parties in a state:

[I]t will immediately be demoralised, diminished, weakened and drawn in on itself; it would be sensibly destabilised and it will finish up by melting away in the hands of whoever might be so foolish as to imagine that they might to grasp its power.[47]

If Bakunin is opposed to the IWA having a political programme, an official philosophy, then this is for tactical reasons. Rather than emphasising the *ideological unity* of the organisation of the mass of workers, Bakunin insists on *organic unity*, as the condition of its power in the face of its class adversary. However this does not preclude that the IWA might one day consider the question of a political programme. Indeed limiting the role of the IWA to economic action alone would imply that the latter should undertake

comparative statistics, the study of the laws of the distribution and production of wealth, that it should busy itself – where and when such things are possible – exclusively with wage claims, the raising of strike funds (caisses de resistance), the organisation of local, national and international strikes, the creation of local, national and international trade unions (corps de metier), the formation of cooperatives societies – for mutual credit, consumption and production.

Bakunin says such an eventuality is not foreseeable:

It would be death for the proletariat to preoccupy itself exclusively with purely economic interests. The organisation and defence of its interests – a matter of life or death – must indubitably constitute the foundations of its current activity. But, it is impossible to stop there, without renouncing its humanity and without depriving itself of the moral and intellectual strength, which it needs, to conquer its economic rights. Without doubt the first question which it has to face – in the miserable conditions to which it is now reduced – is that of its daily bread, of bread for the family. But more than with the privileged classes of today – the worker is a human being in the full sense of the word and as such has a thirst for dignity, justice, equality, freedom, humanity and science – and he fully intends to seize all of these at the same time as he conquers in full the enjoyment of the entire product of his own work. So, even if philosophical and political questions had not been posed at all in the International, the proletariat will infallibly pose them.'[48]

So, a contradiction is apparent: on the one hand philosophical and political questions must be excluded from the programme of the International; but on the other hand they must necessarily be discussed.

In freedom a solution is found that arises from and out of itself. No philosophical or political theory should enter as its essential, official foundation, as the compulsory condition in the programme of the International, because, as we have just seen, all imposed theory would become – for all the federations which are now part of it – either the cause of slavery, or of division and a less disastrous dissolution. But it does not follow that all philosophical and political questions cannot nor should not be freely discussed in the International. On the contrary, it would be the existence of an official theory which would kill the development of its own thinking in the world of workers, by making lively discussion unnecessary.[49]

Bakunin's approach does not consist of denying the necessity of the search for a programme for the International and it is not on this point that the divergence with Marx is found. He believed that such research must result from ongoing collective elaboration, and such research would be the better for it not being imposed as '*official* truth discovered scientifically by some isolated big head exceptionally and – why not – *providentially* provided with brains' (evidently he was thinking of Marx).

On the contrary, although no one has, nor can have the pretension to provide it, the search was on. Who is searching? Everyone, and above all the proletariat, which needs and thirsts for it, more than anyone. Many do not want to believe in this spontaneous search for philosophical and political truth by the proletariat itself.[50]

Obviously there was no magical role for revolutionary militants in this process of elaboration. What many authors pejoratively designate 'Bakuninist secret societies' are nothing other than revolutionary minorities active within the mass of workers.

The Hegelian background common to Bakunin and Marx allows us to transpose divergent approaches to the strategy of the labour movement to the philosophical domain, especially given that the question had already been set out as part of the framework of methodological differences between Proudhon and Marx, in the way that each of them explained the mechanisms of the capitalist system. Fundamentally it concerns the question of the theory of knowledge: *development by concept* or *development by nature.*

Concerning understanding Hegel made the distinction between *development by nature*, (reality is first, thought is conditioned) and *development by concept*, as it appears to reason (empirical reality is the effect of reason). The first considers the real process as it confronts understanding: the empirical and that which can be sensed come first; thought is something conditioned. The second considers logical process as it confronts reason: thought annuls the real conditions on which it seems to depend and therein makes its own result. In the current relations between these two processes, Hegel chooses to accord reality only to the second. Marx – after a fashion – follows in Hegel's footsteps: the programme and the unique strategy which he intends to have the International adopt are an application of development by concept to proletariat politics. The concept (programme) comes first and around it is constituted reality (the International). Bakunin follows an inverse process: he begins with development by nature, and with the living reality of the European proletariat, to arrive by gradual stages at the concept, the programme. In some ways he adopts an experimental method, which all anarchist thinkers have considered as the only method that is really scientific.

There were limits on what could be demanded of the IWA, and however strong the forces that are pulling and pushing a mass organisation like the IWA, these limits were set in place precisely because of its diversity. Bakunin strongly underlined this. It is a substantial error, he said, to demand from an institution more than it could give. There was a risk of demoralisation and death should it go beyond its limits. 'Is this a reason to hope that one might make use of it as an instrument for political struggle?'[51] This is what Marx wanted to do and he ended up with the liquidation of the organisation.

At issue was a practical problem rather one than a theoretical one. The IWA had moved on from supporting isolated strikes to veritable class confrontation – on a European scale. It organised collections, appealed for solidarity beyond frontiers, sent funds to strikers, and encouraged the formation of unions and the regrouping of labour forces. The success of one building workers' strike in Geneva was due to the help of Parisian bronze workers. As strikes became widespread, the IWA's politics became more radical. This radicalisation did not captivate everyone. Bakunin denounced the Marxist current of the Geneva IWA when they made building workers call off another strike in 1870 because, to use the expression of Utin, it would have been 'disastrous' for the election prospects of a certain Amberny, a lawyer.

According to Bakunin the definition of the International's programme should be a spontaneous process – and there should be no misinterpretation of the Russian revolutionary's notion of 'spontaneity' – a phenomenon is 'spontaneous' if it develops through the workings of its internal dynamics without outside intervention. It is therefore the opposite of a phenomenon that develops without a defined cause, through will alone or by chance. In consequence the concept of spontaneity is very close to that of ... determinism, which evidently goes against the grain of much common thinking. In short what was at issue was the question of how workers were to acquire class and revolutionary consciousness? The reply to a second question – what type of organisation was to be adopted? – also depended on how this first question was answered. Conscious awareness of the necessity of social transformation could never result from a purely bookish adherence, without some prior practical experience. Bakunin says, only a very small number of individuals 'are ready to reshape themselves in accordance with an abstract, pure "idea"'. To draw the proletariat into the activity of the International, it needs to be approached

> ... not with abstract and general ideas but with a realistic understanding of real ills. Its everyday woes, which may have a general character for a thinker, though they may well really be the result of particular effects of general and permanent causes, are infinitely diverse, taking on a multitude different facets, and are the product of a multitude of partial and temporary causes.[52]

Workers, 'join the International in the first instance to organise only for an eminently practical goal: to demand together, all their economic rights, against the oppressive exploitation of the bourgeoisie of all nations.'[53] As a result of this single fact, the proletariat placed itself in an eminently political situation, destroying 'political frontiers and all international politics of states'. It also situated itself 'beyond the action and political play of all parties of the state'.[54] Its official programme is *'the organisation of International solidarity – for the economic struggle of labour against capital.'* It is from this base that a new moral, intellectual and social world must arise.

> To ensure that it should be so, all [trends of] thinking – all the International's political and philosophical tendencies should emerge from within proletariat, and should have as their principal – if not exclusive – starting point this economic demand which constitute the very essence and goal of the International. Is this possible?

The programme is formed slowly 'sometimes bit by bit, sometimes all at once', in a three step process: [through]

- international strike solidarity, and the organisation and federalisation of strike funds;
- organisation and the international federalisation of trade unions (corps de metier);
- and lastly through '*the direct and spontaneous development of sociological and philosophical ideas within the International*, which, one might say is an enforced and inevitable consequence and concomitant of these first two movements.'[55]

Thus, this 'self-enlightenment' that each person accomplishes for themselves, as to the reality of their own exploitation, could not be provided by the revelation of some self-proclaimed revolutionary scientist; it could only develop progressively, through personal and collective experience within a group sharing the same way of life. Bakunin described this process with great clarity. When a worker entered an IWA section:

> [T]hey are taught that the same solidarity which exists between every member of one section is established equally between every section, or between every trade union (corps de metiers) of a locality; that the organisation of this wider solidarity, embracing without distinction workers of every trade, has become necessary because the bosses of every trade have come to an understanding amongst themselves.[56]

Practical experiences of solidarity

A strike wave grew and spread all over Europe after 1866. Often its ferocious repression served only to build the influence of the International that had been created just two years earlier. Strikes which hitherto had fortuitous characteristics, became true class conflicts, and helped to give workers practical experience of solidarity. Sometimes they had the benefit of support coming from abroad, as was shown in France, Belgium and Switzerland:

- In France: the strike of Parisian bronze workers of February 1867, funds were collected by the IWA; the strike of the Roubaix weavers and spinners of March 1867; the strike of the Fuveau mining district of Gardanne, Auriol, La Bouillasse, Greasque, of February to April 1867; the commitment shown by the miners of Fuveau to the IWA abroad. From 1867 on the essential activity of the French sections was solidarity action, building support for these strikes abroad.
- In Belgium, the strike of the Charleroi miners and its repression by the army resulted in a strengthening of the IWA; the strike of the Verviers weavers, who wanted to place their solidarity funds with the IWA; the strike of the Antwerp sail makers given monetary support by the IWA. The IWA was making its presence felt in every industrialised area.
- In Geneva, a strike of building workers was declared in a favourable period of full employment, it was well led and ended in success. International solidarity was effective. A delegate at the Brussels Congress of the IWA declared: 'The bourgeoisie, although they are in a republic, have been more malevolent than elsewhere, but workers held out well. Before the strike there were just two sections in Geneva, now there are 24 – and there are 4,000 members.'

International labour solidarity – the cornerstone of IWA life – was a theme constantly promoted in collectivist literature. Bakunin insisted that international solidarity was incompatible with political participation in elections within the remit of the national state. Often the IWA recommended moderation, but it came to be involved in a greater number of violent struggles. Its very existence, buoyed up by some initial victories created a serial phenomenon – a cumulative effect. *Violent repression pushed workers into organising for themselves.* Moderates lost ground with each army intervention and little by little the International became more radical; this radicalisation, it should be noted, was not the result of some ideological debate, but of grounded, practical, international solidarity coupled, simultaneously, with an experience of struggle. Indubitably there was a fissure in the international labour movement and the opposition between Bakunin and Marx was the expression but not the cause of this fissure. It can never be emphasised sufficiently that anarchist theory, as Bakunin formulated it between 1868 and his death in 1876, was largely founded on his observation of the struggles of workers in these times.

If after the Basel IWA Congress of September 1869 it appeared that revolutionary proletarian action was needed to resolve social problems, thus far nothing had been settled as to which practices the working class should choose to rely on. The statutes of the IWA, written in 1864 by Marx, were sufficiently ambiguous that all parts of the labour movement could join. The three years between the Basel IWA Congress and that of The Hague (1872) were crucial and witnessed the creation of German Social-Democracy, the Paris Commune and the birth of revolutionary anarchism. Struggles between tendencies became more pronounced in these three years.

There had been a strong collectivist majority at the Basel Congress. The discussion of the principle items brought out opposing ideological theses. The 'Marxist' propositions on rights of inheritance were rejected by 37 votes to 19, which gives an idea of the balance of forces present. A change to the agenda was proposed, to add the question of taking power within the remit of national states.[57] Bakunin replied that the International through its resolutions had declared that social and political questions were intimately linked, but by definition, these political questions were perforce international rather than national. [See appendix for extracts from this discussion.]

The problem of practical ways and means for the proletarian revolution could no longer be avoided. From this congress onwards conflict erupted. On the one hand there were those headed by Marx who wanted to transform the International into national political parties. Each party would have its own hierarchy, and would present electoral candidates with the objective of taking power. On the other hand there were those, with Bakunin as their main spokesman, who believed that an egalitarian society could result only from a collective takeover of the means of production by organised workers. What would subsequently be called the 'Anti-Authoritarian' tendency did not appear in the IWA before 1868. In later years some libertarians would accept the idea of continuity between the first Proudhonists and Anti-Authoritarian Internationalists. In reality collectivists were in conflict with the first Proudhonists (who were partisans of private property), and the Proudhonists were overcome little by little. Bakunin himself supported Marx in the struggle against Proudhonist 'reformists'. The new generation of Proudhonists who now participated in the life of the International, or became active at the time of the Commune, were revolutionary collectivists and would oppose reformist Proudhonists. *Revolutionary anarchism would establish itself in its fight against Proudhonist reformism as much as in its fight against Marxism.*

Anarchism is often attached to the name of Bakunin, but the real influence of the latter has often been obscured. Before his entry into the

International, Bakunin's positions were generalisations and matters of principle. It is not Bakunin who orientated the Anti-Authoritarian tendency of the IWA through his ideas, rather it was the opposite. Bakunin's texts dating from the few years before his entry into the IWA contained vague statements of principle with a libertarian character, but these remained vague. His thinking about strategy and organisation became clear only after he joined the IWA. Bakunin did not 'invent' the practices of the current that he represented, he described them. Collectivists who aired their views at the international congress had not waited for Bakunin. But it would also be wrong to underestimate Bakunin's role, or that of his close entourage, in working to systematise and spread the good news of the International. What Bakunin observed in the real International confirmed his intuitions, and in Bakunin the Anti-Authoritarian current found someone who could clearly express their views. It was the work of Bakunin's entourage alone that resulted in the creation of the Spanish Federation.

Before he joined the IWA, the Russian revolutionary already had a certain number of ideas (derived essentially from Proudhon) developed in the programmes of various clandestine organisations. Observation of labour movement practice confirmed his ideas. So there was an ongoing and reciprocal dialogue between theory and practice. If Fanelli, someone close to Bakunin, succeeded so well when he went to Spain to develop the International, it was because the practices of the IWA corresponded to the expectations of the Spanish proletariat, but it was *also* because these ideas of the International were clearly formulated.

British trade unions and German Social-Democracy were each preoccupied with their own national problems. So, on the eve of the Commune the federations which were developing and functioning, paid their dues and participated regularly in congress debates. The only federations on which the General Council could rely were the Belgian, Spanish and Swiss and (to a lesser extent) French federations; all termed 'Bakuninists', they continued to send reports and practiced internationalism. Independent of political parties these federations all had their own organisation: sections, trade federations, and federal councils. They developed in close relation to workplace movements, which they tended to organise, in relation to labour associations which they coordinated, as in Belgium, or with which they completely identified, as in Spain (the Spanish CNT, with its million members in 1936, would be the inheritor of the Bakuninist Federation of the International). The latter, declared its anarchist identity immediately, developed at a tremendous rate and soon organised the Spanish working class into trade associations, and local federations. It practiced the control of responsible positions and mandates, as well as direct democracy – something that it alone appeared to respect scrupulously. By 1870 it had as many members as the rest of the IWA put together.

IWA Anti-Authoritarians perceived the International as a vast mass organisation, founded on federalism and internal democracy, offering its structure to the proletariat and poor peasantry. It needed to develop on its own ground, independently from bourgeois organisations. It saw its work as:

1. The destruction of state power through an insurrection of the armed proletariat, organised through sections, trade federations and local IWA federations;
2. The use of its own structures – trade federations and local federations – as a matrix for a future libertarian and federalist society.

This was an agenda for what became anarcho-syndicalism. In these times the 'Anti-Authoritarian' term signified 'anti-bureaucratic' and appeared to distinguish sections and federations opposed to the bureaucratic centralisation of the International operated by Marx and his entourage. What was at issue was not bureaucratisation restricted to growing complexity in the management of current affairs but a bureaucratisation that was intent on a preserving its own power. Thus, John Hales, a member of the British committee of the International, spelt out his vexation faced with the practice of particular officials:

> Someone who did not know the defunct General Council can have no idea of the manner in which facts were distorted and of how information which might have informed us was intercepted. Never was there a secret conspiracy whose activities were more occult than that of the ex-General Council. Thus when I was general secretary of this Council, *I never knew and I was never able to obtain the addresses of federations on the [European] continent*. Another example: one day the English Federal Council received a very important letter from the Spanish Federal Council, but the signatory of this letter, citizen Anselmo Lorenzo, had forgotten to give his address in this letter; so the English Federal Council asked citizen Engels, who at the time was the corresponding secretary of the General Council for Spain, to give it the address[58] of the Spanish Federal Council: citizen Engels formally refused. Later he also made the same refusal in relation to the Federal Council of Lisbon.'[59]

The reader reads correctly: Hales, who for several months had been general secretary of the IWA General Council, could not have access to the addresses of federations on the continent because Engels prevented it.[60] Obviously the officialdom that federalists fought against was not something they imagined. In a period of tremendous intensification of European class struggle, in which there were mass mobilisations of the most radical fraction of the European proletariat, the directing body of the IWA attempted to construct national electoral parties. Because a part of the latter was out of its control it actually blocked the work of the International. The General Council perceived only very tardily what was happening on the continent, namely that the situation was unravelling and would end up in a war. Marxism now seemed incapable of keeping up with reality – in the shape of the movement of labouring classes – as it had done up to the Basel Congress. Hereafter Marxism, an ideology elaborated twenty years earlier in very different circumstances, imposed on the working class a division into national blocks mired in alliances-against-nature with ruling-class political organisms, in complete contradiction of internationalism. Bakunin explained this very clearly:

> I do not hesitate to say that the Marxists' cuddling up with radicalism – be it reformist or revolutionary – can result only in the demoralisation and disorganisation of the nascent power of the proletariat. ... To whoever might doubt this we have only to show what is happening today. In Germany organs of Socialist democracy sing joyous hymns as they see a congress of bourgeois professors of political economy recommend the high and paternal protection of the state to the German proletariat. In those parts of Switzerland where the Marxist programme prevails, ... the International has succumbed – to the point of being nothing more than some sort of electoral post-box serving the radical bourgeoisie.[61]

The Marxist historian Franz Mehring adds in his biography of Marx that 'wherever national workers' parties formed the International began to break up'.[62] In contrast, the IWA's internationalist solidarity was palpable in its living sections and federations.

Action and organisation

Questions about means, as to what course should be taken, always finish up in choices about forms of organisation. With the foundation of the International, with many workers from across Europe joining together, the matrix of patriotism, religion and politics which for centuries had impeded the masses from coming to an understanding of their oppression began to disappear. What impeded their self-liberation now was their 'lack of organisation, the difficulty of coming to agreements and of acting in concert'.[63] The people had immense spontaneous strength, incomparably greater than that of the state. For this reason the primary condition for a popular victory was 'the unity or the organisation of popular forces.[64] This is far removed from the commonly presented petty caricature of Bakunin as a 'spontaneist'.

Organisation was not just some technical necessity, without which the overthrow of an exploitative regime becomes impossible; it was essential for all activity. When one wanted to organise a force, one had first of all to establish clearly one's aims, as 'the very nature and form of one's own organisation depends essentially on the nature of one's aims'.[65]

This is a capital phrase for understanding Bakunin's theory of organisation. Organisation, being linked to a particular goal, cannot contradict that goal; it must contain the goal, it must be of the same nature. The organisational form of the international proletariat in struggle against capitalist exploitation is *at the same time* the form of future society. There is no utopianism here: the form of organisation of a society without exploitation is *deduced* from the manner in which workers organise to struggle.

> Certainly, there is sufficient spontaneous strength amongst the people, indubitably the strength of the latter is much greater than that of the government and that of ruling classes within it; but lacking organisation, spontaneous force is no real force. It is not in a [fit] state to sustain a protracted struggle against forces that are much weaker but much better organised. It is on this undeniable superiority of organised force over elemental popular force that all the power of the state resides. ... Thus, the [real] question is not one of knowing if the people are capable of an uprising, but rather whether they are ready to form an organisation which will assure the success of a revolt, a victory which is not ephemeral, but durable and definitive.[66]

Such thinking can be found again and again across hundreds of pages of Bakunin's writings, from 1867-68 until his death in 1876. They can hardly be cited under the heading of 'clandestine activity'.

The Alliance
Between 1865-67, his years in Italy, and 1867-69 in Switzerland, there was a period in Bakunin's political evolution in which he thought it was

possible to draw bourgeois radicals towards socialism. In September 1867 there took place in Geneva the first congress of the League for Peace and Liberty convened at the initiative of European democrats and pacifists concerned with the threat of war between Prussia and France. The years 1866-7 had been lively ones, engendering strong international tensions. In April 1866 Bismarck presented a projected constitution for a North German Confederation excluding Austria. War broke out between the two countries over control of Schleswig-Holstein on 7 June. On the 15th the Prussians invaded Saxony, then Hanover and Hesse. On 20 June Italy declared war on Austria. On 3 July the Prussians crushed the Austrians at Sadowa. Napoleon III undertook not to intervene in the conflict in exchange for compensation (Luxembourg), which was refused him, creating tensions between France and Prussia. The North German Confederation was finally constituted on 16 April 1867, radically changing the balance of power in Europe.

It was in this context that the first Congress for Peace and Liberty took place, and the League for Peace and Liberty was formed. The congress was organised in Geneva by the French pacifist Charles Lemonnier (1806-1891) and by a French jurist Emile Acollas (1826-1891) with the support of many personalities including John Stuart Mill, Élisée Reclus, Elié Reclus, Victor Hugo, Giuseppe Garibaldi, Louis Blanc, Edgar Quinet, Jules Favre and Alexander Herzen. Ten thousand Europeans signed petitions in support of the congress, which brought together six thousand who were concerned to create conditions for a political and economic peace between peoples, and a United States of Europe. Bakunin saw an opportunity to use the grand stage and participated in its first two congresses. He joined the organisation, he said, in order to 'promote socialist ideas'. He became a member of the central committee of the organisation which in June 1867 voted to support a public declaration of principles. Although the League was composed for the most part of representatives of the radical and liberal bourgeoisie, this declaration contained points with a progressive content which, given the context of the times, should not be underestimated. So, the League asserted that 'religion, a matter of individual conscience, should be eliminated from political institutions and from public education so that churches should not be able to impede free social development'. The League also called for the constitution of a United States of Europe founded on 'popular institutions linked together in a federation, allowing equality of individual rights and with autonomy for communes and provinces in respect of their particular interests'. The Russian revolutionary had had a third paragraph adopted that called for radical change in the social and economic system to bring about 'an equitable sharing of wealth, work, leisure and education as an essential condition for the abolition of wage-labour and the enfranchisement of the working classes'. The text concluded with a rejection of all attempts at reform 'made by any despotic power'. However, there remained the business of having this text adopted by congress. At this particular moment, Bakunin's idea was to bring the League for Peace and Liberty and the IWA closer. He was admitted into the Geneva section of the latter in July 1868. Naturally Bakunin's project failed and he resigned at once, taking with him 84 other members – which suggests that everything had been prepared – and, on 28 October 1868, he founded the International Alliance for Socialist Democracy, which brought together the principal members of the secret society he had founded in 1864, the International Fraternity. This fraternity had itself played a decisive role in the diffusion of socialism in Italy. On 21 November the Geneva section of the Alliance was founded.

Marx, when he was put in the picture, wrote to Serno, a Russian refugee in Geneva, to obtain information. Serno was close to Bakunin and updated him on developments. Then on 22 December 1868, the latter wrote to Marx, a letter in which he paid homage to his activities over twenty years. He recalled that he had said his 'public and solemn farewells' to the bourgeois members of the League and affirmed that henceforth he would know 'no other society, no other company than the world of workers…' He added: 'my country (patrie) now is the International of which you are one of the principal founders. You see, dear friend, that I am your disciple, and proud to be so.'

So Bakunin's real and exclusive commitment to the workers' movement, which defined his activity as properly 'anarchist', is to be dated from the end of 1868. It is symptomatic that things should be done in the form of letter to Marx. The programme of the newly constituted Alliance was sent along with this letter. Bakunin hoped that the General Council of the IWA would accept its application for membership and that was the real aim of his approach. If Marx had written to Serno, it was because the latter had attacked Bakunin previously. This is apparent from a letter of Marx to Engels: 'I thought to use this young man to inform me about Bakunin …' and he complained: 'That Russian – Serno – did nothing other than to rush over to communicate my letter to B[akunin] and B[akunin] rose to it and made a sentimental approach.'[67] Not for a second was Marx taken in by Bakunin's protestations of loyalty. The IWA rejected the Alliance's application; the latter dissolved itself on 22 June 1869 and its sections became sections of the IWA.

In September 1868, a revolution in Spain sent Queen Isabella packing. After resigning from the League for Peace and Democracy, Bakunin returned to Geneva. There he dedicated himself to promoting the principles of the International. On 21 October 1868, at his instigation, the central committee of the Geneva IWA sent out *An Address of the Geneva Central Committee to the Workers of Spain*. Many points from the programme of the Alliance were included. One of its key points was that: 'Liberty without political equality, and political equality without economic equality, is nothing but a snare.'

> In Europe and America, the disinherited of this society, having all to defend a common cause and understanding the necessity of unity have founded the International Workers' Association – across frontiers – and despite the frontiers created by our oppressors. The goal of this great association is the triumph of the cause of Labour over privilege, monopoly capital and hereditary property (an inequitable institution guaranteed by the state as an institution fostering irrational chaos[68] a body that perpetuates unequal relations and social disorder) …
>
> Spanish brothers – come, join our work one and all… do not let yourselves be deceived by those who eternally exploit revolution: generals, bourgeois democrats…
>
> Above all, remember that it is only through their own strength that the people extract reforms, and that never, in any country, do ruling classes make voluntary concessions.[69]

Giuseppe Fanelli, one of the Alliance's founder, travelled to Spain in November. Thus the Madrid section of the IWA was created, followed in May 1869 by another in Barcelona. The nearly-simultaneous creation of Spanish sections of the IWA – such pretty seedlings for the International – and the deliberate withdrawal from the League for Peace, may lead one to believe that it was no coincidence. Rather the attempt to shape the League – in a clearly socialist sense, was made with no illusions, as a last honourable skirmish directed against the radical bourgeoisie.

In Geneva, one week after the drawing up of *An Address of the Geneva Central Committee to the Workers of Spain*, the Central Bureau of the Alliance for Socialist Democracy was created: a local group of 85 members 'of both sexes', as James Guillaume notes. What was envisaged was the coming together of 'the most advanced elements, ready to discuss theoretically the principles of socialism'. James Guillaume felt that the project was moribund from birth. It was, he said:

> A small set, making an effort to draw the mass of workers into public meetings – but failing; moreover a body that occasioned no little distrust

and jealousy and was fated – some months on – to provide certain anglers in troubled waters with a welcome pretext to ferment discord in the Geneva International – serving well those intriguers who wanted to exploit or destroy the nascent organisation of the party of Labour.

From the very start a disagreement appeared within the Alliance. The French and Italians hoped that it would have a public presence and that it should have collective members. Bakunin was wholly opposed to such positions: he hoped to preserve a clandestine form of organisation with individual members. He warned friends against a reaction from the General Council.

The Geneva Alliance group applied to the central committee of the Geneva sections for membership of the International. The matter was examined by the General Council in London in December. It was at this moment that Bakunin sent Marx his letter declaring he was his 'disciple'. The General Council rejected the Alliance's application and drew up a resolution explaining its reasoning. The argument was more or less the same as that which had motivated the IWA's positions in regard to the League. Marx decided that this letter should not be published, and thereby inaugurated the system of 'confidential communications' which [subsequently] would become normal practice.

When the negative response of the London General Council became known in Geneva, it became clear that the Geneva group of the Alliance could not remain a part of the local federation of Geneva sections. James Guillaume wrote that

> ... it was obvious that the reasoning employed by the Brussels Congress [of the IWA] in relation to the League for Peace should also apply with equal force to the International Alliance for Socialist Democracy: given that this Alliance had the same aims and principles as the IWA it had no reason for a specific international organisation to exist.[70]

This was an argument that Bakunin was all the more ready to recognise given that, in Bern, he had sought to avoid the Alliance appearing as a rival organisation to the IWA. This is how Bakunin tells the story:

> When the matter was read out within the Bureau of the Alliance, no one rose up with more vehemence against it [The General Council] than feisty old J. Philip Becker. First of all he declared that these resolutions were completely illegal, contrary to the letter and spirit of the International's

statutes; adding that we had the right and the duty to disregard it, he called the General Council a bunch of imbeciles, unable to achieve anything themselves, wishing only to prevent others acting. The two members who most resolutely continued to argue against him and for the necessity of coming to an understanding with the General Council were Perron and Bakunin.[71] Both recognised that the assertions of the General Council against the regulations of the Alliance were perfectly reasonable; since, given these regulations the Alliance would have formed a new international association within the IWA, independent of the IWA.

Note that in these resolutions – the only ones so far agreed and published by the General Council, against the Alliance, it was only the regulations of the latter that were attacked.[72] The matter of the programme [of the Alliance], was not questioned, moreover these were later plainly reproduced in the statutes of the [Geneva] Section of the Alliance, which were unanimously approved by the General Council.

After a long debate it was decided unanimously by the Bureau of the Alliance that Perron, in the name of all of them, should get in touch with the London General Council. Following this decision, comrade Charles Perron wrote a letter either to citizen Eccarius, or to citizen Jung, in which, after frankly declaring the situation and the true goals of the Alliance and having set out what members of the Alliance had already done for the cause of labour in Italy, France and Spain, as well as in Geneva, he asked him to put the following proposal – in the name of the Central Bureau of the Alliance – to the General Council in London: that the Alliance should dissolve itself as an international organisation, that its Central Bureau which represented this International, should cease to exist; would the General Council recognise the sections founded by members of the Alliance in Switzerland, Spain, Italy and France, *with the programme of the Alliance*, as regular sections of the IWA, henceforth preserving no common links other than a programme, and renouncing all other international organisation other than that which they would have as part of the greater IWA? On such conditions the Central Bureau promised to spare no effort to persuade the Alliance sections already established in various countries to renounce everything in their constitutions that stood in contradiction to the statutes of the International.

So, without delay, the Central Bureau wrote along these lines to all sections of the Alliance, advising them to recognise the justice of the resolutions of the General Council. I should note in passing that this proposition of the Central Bureau found its greatest opposition in the group in Geneva, precisely among members who today so relentlessly combat and insult us: Becker, Guétat, Duval, H. Perret and many others whose faces I recall if not their names. Becker was the greatest recalcitrant. On several occasions he declared that only the Alliance group represented the true International in Geneva and that the General Council – in rejecting us – was failing in all its duties, was exceeding its powers, and this proved just one thing – that it was incurable stupid. After Becker, Guétat and Duval were the most violent, they always had little stereotypical speeches on revolution in their pocket. Mr H. Perret showed greater caution ... but shared their views. Finally it was agreed by the Geneva group to wait for the definitive reply of the General Council.

The Bureau of the Alliance decided, concluded Bakunin, 'to conform to the views of the General Council, which appeared just and right'.[73] In this affair, one sees Bakunin as a moderating element.

At the time of the Brussels IWA Congress strong ties of friendship had formed between Belgian and Swiss militants, and the latter had revealed the Alliance's positions. When the General Council's decision was known these militants sent a letter, in the name of the Belgian General Council, to the Alliance in Geneva. A third of the letter was taken up by a reaffirmation of the Belgians' agreement with the content of the Alliance programme. 'So it is not your programme that we attack. What we cannot approve, what we regret, is that in the pursuit of this programme, you have thought it needful to found a separate branch rather than remaining mixed in within the great popular mass – which composes the International Workers' Association.' Bakunin had already grasped the necessity of dissolving the organisation when the Alliance of Geneva received this correspondence from Belgium, dated 16 January 1869. But the Belgian General Council's text is of interest because from it Bakunin would draw lessons and reasoning that he would integrate into his own thinking. He had learned quickly from his mistakes.

So the Belgians' letter reproached the Alliance for wishing to 'make a step forward, posting a programme that was more advanced, more radical perhaps, than that of certain sections'. However, Bakunin would relentlessly defend the idea that the IWA did need to develop progressively its own programme through debate within its varied structures. The letter reproached the Alliance for wanting to 'bring about division within our IWA'. Bakunin would insist on the real unity of workers, formed through everyday struggle against capital. The letter declared that if the Alliance developed 'a particular programme, tomorrow, some others will do the same'. Bakunin would go on to say that the multiplication of programmes would bring with it: 'As many Internationals as there are different programmes.' The letter reproached members of the Alliance for setting themselves up as 'moral guides for other workers'. Bakunin would struggle against those pretending to be guides of the proletariat: he would declare that he was 'the general enemy of all possible forms of *well-meaning* tutelage exercised over the popular masses by *intelligent* minorities, from low to high'.[74] The Belgians' letter concluded:

> We must declare, notwithstanding the special friendship that links us to those we met at the Brussels Congress, that we unreservedly approve the resolutions agreed by the General Council of London in respect of your Alliance.

This letter is particularly important. In the years that followed Bakunin would take in all the themes it touched on, and would thoroughly develop them. One might say that Bakunin's anarchism was unblocked and released by this letter, from the Belgian General Council – in which César De Paepe played a crucial role – more than by his own letter to Marx.[75] In January 1869 there took place a Congress of the International Fraternity, which had been created in 1864, and which ended with the withdrawal of Bakunin. The Fraternity was dissolved shortly afterwards.[76] Among the reasons for its dissolution, it appears that there were incidents provoked by Elié Reclus and Aristide Rey, which had occurred in the course of Fanelli's journey to Spain and which had obstructed his mission.

> Some of our [friends] went to Spain, and, instead of proceeding to bring together socialist elements, which – as we know from material proofs – are already quite numerous and even quite developed in towns and rural areas of this country, they have become greatly engaged with radicalism and a little with bourgeois socialism. ... These brothers, forgetting the goals that they were pursuing and that they had been intended to pursue, have embraced the poor cause of bourgeois republicanism which is agitating Spain with so much noise and so little effect...

The dissolution of the Fraternity did not trouble Bakunin unduly. He believed that it was 'formed of men who for the most part believed themselves so little committed, that they have thought that they were right to act in opposition to those duties, which were incumbent on each brother in accordance with the Fraternity's principles and statutes', – a reference to Reclus and Rey. The organisation was not an end in itself, it was only a means. The time for the Fraternity had passed; serious matters were in progress and, as we shall see, Bakunin was right to give priority to Spain and to be preoccupied with events there.

On 20 March 1869, the General Council replied to the Central Bureau of the Alliance that it had no objection to it developing its own programme and that sections of the Alliance could transform themselves into IWA sections. Nevertheless, this letter made an exception regarding the expression 'equalisation of classes', suggesting that this was a slip in place of 'abolition of classes', and it requested that this error be rectified. The Central Bureau dissolved itself and Alliance groups were transformed into regular IWA sections. In April 1869 the Geneva section modified its statutes. The new statutes included in their first part 'The General Statutes of the IWA adopted at the Geneva Congress of 1866' and were followed by 'The programme of the section of the Alliance of Socialist Democracy in Geneva'.

Article One of the regulations of the section set out that the 'Geneva group of the Alliance for Socialist Democracy, wishing to belong exclusively to the great IWA, constitutes a section of the International, under the name of the *Alliance for Socialist Democracy*, but with no organisation, bureau, committee or congress, other than those of the IWA'.

On 28 July 1869, the General Council of London unanimously recognised the Alliance section in Geneva as a regular section of the International. On 31 July the Alliance section decided to send dues for 104 members to London. It remained for the new section to request its admission into the hostile Geneva Cantonal IWA Federation which, on 16 August, resolved to reject its application. On 13 August Bakunin had announced to the committee of the Alliance section that he intended to leave Geneva immediately after the Basel IWA Congress.

There had been a marked deterioration in the Geneva IWA section. The social composition of the section was very mixed. At first a fundamental part of it was drawn from workers of the 'Fabrique' – this was the name applied to clock and watch workers who were very close to the bourgeoisie, and they were in favour of electoral alliances with the latter. Within the same section were poorly qualified construction workers, mostly super-exploited foreigners. The former disrespected the latter and would not let them forget that they were not Swiss citizens.

> The circle[77] had little by little become an exclusively Genevan institution, administered and governed only by natives of Geneva, and therein construction workers, mostly foreigners, were considered, and ended up considering themselves as foreigners. Often, too often, the Geneva citizens belonging to the Fabrique made them listen to such words as:

'Here we are at home, you are just our guests'. The spirit of Geneva, a bourgeois-radical spirit, one excessively narrow as is well-known, ended up completely dominating everything – there was room neither for international thinking, nor for international fraternity. The result was that, little by little, construction workers, tired of this subordinate position, ended up no longer attending the circle, which today has become an exclusively Genevan institution.[78]

The most exploited workers quite naturally became close to those IWA militants who would listen to them, and thus was justified the existence of the Alliance as a section of the International. This was the initial cause of hostility from the Fabrique: its leaders began to worry when they realised that the Alliance was not content to be some 'sort of academy' and that it did not intend to 'develop abstract pure theory' only, but rather to study the principles and the workings of the International. They were concerned when they saw the Alliance developing some resonance among construction workers – this threatened to diminish their influence.

Thus the Geneva International harboured two tendencies, one of 'bourgeois radicalism and socialism represented by the Fabrique', and one of 'revolutionary socialism drawing on the support and healthy instincts of construction workers'.[79] These two tendencies were in conflict in every assembly, with the revolutionary socialists enjoying a slight predominance given that the construction workers had the greater numbers. The counterpart of this situation was that leaders of the Fabrique had little taste for general assemblies, where some of their intrigues might be undermined, and preferred secret committees. General assemblies, however, did not achieve a great deal. For much of the time it was the same leaders who spoke for each camp, 'repeating the same stereotypical speeches'; the majority were silent. 'There were only superficial discussions, happily or not so happily the dramatic or sentimental side of things was addressed, whilst the real and deeper problems were not touched on. Often there were dazzling fireworks, but the public was left without warmth or explanation; rather, people were left totally in the dark.' This explains why Bakunin, who did not hesitate when it came to speaking in larger forums, preferred meetings with twenty or thirty persons. Bakunin's description of the bureaucratic side of the Geneva IWA is of interest in the sense that it is perhaps the first of its type, and because it highlights that there are some surprising constants in the labour movement.

At first Geneva's central section had also involved construction workers. It was the original founding section of the International in Geneva and was by definition an all-trades structure. Some workers from the Fabrique joined. 'For some considerable time it was the construction workers' unfettered, instinctive socialism that dominated. It was a truly united section, fraternity was not an empty word, but reality.'

The construction workers' strike in 1868 owed its success, as Bakunin recognised very readily, to the support of workers of the Fabrique, who then entered en masse into the central section. They had brought with them: 'Their Genevan, radical-bourgeois, political spirit.' Thereafter the central section was divided into two parties. The Genevans were at first in the minority, but, says Bakunin, they 'were organised, whilst the construction workers were completely disorganised'. Furthermore construction workers were 'paralysed' by the gratitude they felt they owed to the 'citizen-workers of the Fabrique' for the decisive role they had played in their construction strike. For a time there was equilibrium between the currents, but little by little trades' sections came together (in reality trade unions). Lacking the means to pay dues to their trade sections and to the central section (the [rough] equivalent of a trades' council), construction workers retreated into their trade union. So the central section became 'a section exclusively for citizens of Geneva'. The International was composed of two structural forms: the central all-trades section corresponding roughly to local or district trades' councils, and trade sections corresponding to unions. The observation of the functioning of these two structures, and of how they played different but complementary roles, would be a crucial factor in the development of Bakunin's theory of organisation.

Given local circumstances in Geneva, construction workers were confined to their trade sections and they only came together in these to deal with current business.

> In these meetings there was no space for the discussion of principles; and worse, little by little these trades sections became habituated to restricting their role and activity to that of controlling spending, leaving other matters to the care of their committees, which became more or less permanent; and omnipotent with the natural consequence that sections became non-entities – and committees decided things.

These committees became composed of members who could not be dismissed, such that they ended up seeing themselves as 'so many collective dictatorships within the International', holding their meetings behind closed doors, making decisions on all matters, forming 'an occult, invisible government, more or less unaccountable to the greater International in

Geneva'. So, Bakunin provides a first-hand analysis of the phenomenon of bureaucratisation in a labour structure, observed practically from the inside.

The Alliance set itself the task of combatting this tendency to make of the International 'a political instrument for the bourgeois radicalism in Geneva'. Bakunin rejected accusations of sectarian behaviour, affirming that the action of the Alliance group prioritised 'public discussion of the International's principles'. 'Meeting once a week, inviting all to its discussions, working precisely to make those speak who, in meetings of the central section and General Assemblies, had always been silent.' The central section was displeased by such egalitarian manners. As for the construction workers' section, the Alliance section gave them the means '*to formulate their thinking and to express their concerns,* no doubt greatly displeasing the Fabrique'.[80] Bakunin added: 'It achieved more, it gave them the means to understand themselves, so that somehow, in a short time, the Alliance section developed as a small convinced workers' group with real unity among themselves'. Moreover there was another reason behind the 'determined antipathy of the ambitious Fabrique leaders towards the Alliance section':

> Through its programme, and through all later development of its programme, the Alliance had declared against any adulterous marriage of proletarian revolutionary socialism[81] with bourgeois radicalism. It took as a fundamental principle the abolition of the state, with all its juridical and political ramifications. This was worthless for the radical bourgeois men of Geneva – who had experienced the fiasco of the November 1868 elections and who had begun to think of using the International as an instrument for their struggle and success. The same obtained for certain leaders of the Fabrique in Geneva; they aspired to nothing less than coming to power – with the help of the International.

The *Rapport sur l'Alliance* was a document that explained the role of the group within the International. It showed, in the face of the intrigues by Marx and his entourage against Bakunin, that the Alliance was no fractional organisation, and that it had had a decisive role helping to expand the IWA. Bakunin also endeavoured to recap the group's activity, particularly in other European countries. He recalled that members of the Alliance had founded the first sections of the International in Italy and Spain: Gambuzzi in and around Naples, Friscia in Sicily, Fanelli in Madrid and Barcelona. The programme of the Alliance was accepted in Lyons, Marseilles and Paris. And, says Bakunin, note well:

all these comrades far from wishing to organise hostile, separate sections, or ones outside the International, strictly obeyed its statutes; and in the interest of the [better] organisation of the power of labour they everywhere recommended more than was demanded by its statutes, the most rigorous subordination of these new sections to the central direction of the London based General Council.[82]

It was thanks to the influence of the Alliance 'that the first frankly revolutionary socialist voices were raised in Geneva', said Bakunin, referring to the *Address of the Geneva Central Committee to Spanish Workers*. It was also through Alliance influence, and despite the Fabrique's intrigues, that Brosset, representing construction workers 'was elected President of the Federal Council instituted by the Romande[83] Congress held in Geneva in January 1869, and that the majority of that council was composed of non-Genevan workers'. It was through Alliance influence that the journal *l'Egalité*, 'the first frankly revolutionary socialist organ of francophone Switzerland', was created, and that later the programme of *le Progrès* of Le Locle was modified.

In a word, and without any exaggeration, one can say that it was the timely activity of the Alliance which for the first time set out a frankly revolutionary socialist programme in Geneva and constructed a chasm between the proletariat and bourgeoisie in Geneva, a chasm which all the International intriguers were unable to bridge.

When the General Council in London made known that the Alliance had been given conditional admittance into the International, these conditions were accepted and the Alliance sections established in various countries were dissolved. The Naples section and the majority of its members joined the IWA individually, as did the Spanish and French sections. Thus, said Bakunin, the International Alliance of Socialist Democracy died:

through a voluntary death. Wishing, above all, the triumph of the great cause of the proletariat and considering the IWA as the only means to achieve its goal; it made an end to itself, not as some concession in mean spirit, but rather in the spirit of fraternity, because it was convinced there was complete justice in the resolutions that the London General Council had published against it, in December 1868.[84]

Lastly, in the battle within the Geneva International between the 'bourgeois-radical' and the 'revolutionary socialist' tendencies there was an important programmatic foundation. In their publications, the revolutionary socialists, or collectivists, talked of the 'abolition of political and patriotic frontiers, and of states', of the abolition of the right of inheritance, of the organisation of property and collective working. Such things did not suit the worker citizens of Geneva: 'all this could not serve as a bridge to unite in just one party in Geneva the radical bourgeois with the internationalist [IWA] bourgeois.' says Bakunin in *le Rapport sur l'Alliance*.[85] Intrigues amongst the Fabrique section committees resulted in the resignation of Brosset – the representative of the construction workers – from the presidency of the [Romande] Federal Council.

Two questions – on collective property and on rights of inheritance – were to figure on the agenda for the upcoming Basel Congress of the IWA: 'two questions which had the effect of arousing the worst of tempers amongst the leaders and star performers of the Geneva Fabrique.' The question of collective property had been discussed once before, at the Brussels Congress, to the annoyance of representatives of the Fabrique. This time they were resolved to prevent the discussion of these two matters in Basel.

> For them, given their political position, this was a necessity. It was not merely something that they needed in their heart and soul. They had come to a firm understanding with the radical bourgeoisie and their allies in Geneva. They worked on all the sections that were really Genevan, i.e. those of the Fabrique's citizen workers, to organise them around the flag of the radical party, for the forthcoming elections, due in November.[86]

Obviously from this perspective any discussion of the question of inheritance or of collective property was something to be prevented, to avoid 'upsetting the sensitivities of their new allies – the radical bourgeoisie of Geneva'. So they arranged that commissions should be nominated to prepare reports on all points coming up on the congress's agenda – except these two burning issues. In a popular assembly, the Alliance played the spoilsport and had commissions nominated to prepare reports in time. The collectivists had taken care to mobilise all their supporters, and so the venue, the Temple Unique,[87] was full of construction workers. Fabrique orators followed one another on the tribune saying that 'for workers to consider such questions was scandalous, it was a useless waste of time, [or] a subversive activity... practical and achievable matters should be considered, such as co-operation with the bourgeoisie, etc.' Nevertheless, they were defeated.

By an immense majority the General Assembly decided that it would designate committees without delay for these two annoying issues – Bakunin was elected onto the committee on inheritance, and Robin to that dealing with collective property.

The reply of the Fabrique was not slow in coming. It had been decided that the costs of sending delegates to the Basel Congress would be shared, which was 'obviously in the interest of the construction workers' sections, these sections being much less well-endowed than the Fabrique sections'. In the ensuing popular assembly representatives of the Fabrique made it known that they would only share expenses if these two controversial issues – inheritance and collective property – were supressed. The Alliance's orators made great play, protesting indignantly:

> We went up to the tribune, to explain to the construction workers, that in the making of such a proposition they were being insulted, their rights and freedom of conscience was being attacked; that it would be better to send just one delegate, or none, rather than to send five or more on the basis of the unacceptable conditions that would be imposed on them for the sake of the Fabrique sections. The orators of reaction then returned to the tribune singing that eternal refrain of unity that was so necessary, if the power of the working class was to be built; they reminded construction workers that they owed eternal gratitude to the Genevan citizens of the Fabrique for the support that they had given them during the great strike in the spring. They warned them against certain foreigners, who had come to sow division in the International in Geneva. Brosset, Robin, Bakunin and others replied: there could be no foreigners in the International, that gratitude and unity were no doubt very lovely things, but such things should not create servitude; and that it would be better to separate, rather than to become a slave. On this occasion too, victory was ours. There was an immense majority in favour of these issues [being addressed] and for committees [to prepare discussions].[88]

In the end the Fabrique sent just one delegate mandated to abstain from voting on these two controversial issues' while the construction workers, together with shoemakers and tailors, sent three with a mandate to vote for these resolutions. The Alliance section nominated a Spaniard, Gaspard Sentiñon, as its representative; he was also the delegate of the Barcelona section. Bakunin had a mandate from the Lyons silk workers, who had recently joined the IWA, and from the Naples mechanics section.

Before the Basel Congress there was another matter that made the worker-citizens of Geneva look ridiculous. A commission on comprehensive education[89] had been charged with making a report and a man named Cambassedes had been given the task of preparing it. He was a member of the bourgeois Radical Party and was not even a member of the International, but he was Chief Inspector of Schools in Geneva. His report was written in an eminently bourgeois spirit. It defended a separation in schools by [social] class, says Bakunin, 'on the charming and touching pretext that the bourgeoisie would never consent to have its children sent to schools frequented by the children of the people'. The rest was in the same vein. Fritz Heng, charged with reading the report – and not having had knowledge of it first – stopped in the middle of his reading and naively declared that it had no value and could not suit the International.

Apart from activities with contacts in various countries – Spain, France and Italy – the Alliance, as we shall see, was dedicated to grass-roots militant activity encouraging the most miserable workers to organise themselves autonomously to fight bourgeois influence in the Geneva working class. This would have obviously been impossible without a minimum of cohesion within the group. Their activity strangely resembled that of Bolshevik fractions some forty years later. Given the Fabrique's organisation, it was not easy to make one's presence felt within general assemblies without prior preparation. But this activity was aimed at removing construction workers from the influence of bourgeois and electoralist socialists, rather than as Marx tried to have one believe, as a 'plot' against the International. Bakunin, as he had announced, left Geneva after the Basel Congress.

The Alliance asked for its incorporation into the Romande Federation. The Federal Council did not positively refuse, but suspended making a decision to some more opportune time; and Bakunin believed they had no intention of ever accepting the Alliance. Heng, who was close to the Alliance, and a member of the Federal Council, reported on the reaction of the latter. He had presented the two letters from the General Council admitting the Alliance into the International: it was therefore impossible to deny the legitimacy of its request. Further, the Alliance had, as an IWA section, sent a delegate to the Basel Congress. The Fabrique representatives dithered and decided, on 16 August 1869, to postpone any decision.

In 1872 the Alliance was one of the pretexts invoked by Marx to justify the exclusion of Bakunin from the IWA. The main item in the 'dossier of accusations' written up as a document – in fact a pamphlet – was edited by Marx, Lafargue and Engels and was entitled: *The Alliance of Socialist*

Democracy and the International Workers' Association. Bakunin was accused, along with the Alliance, of wanting to destroy the International. This text only developed and recycled the thesis of another document, a confidential communication of the General Council, *The pretended splits in the International.* On this subject Franz Mehring, Marx's biographer, says that if one had to examine the components of this pamphlet 'to check or invalidate the exactitude of the accusations that it contained' point by point, one would end up with a document of at least a dozen notebooks, a labour that Mehring admits he had no desire to accomplish. 'But little has been lost by readers, he adds, noting that 'this document is much inferior to everything else that Marx and Engels were able to publish;' it 'offers not a word on the internal causes that were responsible for the IWA's decline.' 'This pamphlet has no historic value; it is a one-sided accusation, on every page its tendentious character breaks out. Moreover its German translator judged that it was useful to add to it, giving it a title that would have been the envy of any prosecuting council: *The Plot against the International Workers' Association.*'

> The decline of the International had quite different causes than the existence of a secret Alliance, but even so, the Alliance pamphlet does not offer even elementary proofs that such an Alliance existed. Even the committee of inquiry set up by The Hague congress had already had to be content with possibilities and probabilities.[90]

In the documents drawn up by Marx and Engels to have Bakunin excluded from the International the presence of the Alliance becomes an obsession and turned to paranoia. If, as Mehring, says, no serious document could be produced in the actual trial of Bakunin and his entourage at the Hague Congress, nevertheless the Alliance had a real existence. But it was not as Marx and Engels had imagined it; it was only a small coherent group of militants, friends who had dedicated themselves entirely to the development of the International.

Bakunin had sided with Marx in the struggle against Mazzini. He had acted likewise against followers of Proudhonists who defended private property. Also, in other circumstances, he declared to Slav workers in the Austrian empire that if they had no other possible choice, it would be better to join the party of German workers rather the Slav nationalist parties. Bakunin had foreseen the possibility that Marx and his entourage might provoke a split even before the wave of exclusions that would fall on the international workers' movement at the instigation of a handful of men. He declared: if

German workers go on strike, if they rebel against their boss's economic tyranny or against the political tyranny of their government, 'would the proletariat of countries excommunicated by Marxists sit back with arms folded, as a disinterested spectator of the struggle?' Of course those excluded should support German workers, 'without asking, as a precondition, what might be the political system they believed in for their deliverance. This is where true unity of the International lies.'[91] So class criteria remained key for Bakunin. This was Bakunin's answer to accusations of Germanophobia. The Russian revolutionary might show ferocious hatred towards political and bourgeois Germany but his esteem for the German proletariat could not be denied.

Organisation and the proletariat

Bakunin wrote of bourgeois exploitation as the principle enemy of the proletariat. Whatever form it might take, the state, with all its repressive power, had become in these times both a consequence and, simultaneously, a guarantor of that exploitation. This is why the proletariat must seek 'every ounce of its strength within itself alone', it must 'organise that strength entirely out of reach of the bourgeoisie, against it, and against the state'. In Bakunin's view there was a direct and determining link between objectives and whatever means were used to obtain them. This implied serious reflection as to the form and nature of objectives. Marx had declared that he did not aim to provide a recipe for the revolutionary cooking pot. Bakunin was completely aware of his differences with Marx and the Social-Democrats on this point. Bakunin expressed perfectly their different projects when he wrote: 'a political programme has value only when, going beyond vague generalisation, it outlines very precisely those institutions that it proposes to take the place of those that it wishes to reform or overthrow.'[92]

In Bakunin's eyes German Marxists' organisation and the forms of activity that they promoted were adapted quite simply to the goals that they were seeking: the constitution of a German republican and 'so-called popular' state. To achieve these they were obliged to ally themselves with the progressive bourgeoisie, just as associated sections of the International in Zurich had done when they adopted the programme of German Socialist democrats and became 'instruments of bourgeois radicalism'. In his critique of Marx Bakunin cited the case of a certain Amberny, a lawyer in Geneva belonging to the Radical Party and to the IWA who, in 1872, had made a public promise 'in the name of the IWA and in front of his bourgeois fellow citizens, that there would be no strikes this year.' James Guillaume noted that Amberny, a candidate for the legislature, had obtained from the cantonal

IWA committee a commitment that it would do all could to have working-class voters vote for him. Construction workers were then considering taking strike action because their employers had reduced wages. The Jura Federation protested against such wheeler-dealing. Kropotkin, who was then in Geneva, wrote: 'It was Utin himself who made me understand that a strike at this moment would be disastrous for the election of the lawyer Monsieur A[mberny].'[93] So, it was not without some justification that at this moment Bakunin wrote a long letter, 'to comrades of the Jura Federation' in which he said that: 'on every occasion that workers' associations ally themselves with bourgeois politics, whether they like it or not, they can only become its instrument.'[94]

The strategy advocated by German Social-Democracy – parliamentary action – led inevitably to the construction of alliances, to 'a new political pact between the radical bourgeoisie (perhaps constrained to pass itself off as radical) and a respectable, intelligent, that is to say properly gentrified,[95] urban minority of the proletariat'.[96]

Considering the form that workers' organisations might take, Bakunin's general idea was that they should not be modelled on the organisations of bourgeois society but rather be based on the internal dynamics and requirements of workers' struggle and, as such, prefigure a socialist society. The proletariat organised in ways dictated by particular forms of workers' struggles where they were exploited. The basic unity of workers' organisation was located in the place where they were exploited – in the workplace. From there it expanded horizontally (or, if one prefers, geographically) through areas and regions, and grew vertically by industrial sector. Such thinking would obviously provide Marx and Engels with opportunities for considerable sarcasm at Bakunin's expense. He was accused of being indifferent to political matters, insofar as in this view the proletariat's activity lay entirely outside of any parliamentary perspective, and the latter was considered as the only conceivable form of political action. However Engels, over and above polemical misrepresentations, had perfectly understood what lay at the base of Bakunin's thinking. He had written to Theodore Cuno:

> Now since, according to Bakunin, the International is not to be formed for political struggle but to facilitate through social liquidation the replacement of the old state organisation, it follows that it must come as near as possible to the Bakuninist ideal of future society.[97]

So Engels summarised perfectly Bakunin's point of view – and that of the anarcho-syndicalism that would develop thereafter. If one puts aside the habitual amalgam, by which Bakunin's opposition to parliamentary action can be confused with an opposition in principle to political struggle, Engels, in this passage, said just this: (1) Workers' organisation should be based as closely as possible on the society that the working class carries within itself. (2) Workers' class organisations, which under capitalism are their instrument of struggle, constitute equally an organisational model for society after the overthrow of the bourgeoisie. That is the meaning of the expression 'destruction of the state'; the destruction of the state is nothing other than the replacement of the class organisation of the bourgeoisie – the state – by that of the proletariat.

This class organisation brought together individuals as workers, on the one hand in their workplaces and on the other in all-trades structures. This double structure, vertical and horizontal, developed as a federal model on the national and international level. To sum up, workers' class organisation – an instrument of struggle under capitalism – was a model for the political organisation of society after the revolution. This was a fundamental idea of Bakuninism and later also of anarcho-syndicalism, when the horizontal, geographic structures (Bourses du Travail) were brought together with the trades' structures (syndicates). Such an approach would be rejected almost unanimously by all Marxist theoreticians, with the notable exception of Pannekoek, who frequently took up the idea in his writings:

> Since revolutionary class struggle against the bourgeoisie and its organs is inseparable from the seizure of the productive apparatus by workers and its application to production, the same organisation that unites the class for its struggle also acts as a form for the organisation of the new productive process.[98]

In Bakunin's view the proletariat developed as a class through everyday struggle and this is why the nature of workers organisation had to be in keeping with that necessity. On the other hand, Marx looked to the constitution of national political parties having as their objective the conquest of parliaments. Here, said the Russian revolutionary, is where we separate ourselves completely from the Social-Democrats of Germany: 'The goals that we propose being so different, the organisation that we recommend to the working masses must be essentially different to theirs.'[99]

This idea was not an 'invention' of Bakunin. The quote dates from 1872 but one can find it in a short text of César De Paepe from 1869, significantly entitled *The current institutions of the International from the viewpoint of the future*.[100] The Belgian militant began with the idea that institutions that the proletariat constructed under capitalism prefigured the institutions of the future: 'We want to demonstrate that the International already offers a model for future society, and that its various institutions, with some deliberate modifications, would form future social order.' One should recall that while the Belgian Internationalists had opposed the Alliance, they did express support for their programme. Between them and the Bakuninists there was a real closeness of views, and the common factor was surely Proudhon. So the section – which was, as we have seen, the all-trades structure based in one locality – brought together 'workers of all trades without distinction. Here matters of interest to all workers whatever their trade were to be considered.' The section, said De Paepe, 'is the model for the commune'. Bakunin called it the 'central section'. The Federal Council would bring together what De Paepe called 'resistance societies', which Bakunin called 'trade sections'.[101] These were in fact syndicates (unions). Workers of the same trade were brought together within them, in everyday conditions they were taught 'to discuss their interests, to calculate factory prices and the sales price, and, in the light of that, to draw up their expectations [for wages and salaries]; in the future resistance societies are destined to organise work.' Resistance societies, says De Paepe, would transform themselves into co-operative workshops. The Belgian militant reviews every sort of body created by the working class: co-operative societies for consumption will replace existing commerce; contingency and mutual assistance funds will become universal insurance societies. Relations between countries would be entrusted to an International General Council; so no more diplomats and no more wars.

Since one could be a whole person only when one was, at one and the same time, a worker and a thinker, the workers who met in the Brussels Congress demanded comprehensive education, taking in both science and trade apprenticeships – an idea that Bakunin would take up in an article in *l'Egalité* entitled 'Comprehensive education'.[102] In the view of De Paepe, sections would be grouped together in federations, by region and country. Federations would take in both groupings of [central] sections, and trades' organisations, in the same way such structures existed within communes. So, labour might be organised in this way within communes and within the country as a whole. 'We have now shown, we believe, that the germ of all future institutions is coming together in the International. In every commune, a section of the International is being established. In the same breath a newer society would take shape and the older one would crumble.'

What De Paepe was doing was nothing less than defining a model for the abolition of the state. Bakunin used the same language as De Paepe: there is no sense in asking who copied what from whom. Bakunin's anarchism was founded on Proudhon's federalist ideas, and it arose directly from his observation of Swiss workers while living among them. But, on a wider scale, the ideas developed by both men about proletarian organisation as a prefiguration of organisation in an emancipated society were simply elements in the air of these times. After a fashion Lenin would confirm the logic of both Bakunin and César De Paepe. The Bolsheviks were opposed to 'natural' proletarian structures – workers' councils, developed in periods of conflict. They even accused the latter of doubling up on the work of the party and, in the midst of the 1905 revolution, they called for their dissolution. The Petrograd party committee issued the following ultimatum to the councils: 'Workers' and deputies' councils cannot function as political organisations and Social-Democrats should withdraw from them given that the latter, in view of their role, obstruct the developing Social-Democratic movement.' Nevertheless, in the end, the Bolsheviks understood their potential. After Lenin's arrival in Russia, things reached a point where their slogans made them appear as anarchists in the eyes of European worker militants. Lenin's *April Theses* imposed on the party policies that were completely opposed to those that they had previously developed. Thereafter the agenda became anti-parliamentarianism, the arming of the proletariat and all power to the Soviets. Lenin's closest allies could not believe their ears. Goldberg, a former member of the central committee and an old friend and collaborator of Lenin, said: 'The place left vacant by the great anarchist Bakunin is occupied anew. What we have just heard constitutes a formal negation of all scientific Marxist theory and of Social-Democratic doctrine. It is the most blatant and grand apologia for anarchism.'[103]

Lenin had understood that in organisational structures such as Soviets and factory councils the energy and action came from the people where they were in direct contact with problems and struggles. If the party had followed orthodox Marxist polices, the Bolsheviks would have been only the left wing of the Russian parliamentary left. Kamenev went so far as to declare that Lenin's position was unacceptable: 'because it was based on the premise that the bourgeois democratic revolution had ended and counted on its immediate transformation into a socialist revolution'. Some years later, the 9th and 21st conditions of admission of the Communist International showed again some de facto recognition of Bakuninist conceptions. They stipulated that every communist party should build cells in the mass organisations of the working class, and these cells 'through persistent deliberate work should win over the unions to the communist cause'.

A system of workplace cells was introduced in France in the years 1924-25 with the 'Bolshevisation' of the French Communist Party. Hitherto, the structure at the base of the party organisation had been the section, working within a commune[104] as a forum for electoral activity; thereafter within the Bolshevised party, it was the workplace – the terrain for the confrontation of the 'two fundamental classes' of capitalist society – 'the factory is the nerve centre of modern society, it is the home of class struggle. For you communists, the factory must be the centre of your work, of your communist activities.'[105] In Lille, at the fifth congress of the French Communist party, Pierre Sémard, declared: 'The section is a little distant from the bosses, somewhat removed from capitalism, but the cell is much closer.' If the establishment of workplace cells as the 'fundamental strength of party organisation' looked towards the elimination of the electoralism that had come over from the Second International and from the Marxist wing of the IWA, then also on the agenda was the creation of an instrument of struggle against revolutionary syndicalism, which was in part a legatee of the Bakuninist wing of the IWA. At the third party congress in 1924, where there was a discussion of the eventual creation of workplace cells, Pierre Monatte – at that time a member of the party – was firmly opposed to them, demonstrating that this was a measure destined only to subordinate unions to the party. Thereafter, periodically, the party had to condemn a tendency, appearing frequently amongst militants at the grass-roots, to prioritise work in unions: 'Such practices – based without doubt on the incomprehension of the decisive role of the party in the workplace and on the old conception, frequently condemned, that advocates that "the union can do it all" (le syndicat suffit à tout) – are hugely detrimental.'[106] So, it was only in the mid-1920s that the legatees of Marx understood the elementary Bakuninist principle that exploitation and workers' struggles takes place first of all in the workplace; as regards conflict this was the centre of gravity, the fundamental structure of labour organisation.

Trades Sections and Central Sections

It became clear in the various texts in which he touched on this question that Bakunin perceived labour organisation in the form of two complementary structures: one vertical, the other horizontal, the first an industrial structure, the second having an all-trades character. In the first, workers come together and were organised 'not by ideas, but by the actual necessities of their common labour'.

> This economic reality – of a distinct industry with particular industrial conditions of exploitation by capital; the particular, close solidarity of aspirations, situations, needs and interests between all the workers who are involved in this trade section – all this forms the real basis of their association. Ideas come afterwards as an explanation or expression, something that goes hand in hand with the developing and circumspect consciousness of these realities.[107]

Trades' sections followed a natural path of development, beginning with realities and coming on to ideas. In fact, said Bakunin, only a very small number of persons are open to being shaped by pure, abstract ideas. The majority – be they, proletarian or bourgeois – allow themselves to be drawn on by the logic of reality alone. In order to interest the proletariat in the work of the IWA, it must be approached not with general ideas but with 'a lively and real understanding of its real ills'. Of course, thinkers might present these everyday ills in terms of generalities; they understand that such ills are the particular effects of ongoing, general causes. But the mass of the proletariat, forced to live from day to day, those who 'barely find a moment's leisure to think about tomorrow' grasp the ills they suffer from precisely and exclusively within this reality, and almost never as a whole. To obtain their confidence, to win the support of the proletariat, one has to begin to talk to them 'not of the general woes of the whole international proletariat, but of its everyday woes'.

> One has to talk of their own trade and its working conditions precisely in the places where they live, of the excessive length of the hard working day, of inadequate pay, of how malign the bosses are, of the high price of everyday necessities, and of the impossible difficulties they face feeding and bringing up their family decently.[108]

One has to suggest how they might improve their situation while, in the first instance, avoiding calling for revolutionary means. Sometimes, under the influence of religious and political prejudice, they might reject such ideas. On the contrary, one should 'suggest such means that natural good sense and everyday experience cannot fail to recognise as being useful, and which cannot be rejected'.[109] Revolutionary consciousness was not a natural fact, it was not spontaneous. However, for Bakunin this word had a particular sense, one which has provoked a deal of misunderstanding. For him a spontaneous social phenomenon is a phenomenon which develops as a result of its internal determinants, without outside intervention. Revolutionary consciousness was acquired gradually, though daily experience; to become effective, workers needed to rid themselves of religious and political prejudice. It was impossible to instil such revolutionary consciousness through some brutal mechanical process, education was needed. It arose out of living experience and through contact with a collective of organised workers. A newcomer learns only through contact with others that the solidarity that exists between workers in one section exists also between sections or trade bodies of the same locality; that the organisation of this wider solidarity 'embracing without distinction workers of all trades, has become necessary because the management of all trades have come to a mutual understanding amongst themselves'.[110] The practice of solidarity constitutes a first step towards class consciousness; once this principle was established, all the rest would follow as a natural and necessary development, arising from 'the tragic and living experience of the struggle which daily becomes wider, more profound, more terrible'.

Bakunin's viewpoint summarised

1. In form and in kind workers' organisations were the product of history, they were born in practice, in the daily experience of struggle. All rising classes constructed their own organisational forms within regimes which ruled over them.
2. The organisational form suited to the bourgeoisie brought together citizens within an electoral constituency, corresponding to a capitalist system of production which sought only to deal with isolated individuals. Thus real power, arising from control over the means of production, remained in the hands of the owners of these means of production.
3. Workers' class organisation draws together producers not citizens. Whatever the name might be given to this organisation – union, workers' council, factory committee – the framework that remains is a class organisation.
4. Federalism is the basic principle of such organisation.

The logic and nature of transformation, from an exploitative society to a non-exploitative society, cannot be the same as it was with transformation from one exploitative society to another – this is one of Bakunin's greatest lessons, drawn from his reflection on Marxist analysis of the French Revolution.[111] All past revolution, including the great French Revolution, notwithstanding being accomplished in the name of grand programmes, were nothing but 'struggles between these [privileged] classes, amongst themselves, for the exclusive use of state guaranteed privilege, and struggles for the exploitation of, and domination over, the masses'.[112] For Bakunin, the working class did not have the possibility of choosing the same transformative logic because the state was the specific organisational form of exploiting classes. This explains the frequently misunderstood notion of the abolition of the state. What was on the agenda was evidently not the abolition of all forms of organisation, but rather the replacement of the state as a specific form of bourgeois class organisation – and thus, in consequence, there could be no question of its 'conquest' – by a workers' class organisation. Thus arose the full meaning of Bakunin's dictum on the working class's project 'the form and even the nature of an organisation depends essentially on the nature of its goals'.[113] If this workers' class organisation is still to be created, it is not something to be 'invented'. It is not a utopia, meaning some intellectual creation of a perfect system which one might *desire* to come into being. It is *deduced* from the real practice of the working class. Thus the concrete experience of the working class created this organisation, initially in embryonic forms. It was to such work that Bakunin dedicated himself to in the last years of his life – in his 'anarchist' period. Bakunin's developing ideas on workers' conscience and organisation did not arise from a priori constructions but as a result of the observation he was able to draw on from experience obtained through his frequent relocations from place to place.

The IWA of these times was in a period of extraordinary expansion that followed on from a rise of social movements throughout all of Europe. On each occasion the result of savage repression was real international support, and a growth in membership. It was his observation of workers struggles in these times which enabled Bakunin to formulate the elements on which he based his theory of labour organisation. His objective was – in his own words – to *'articulate their thought and express their words'*. When he left the League for Peace and Liberty, the general principles of Bakunin's political thought had already been defined, but it lacked essentials: an organisational, strategic and tactical vision for the labour movement. This void would be filled through his observation of workers' practices, which he would conceptualise in his writings.

Attempts have been made to present the division between Bakuninists and Marxists in the IWA either as the expression of personal conflict or as the expression of the different levels of conscience within the working class with German and British workers, the most conscious being with Marx, and others being with Bakunin. The level of capital concentration has also been considered – workers in large-scale industry with Marx, workers in small artisanal workplaces with Bakunin. But understanding who is with whom was not the real problem; that was elsewhere: one had to consider which fractions of the working class were able to hope for improvement in their condition through parliamentary action, and which had no such hopes. These realities were only supplemented by the strategic, organisational and theoretical developments of particular thinkers.

Moreover, one can understand that it was only after some tragic experience of struggle that Bakunin was able to write:

> the worker, even the most malleable, with little education or experience, drawn ever further forward by the very consequences of struggle, ends up recognising themselves as a revolutionary, an anarchist or an atheist, often without themselves knowing how this came about.

In Bakunin's eyes, only trades' sections (one should think of a structure rooted in the workplace rather than a narrowly defined professional grouping) had the capacity to provide a practical education to its members. They alone could make the IWA into a mass organisation, and 'the triumph of the social revolution would be impossible without their powerful support'.[114] Central sections on the other hand, represented no particular industry: 'because within them the most advanced workers of all industries comes together'. They are, to use the language of today, all-trades structures and they represent the very idea of the International. Their role is that of developing ideas, making propaganda for the emancipation of workers not just in one industry, or of one country, but of all countries. They are active centres in which: 'the new ways of thinking (beliefs) are remembered, concentrated, developed and explained.'[115] One joins in their activity as a worker, not as the specialised worker of a particular trade.

In contrast with trades' sections, which begin with realities in order to come to ideals, central sections follow a path of abstract development; they arrive at reality but start with ideals. Bakunin recognises that this is the same method as that used by idealists and that their 'final powerlessness is a fact noted by history'.[116] This is why – if it had only central sections – the IWA would not have developed into a real force.[117] Central sections would have been only 'labour academies' where all social questions would be debated endlessly, 'but without the least possibility of them being realised'. If central sections alone existed, they might perhaps have been able to form 'popular conspiracies', they might perhaps have brought together a small number of the most conscious and convinced workers, but the mass of workers would be left outside, and, Bakunin says, to overthrow the social and political order of the day 'one needs the participation of millions'.[118] The central section has an eminently political role. Rooted in a locality on the basis of geography, it brings together workers with no consideration of their profession to provide trades' sections with perspectives and a vision going beyond the narrow confines of the workplace. In the first place it helps all workers in an area to be informed on each other's circumstances and, where needs arise, to organise support. It is also the forum in which there is a natural pace for reflection. Lastly, it is a centre from which the organisational impulse can spread.

Historically, central sections were, says Bakunin, the product of the founding centre which had developed in London.[119] They allowed the IWA to seek out the masses wherever they were to be found, 'in everyday reality, and this reality is in everyday work, separated and specialised into trades' organisations'. Those who founded the central sections had to address workers who, given the necessity of collective work in each particular industry, were already more or less organised, and sought to create around themselves 'as many trades' sections as there were different industries.'[120] So, central sections, which everywhere represented the heart and soul of the IWA, became real and powerful organisations.

The central section – and by extension the general organisation of central sections on an international scale – was therefore the structure which helped provide labour organisation with its deepest meaning, offering wider perspectives to member workers. They constituted and defined the proletariat as a class as they affirmed and practiced the principle of the solidarity of workers' interests. It was the trades' section that united workers on the basis of the material principle, whilst the central section united them according to the principle of knowledge.

Bakunin asserted that there was a corresponding relationship between these two processes, between these two organisational entities, and it was their synthesis that would constitute class organisation in forms fitting enough to substitute for the organisation of the state. Whilst in bourgeois society there was a separation between vertical (productive) structures and those that are horizontal (political, decision-making), which of necessity meant the subordination of the latter to the former, and while in state-communism they would be completely fused and concentrated, which would imply the subordination of parties to the centre, Bakunin envisaged such structures as complementary – as federalism – in which each level was autonomous within the norms of its attributes and wherein there were balancing forces countering the monopolisation of power by the centre (since the principle of autonomy deprived the centre from having the *matter* over which it might exert its authority), and guaranteed against centrifugal movements through the affirmation of the principle of solidarity of the parts for the whole. It was in this way that Bakunin defined 'anarchism' – or to be more exact 'revolutionary socialism' – which was the term he used.[121]

Bakunin noted that many believed that central sections should dissolve themselves once their mission – the creation of powerful organisations – was accomplished, leaving only trades' sections. That, he said, was a grave error because the task of the IWA 'is not just some economic or a simply material creative activity, it is at the same time and to the same degree an eminently political process'.[122] In other words, Bakunin does not restrict the role of the mass workers' organisation simply to economic struggle. If the IWA was left without its central sections, it would be deprived of a place where it might elaborate its policies, an indispensable space for workers' to develop and reflect on the aims and goals of their activities. While, in the first instance, uniting workers on the basis of their immediate interests, class organisation is also the place in which the politics – which will lead to their liberation – will be elaborated and developed. Can Bakunin still be accused of being indifferent to politics?

In articles published in the labour press of the era Bakunin expounded his point of view with extreme clarity. His positions were never refuted in any detail by Marx. He faced only polemical responses. Moreover the London-based exile understood perfectly what was on the agenda. His letter to Lafargue of 19 April 1870 should be remembered – here he called the Russian revolutionary a 'donkey' and summarised Bakunin's ideas, declaring that the role of the working class 'should be limited to organising unions. One fine day, with the aid of the International, they will supplant every existing state.' This is certainly a very curt summary, but it was perfectly exact as to Bakunin's way of thinking. However, the general principles which Bakunin developed were partially contradicted by what he said about the effective capacity of the IWA, for revolutionary action, *at that particular moment*. The IWA had given workers the beginnings of an organisation beyond the frontiers of the state and outside the bourgeois world. Furthermore, it contained 'the first germs of future unity and organisation'. But, thought Bakunin, it was not yet an institution ready to lead and organise revolution. 'The International prepares elements of revolutionary organisation, but it does not accomplish it.'[123] It organised workers' public and legal struggles. The IWA made theoretical propaganda for socialist ideas and was a place that was conducive and necessary for the organisation of revolution, but 'it is not yet that organisation'. It brought together workers without distinction, whatever their opinions or religion, as long as they accepted the principle of workers' solidarity against the exploiter. Within itself, this condition was enough to separate the world of workers from the world of the bourgeoisie, but, it was not sufficient to orientate the proletariat towards revolution.

In view of this, it was obvious that an organisation of revolutionaries should exist *somewhere*. That organisation – the International Alliance for Socialist Democracy – had a role, not so much of taking control of mass organisations, but rather of inciting them to develop according their internal logic – which is to embrace society as a whole. It should be remembered that in 1870, *the form of this organisation had not yet been discovered*. One should not analyse this in an anachronistic manner, projecting onto the context of these times the results of experience of a later century. However tempting, it would be wrong to see the Alliance as providing a model for an 'Anarchist Party', or as a model of a 'specific' anarchist organisation, such as one might consider today. *The Alliance was an organisation built within a mass organisation by militants who were members of the latter*, and who strove to develop strategies which this mass organisation would need to consider.

One of the documents in which Bakunin most clearly exposed the functioning of the Alliance was a letter to a Spaniard – no need for astonishment – Tómas González Morago,[124] who was, alongside Lorenzo and Mora, one of the three founders of the International in Madrid. On 21 May 1872 he wrote that the Alliance was the 'necessary complement to the International'. They have identical goals, but they have different priorities. The mission of the International was to 'bring together the labouring masses, workers in their millions, across various trades and countries, across frontiers and states, in one compact and immense body'; the mission of the Alliance, for its part 'is to give to the masses a truly revolutionary direction'.[125]

> The programmes of the one and the other, without in any way being opposed, are different in keeping with the extent of the development of each. That of the International, if it is taken seriously contains, in germ – but only in germ – the whole programme of the Alliance. The programme of the Alliance is the elaboration[126] of the programme of the International.

One might be tempted to see in this a Social-Democratic model of a division of labour between a political struggle managed by a party and an economic struggle managed by a union. All the more so since in this letter Bakunin returned again to the idea that the IWA should not impose doctrine If the founders of the International had done so, they would have 'created a very small association, a sect, but not the stronghold of the world proletariat against the ruling and exploiting classes'. In his letter Bakunin repeated that: 'If the programme of the Alliance were imposed on the International, the International would count in its ranks in all of Europe, barely two or three thousand members.' We shall see that this was precisely what would happen to the so called 'Anti-Authoritarian International'. Formally then the same type of relations are in evidence. However there is an essential difference: in the Social-Democratic relationship, the division of labour between mass organisation and political organisation is arrived at by the subordination of the latter to the former, only the political organisation having the competence to develop strategies and a programme. The mass organisation is considered to be like a 'school' in which future member of the party are formed. The Alliance, in contrast, saw itself as an organic extension of the mass organisation and only expressed the programme that was implicit in the IWA. Between the two there was only a difference of degree, which is what Bakunin meant when he wrote that 'the programme of the Alliance is the elaboration of the programme of the International.' The objective of Social-Democracy was the conquest of political power by the party,[127] whilst preserving this division of labour. The objective for the Alliance was the conquest of social power through the class organisation – the function of the Alliance being precisely to guarantee that the IWA did not lose sight of this objective.

The letter to Morago has real interest because it was addressed to a militant in whom Bakunin had confidence, and he expressed himself candidly. It was written by the Russian revolutionary some months before his exclusion from the International. Of course he was aware of what is being plotted in London against him and his friends. One has the impression from his unrelenting insistence and hammering away at the necessity of maintaining the basic unity of the International, on the basis of *practical necessities*, that he was motivated by awareness that this unity was being undermined. But this should not be taken to say that he thought, out of regard for the unity in practice of the organisation, that 'comprehensive education, the abolition of states or the emancipation of the proletariat by the state, the emancipation of women, collective property, the abolition of the right of inheritance, atheism, materialism or deism' were 'very interesting questions and their discussion is very useful for the moral and intellectual development of the proletariat,' but that in the end these were [merely] ancillary points. Bakunin was particularly committed to discuss these matters at the time of the IWA congresses in 1868 and 1869, notably the question of comprehensive education. One also knows that Bakunin *was particularly attached to the question of the liberation of women.*

This then is the sole explicit goal, the sole obligatory supreme law of the International – the organisation of practical economic struggle of labour against capital, day by day, internationally.[128]

Those who do not submit themselves to 'the practical necessities of solidarity in this struggle should leave or be expelled from the International'. Clearly Bakunin was thinking of Marx, who was intent on imposing on the IWA the principle of conquest of political power.[129] While at one time the IWA was the instrument through which the working class would achieve its global emancipation, Bakunin now restricted the field for his interventions to that of an international of [workplace/ labour] unions,[130] and he was perfectly aware of this:

> To those who might observe me – and say that I restrict the character of the International, setting the limits to its compulsory [official] programme and goal to organising this purely economic struggle – I would reply that an attempt to introduce into it one uniform and compulsory-for-all philosophical or socialist political policy, would destroy it, kill it. Because I defy you to formulate a single clear doctrine which might bring together millions under its banner; no, I should say workers in tens of thousands! And, unless the beliefs of one sect are imposed on all others, one would end up with the creation of a multitude of sects, or one might say the organisation of a veritable anarchy within the proletariat – a mighty triumph for the exploiting classes.[131]

This declaration puts Bakunin completely beyond the 'anarchist' problematic in which he is commonly placed. Without doubt this is a prefiguration of what would become, thirty years later, revolutionary syndicalism. In this letter to Morago, written five months before the Congress of The Hague, one feels a singly defensive attitude. Bakunin seems to wish to preserve at all costs what appears to him as essential – the unity of the International – and this unity was possible only on the basis of economic solidarity. The stakes are no longer the same as they were at the time of the Congress in Brussels, or the Congress in Basel, when collectivism seemed to have the wind behind it. The stakes have changed now. After the Franco-Prussian war, after the Commune and the unification of Germany the balance of forces has changed. Furthermore, the hold that Marx and his entourage had on the apparatus of the International appeared to be unshakeable.

Bakunin saw the International in danger and this fear was apparent in another passage of his letter. He remarked on the effective separation between the British, Americans and Germans on the one hand, and the French, Belgians, Italians, Slavs and the Spanish on the other hand, he asks: 'Should two Internationals be established? One Germanic, the other Latino-Slav?' That would be a triumph for the bourgeoisie. He asks another question: 'Is there a possibility of achieving some accord between the Marxian programme and our own? No, he replies. A third question: 'To preserve the unity of the International and for the love of peace should one of these two programmes be sacrificed to the other?' Again, he replies, no.

> What then is to be done? One should seek out this unity there where it can be found, and not where it cannot. It is not to be sought for in theories – be they philosophical or political – but rather in the aspirations of the proletarian of every country for solidarity, for material and economic liberation – on the terrain of everyday practical economic struggle of labour against capital.

Concrete solidarity between the members of the International is the sole truly essential point; therein is founded the unity of the organisation. Everything else is supplementary. The organisation of practical economic struggle of labour against capital, day by day, internationally, is the sole explicit goal, the sole obligatory supreme law of the International.

Five months before his expulsion from the IWA, Bakunin is affirming that the solidarity that unites workers is 'completely independent from the different philosophical and political currents that are followed by the mass of workers in various countries. For example, if German workers go on strike, if they revolt against the exploiting bourgeoisie, you do not ask them if they believe in God or not, or if they are for or against the state? You support them as strength permits because they are workers who have risen against their exploiters.'[132] *As if to show that he does not confuse the German leadership of the General Council with the German proletariat, several times Bakunin returns to the necessity of supporting Germans workers in conflict.* For him class criteria always came first.

The terms of Bakunin's reservations, concerning the capacity of the IWA to direct, on its own, the proletariat towards social revolution would fuel a debate. Was this a particular circumstance reflecting the lack of historical experience by the working class of these times, or was this a situation that flowed from the very nature of the International? To put things another way, if circumstances suit it, can the working class, in an autonomous manner, develop a practice and establish a doctrine, or is it intrinsically incapable of doing as much? In the first case one would have revolutionary syndicalism and anarcho-syndicalism; in the second case one would have Leninism. There can be no doubt that for Bakunin an organisation bringing together an organised revolutionary minority was indispensable. Such an organisation was the International Alliance for Socialist Democracy. But any reflection about the organisation of a revolutionary minority, in the era of Bakunin and Marx, must avoid the anachronism of approaching the matter in terms that would become current at the beginning of the twentieth century when the radical wing of Social-Democracy – Bolshevism – appeared. One has to keep in mind that those debates which marked the break between revolutionary Marxism and the Second International had not yet taken place and that the Marxism that appeared in these times was essentially parliamentary.

Between 1860 and 1870 unsuccessful attempts were made to create a revolutionary organisation. No one in these times found an acceptable solution. If Bakunin oscillated between secret and public organisation – it should be remembered that workers' organisations were illegal in France, Italy, Spain, and Belgium – these secret organisations were more like networks of militants who corresponded between themselves rather than a body with an ambition to take on the leadership of the international proletariat. Their main objective was to bring together active and resolute militants, to develop revolutionary cadres, a task that seems natural chronologically, when one wishes to promote a particular orientation in a mass organisation.

Bakunin posed the problem of an organisation of revolutionaries and of its relation with the masses, in opposition to Marx's parliamentary and electoralist political strategy. Marx's successors easily forget that throughout the 1848 revolution in Germany there existed a revolutionary organisation, the League of Communists that Marx and Engels had [later] dissolved. This was largely a time of trial and error, and the organisational typologies of revolutionaries did not appear then with either the evidence or the certainty that would later be developed by the likes of Lenin.

Moreover, essential elements of the Leninist critique of German Social-Democracy – which would become the foundations of Bolshevism – had already been made thirty years earlier, by Bakunin. Bakunin found no solution to the problem he faced. Now, one knows that Lenin also found no solution. Indubitably, Bakunin was able to develop a theory of proletarian organisation through his attentive observation of the practice of the labour movement in the years in which he was an IWA militant. There was greater merit in his theory in comparison with that of his adversaries – with their reductionist simplicities – and also, it must be said, often also with the ideas of those who claimed to be of the same current as him.

AFTER THE COMMUNE

Marx, as the correspondent of the IWA General Council for Germany, sent a 'Confidential Circular' to Dr Kugelmann on 28 March 1870, to be distributed to the leaders of the German Socialist party. This text is one of the innumerable writings to be placed in the dossier of the campaign of defamation orchestrated against Bakunin, to politically discredit him with accusations of his being an agent of the Tsar, a swindler, an inheritance hunter, etc. At the Basel IWA congress (September 1869), Liebknecht, who had accused Bakunin of being a Russian agent, faced a Tribunal of Honour and acknowledged that he had 'acted with culpable frivolity'. This did not prevent Marx from repeating this accusation in his 'Confidential Circular', wherein one can learn moreover that Bakunin has fanatical partisans in his service, that he wished to establish his dictatorship over the International and that he sought to acquire Herzen's inheritance. This circular has a curious status, since although it was written in the name of General Council, on the IWA letterhead and so had an official character, it was, by the wish of its author, Marx, confidential. Bakunin was never able to defend himself against the accusations made against him in this circular since he never had any knowledge of it.[133] So well was the secret of this document kept that James Guillaume only found out about it when it was published in *Neue Zeit*, the magazine of the German Social-Democratic Party, on 12 July 1902. This was an anticipation of truly Stalinist methods.[134]

For his part, Engels launched a campaign to discredit Bakunin in Italy, looking to Cafiero for assistance. He managed things so well that the latter broke with him abruptly and went over to Bakunin. Lafargue tried the same game in Spain where the International had developed hugely: in 1873 it would count 25,601 members in 331 sections. Lafargue attempted to sabotage the activity of Spanish Internationalists but failed miserably. He too managed things so well that militants who had at first followed him ended up by going over to the Bakuninists.

The 'Anti-Authoritarians' opposed both the establishment of a compulsory programme – of no use anywhere – and excessive organisational centralisation. Their viewpoint reflected basic, practical concerns. There was an extremely variable level of development amongst the various sections and federations of the IWA: 'conditions that were so different: in economic development, culture and temperament.'[135] So it appeared there was precious little use or desire for an imposed uniform programme. Furthermore, federalists opposed Marx's project of forming political parties tasked with taking power through parliamentary activity.

Bakuninists looked to resolve to their advantage what they considered as a simple conflict of ideas. But Marx himself was incapable of engaging in open public debate where there were conflicting perspectives. He had never intervened directly in an IWA Congress. Above all he feared another Congress where Bakuninists might have a chance to express their views. He wanted to avoid open debate at all costs. He consented to present his views in September 1871, but only before a carefully selected audience.

The London Conference, 17-23 September 1871

With the defeat of France in the Franco-Prussian war Marx and Engels looked with some satisfaction towards the transfer of the centre of gravity in the labour movement to Germany. They also pushed things along a little. In January 1870 Marx had distributed the famous *Confidential Communication*, an anti-Bakunin text, within the IWA. Evidently one day the two currents of the International would have to confront each other openly. The London conference met three months after the defeat of the Commune, from 17-23 September 1871. IWA statutes set out that any decisions of conferences were subject to confirmation by a Congress, in this case The Hague congress, which would meet in the following year.

Marxist theses carried the day in London, by virtue of a fake majority obtained by rigged mandates given to trusted men through delegates co-opted by the General Council, while some Federations were kept in the dark. Overall an arsenal of measures were invoked such as would be used only in the worst moments of the labour movement. The Jura federal committee in particular, received no notification. Bakunin would say later:

> It is [well] known that it was a botched conference; it was composed of Mr Marx's intimates, carefully selected by him, plus a few dupes. The Conference was good enough to vote for every proposition put to it, and the Marxist programme, [now] transformed into official truth, was imposed as a compulsory principle throughout the International.[136]

According to James Guillaume the conference had brought together 23 members, six Belgian delegates (one of whom was also a member of the

General Council), two Swiss delegates, one Spaniard, thirteen members of the General Council nominated by the Council itself, and one unknown with no credentials. Of the thirteen delegates-and-members of the General Council – nominated by the Council – there were seven who were present by virtue of their titles as corresponding secretaries for the various countries not represented at the Conference. These were Engels for Italy, Marx for Germany, Eccarius for America, Hales for England, Rochat for the Netherlands, Cohn for Denmark and Zabicki for Poland. Further, Marx had six others designated to represent the General Council. 'These thirteen members of the General Council, *who had no mandate at all*, between themselves constituted a majority in the Conference of 23 members.'[137]

It would be correct to add to this list: the daughters of Karl Marx, who were admitted to take a place in the last session of this secret Conference. Records do not say if the Conference gave them a deliberative voice; it would not have been irregular, these young women had as good a title to represent the international proletariat as the greater number of delegates.[138]

In Switzerland, it was evident that a split had been prepared in the Romande Federation. The influence of the Alliance had declined. Bakunin had left Geneva. Socialists had gained ground and had taking over the organ of the Romande Federation, *L'Egalité*, whose editors had been collectivists. Differences had grown between Geneva and the Jura, and the General Council took up a clear position for the Geneva socialists. In contrast, in the Jura mountain region sections were doing well. New sections had been created in the valleys around Ruz and Saint-Imier, in Neuchâtel, and elsewhere. In La Chaux-de-Fonds, a newly founded propaganda section was preparing the way for a local federation. 'Thus, in the years 1869-1870, the International was reaching the apogee of its development. It enjoyed a moral power, by virtue of the devotion of its members, through the eminence and prestige that they enjoyed amongst workers who had begun to wake up to the idea of organisation.'[139]

The split had taken place at the second congress of the Romande Federation, in early April 1870 at La Chaux-de-Fonds. It was a definitive parting of ways between the Anti-Authoritarian collectivists and socialists of the Jura, and the socialists of Geneva. Anti-Authoritarians and socialists diverged from each other not only on the basis of their respective political projects and programmes, but also in terms of their practice. The former always demonstrated that they were ready to be conciliatory towards socialists; the latter showed themselves to be petty-minded in the extreme. The Anti-Authoritarians considered socialists as comrades, the latter considered Anti-Authoritarians as adversaries. For example, when Schwitzguébel formed an IWA section in the Saint-Imier valley and asked for admission into the Romande Federation, the latter refused to admit this collectivist section. *L'Egalité*, once it passed into the hands of socialists, published articles attacking the collectivists and their sections.

The Geneva socialists were in the minority as compared to the Anti-Authoritarians. They looked with some apprehension towards the annual congress of the Romande Federation, due to take place in La Chaux-de-Fonds. There were three principle points on the agenda: 1. The organisation of strike funds [caisses de resistance]. There was no difficulty concerning this point, all were agreed on creating funds to help workers in struggle. 2. Co-operation: for socialists, this was the only means by which workers were to be emancipated. For collectivists, it was only the form of labour for the future. 3. In the matter of political activity, socialists supported parliamentary activity, whilst collectivists, prior to a social revolution, favoured electoral abstention. In fact the congress of La Chaux-de-Fonds was unable to deal with these matters. After mandates were verified, and a bureau elected, Adhémar Schwitzguébel hastened to demand the admission of the section of decorators and engravers of the Saint-Imier valley into the Romande Federation, to the great displeasure of the socialist fraction in the assembly. Delegates of this new section were soon admitted and took their place in the congress, reinforcing the libertarian majority of the congress. Further, the anti-electoralists (anarchists) called for the admission of the La Chaux-de-Fonds Alliance section for propaganda.[140] A violent discussion took place. One after another the Genevans took turns to speak, accusing Bakunin and the Alliance. Soon the congress had to come to a decision on the admission of the Alliance into the Romande Federation. There being an anti-electoralist anarchist majority in the assembly, the Alliance was admitted by a vote of 21 to 18. Delegates from Le Locle, the Courtelary area, from Moutier, Bienne, Neuchâtel, Granges and Vevey voted yes, whilst the followers of Dr Coullery from La Chaux-de-Fonds and the Geneva socialist voted against the Alliance's admission.

Reactions to the London Conference

The Jura federal committee decided, at a meeting held in Saint-Imier on 30 October 1871, to convene a regional congress to meet in Sonvilier on 12 November. It was timed shortly after the destruction of the Paris Commune and after the London Conference. Notification for the Congress addressed these two events:

1. ... we consider that the IWA is now entering a new period, and must organise in such a way as to use any partial struggle that may break out between the latter and the bourgeoisie, for the benefit of workers.'

2. ... the dictatorial attitude of the General Council towards sections. The conference held lately in London has adopted resolutions which greatly concern us. You are aware that a split came about at the congress of La Chaux-de-Fonds in 1870. The dissident minority [the Genevans and the Coulleryists of La Chaux-de-Fonds] took for themselves the title of Romande Federation. We had relied on the spirit of impartiality prevailing amongst members of the General Council, and for some time we hoped that they would put an end to this conflict, recognising at least our right to exist as a federation, also as the equal of the confraternity in Geneva. Well, the General Council has enclosed itself in inexplicable silence. Only one way was left open to us – to wait for the convening of a General Congress which would put an end to this conflict.

The Jura Federal committee protested to the General Council that it had not been invited to this Conference, and challenged any decision that the latter might make in the matter of the split in the Romande Federation, one of the parties in the conflict not being represented in London whilst the other was allowed to be both a party to the conflict and a judge.[141] Moreover, concerning the powers of the annual [French-Swiss] Congress, the Conference had no competence to decide matters.

So the Sonvilier congress was convened expressly, to reorganise the federation on a new basis and to make plain to other IWA federations the position of the federalists regarding the 'Acts of the London Conference'. The Federal Committee report presented to the congress noted the state of disorganisation of the International in Switzerland. Certain sections no longer existed; as for trades' bodies, they appeared to be uninterested in the activity of the IWA. The congress designated commissions to report on the acts of the General Council and the London Conference, on the reorganisation of the federation and on a revision of its Federal statutes, and on proposals for a congress of Swiss labour. Congress voted unanimously for a resolution designed to end the quarrel with the representatives of the Temple-Unique [the central section in Geneva]:

Considering *that this present congress is the only legitimate representative of the Romande Federation,* and that the latter, through the withdrawal of some sections that had constituted it, has lost its original character, this congress believes the time has come to dissolve that Federation, and declares it dissolved.

Considering also that a congress of Romande sections, meeting in Saint-Imier in October 1870, discussed proposals to create a new Federation, to be named the Jura Federation; that this proposition – put aside at that time as being premature – but now again represented by many sections, congress decides to found between those sections represented at this congress and those who will join it a new Federation which will take as its name the Jura Federation.

These proceedings gave birth to the Jura Federation, a federation that would be targeted with thunderbolts by Marx. The congress confirmed the decisions of the previous La Chaux-de-Fonds congress. Federalists constituted the majority – the Jura sections were the legitimate Romande Federation – in consequence it was truly the Romande Federation that decided to transform itself into the Jura Federation. Congress adopted the set of statutes proposed by the Neuchâtel section:

Delegates voted in favour of these proposals, subject to the condition that subsequently, they would be agreed by each section. The principle of the autonomy of each section was recognised; and thus was furnished the proof that, through a reduced and very small number of articles, one could do without the baggage of exacting and weighty regulation, such as commonly burdened the statutes of such associations.[142]

The Sonvilier Congress considered the activities of the General Council and resolutions of the London Conference. Delegates all agreed to condemn the manoeuvres of the Council and the conference's resolutions. Congress called for a General Congress to be convened as soon as possible, to confirm the preservation of the principle of autonomy within the IWA. A circular was written to IWA Federations, explaining the motivation behind the establishment of the Jura Federation, its condemnation of the London resolutions, and why the convening of a General Congress was a necessity. The most delicate matter in the circular, from Marx's viewpoint, was doubtless the emphasis placed on the fact that it was only by chance that the IWA's head offices were located in London and that there was no obligation to keep them there. Doubtless this explains why Marx, fearful of the offices of the General Council escaping him, and being moved to Geneva, would do all he could to ensure they were transferred to… New York!

The circular recalled, in relation to the activities of the leading offices of the International, that nothing in the statutes permitted the General Council to take any sort of power over federations and that it should serve only as a central correspondence bureau between sections. The circular declared that up to now the composition of the General Council had been decided 'as a matter of confidence', on the basis of lists presented to each congress – lists 'which for the most part contained names of persons absolutely unknown to delegates'. Their confidence went so far as to allow the General Council the option of co-opting whoever seemed good to them; and through this disposition in the statutes, nomination of the General Council by congress had become something of an illusion. Indeed the Council could at a stroke take on a set of persons who would completely modify majorities and tendencies.'[143] It was in this way that at the Basel congress the blind confidence went so far as to validate a voluntary abdication into the hands of the General Council. Through *administrative resolutions*, the General Council was given powers to suspend federations.

Here James Guillaume makes an extremely important comment, showing that at the time libertarian thinking was only embryonic. He explains that the composition of the General Council was practically immutable:

> Composed five years since by the same men, who were always re-elected, and given – through the Basel resolutions great power over sections, it ended up seeing itself as the legitimate head of the International. A mandate of membership of General Council became, in the hands of some individuals, like private property, and to them London appeared as the irrevocable capital of our Association. Little by little these men, who were only our designated agents, – and most of them are not even agents regularly nominated by ourselves, given that they were not elected in congress, – we say, that these men, being used to marching at our head and speaking in our name, have been carried away by the natural pressure of things and through the dynamics of this situation, to desire to have their personal doctrine and their special programme predominate in the IWA.[144]

Federalists opposed organisational forms which produced divergent forces and completely undermined federalism; they were confronting the centralisation of the International, (and – in the eyes of the Jurassians – Marx was its personification) and the General Council's bureaucratic manoeuvres. They defended thoroughgoing decentralisation. So – as underlined by James Guillaume – a set of measures would be set out against bureaucratic drift. In these the emphasis would doubtless be placed not so much on thorough structural decentralisation but rather on a simple rotation of responsibilities – one might say a strict limitation of the length of any mandate. But this rather basic measure did not appear to have been within the arsenal to hand among the 'Anti-Authoritarians' of the day. Perhaps because, at the time, it would have been difficult to implement.

In underlining that the continuation of the General Council in London was only the consequence of a decision of each [General] congress, the Congress of Sonvilier drew attention to the fact that the seat [of the IWA] might be changed at any time. The call for a General Congress was therefore an open threat against Marx and his friends. They would therefore have to react vigorously.

The Fifth Congress of the International, The Hague, September 1872

As the London conference had no decision-making power, a Congress was convened, one that would be equally rigged. It was convened in The Hague in September 1872 and confirmed the expulsion of Bakunin and James Guillaume, with Schwitzguébel narrowly escaping this sanction. The General Council was endowed with complete powers. Bakunin had written of the General Council: 'it was given the right to censor all the press and every section of the International. The urgent need for secret correspondence between the General Council and all regional councils was recognised; further it was given the right to send agents to every country to pursue intrigue in its own interest.'[145]

The General Council was given the right to 'suspend branches, sections, federal councils or committees, and IWA Federations until the next congress' (Article 6 of the modified general regulations). It was by virtue of this modified article that the Jura Federation would be suspended. To ensure reliable mandates for the congress to be convened in September 1872 in The Hague, the London Conference had voted for a resolution prohibiting the creation of IWA sections in the form of secret societies. Evidently this was a measure against the Bakuninist Alliance, but as a principle it also acted against any IWA section formed in countries where the right of association was generally prohibited.

Nonetheless, at The Hague, French delegates would be present, having mandates from persons unknown which it was impossible to verify. Serraillier – the General Council's corresponding secretary for France (where the IWA was proscribed) – arrived in The Hague with pockets full of mandates. Six French delegates were known only by pseudonym, with no indication of the town from which their mandate was derived. The only one mentioning a town – Rouen – was disavowed by the Rouen Federation, after the event, because he had voted with the General Council, although he been given an imperative mandate to vote with the federalists. The Bordeaux Internationalists found that their delegate, who had received an imperative mandate to vote for the federalists, had voted for the General Council. Two other French delegates, with the pseudonyms 'Swarm' and 'Walter', were arrested shortly afterwards and put on trial, one in Toulouse, the other in Paris. It was learned that 'Swarm', the agent of the General Council in Toulouse, was a police operative. As for 'Walter', the agent of the General Council in Paris, he repented and swore to become a relentless adversary of the International.[146] After the congress of The Hague had finished the English federal council realised that the delegate representing it was not even a member of the International!

Germany had not a single IWA section and only a small number of individual members. Thus it could not send proper delegates to the congress. But to provide reinforcements for Marx and his side, nine Germans were introduced as delegates of non-existent IWA sections. To vote at the congress, sections had to have paid dues. But on 16 March 1872 Bebel had written in *Volksstaat* that the German Internationalists had *never* paid London any dues! Engels, in a desperate attempt to obtain some German presence at the congress in The Hague, had written to Wilhelm Liebknecht:

> Does the Social-Democratic Workers Party wish to have itself represented at the congress? If yes, and as a prerequisite, how then does it think that it should act to regularise its position so that its mandates cannot be susceptible to being challenged at the congress? To do so it must: 1. announce, not just symbolically but really and practically that it has joined the International as its German branch, and 2. that as such, it should pay its dues before the Congress. Things are getting serious, and we need to know where we are, if not, you will force us to act in our own behalf, considering the Social-Democratic Workers Party a stranger to the International, and we will treat it as a neutral organisation.[147]

Reading these lines, it becomes clear *that there were no German sections in the IWA*. At best one can speak only of verbal support from a few Social-Democratic leaders for the political sensibilities of their London mastermind, but *there was not a single instance* of the membership of organised workers in the International. The argument that seeks to justify the absence of German sections because of laws prohibiting membership of the International cannot be accepted. Effective sections existed in France despite law and repression. In Spain, internationalists faced ferocious repression, but this did not prevent them for building a membership of over 20,000.

Taking advantage of the absence of any opposition, the Congress of The Hague introduced important changes to the statutes and added an article 7a. Marx had always been obsessed by the idea of introducing into the statutes an article calling for the conquest of power and for workers to constitute themselves as national political parties. 'Anti-Authoritarians' opposed the introduction of this clause into the statutes, thinking that article 7 was sufficient and that IWA federations should choose for themselves their own positions on this matter. Marx and Engels used the Conference and the rigged Congress to include an article saying that: 'the proletariat can act as a class only by constituting itself as a distinct political party' and concluding with: 'the conquest of political power has become the chief duty of the proletariat.' Technically, insofar as the all IWA federations[148] repudiated the decisions of the congress of The Hague, this article 7a has no status. Yet Marxists consider it as an accepted norm and see this article as an integral part of the IWA statutes.

The Basel congress (September 1869) where 'Anti-Authoritarians' were moreover in the majority had naïvely and foolishly given the General Council the right to suspend *sections*. Marx noted at The Hague that the extension of this right to suspend *federations* was something entirely in conformity with the statutes, since the General Council could already suspend one by one every section within a federation, and thereby could suspend an entire Federation.[149]

The member federations of the IWA, when they became aware of its abuses and manipulations, disavowed the decisions of this rigged congress: the Jura Federation on 15 September 1872; delegates of French sections in October; the Belgian and Italian Federations in December, the Dutch, English and Spanish Federations in January 1873.

To be sure, these federations were not all 'Bakuninist' and their disavowal of the practices of Marx and his friends did not mean that they had rallied to an 'anarchist' viewpoint. But this disavowal clearly expressed that the international unity of the Labour Movement was possible only on the basis of real concrete solidarity, as Bakunin had proposed, and that the 'powerful centralisation of all strength in the hands of the General Council' had resulted in the effective dissolution of the IWA.[150]

The Alliance for Socialist Democracy and the IWA

At The Hague, a commission of five persons was nominated to draw up a charge sheet against Bakunin and to publish the conclusions of their enquiries. Sadly for Marx, one person declared Bakunin innocent of the charges made against him and another was unmasked and found to be an informer in the pay of the police. Therefore, when it came to editing the enquiry's conclusions, this commission was somewhat discredited. Thus it was the bureau of the Congress, composed of six members – Marx and Engels included – which published a memorandum, some weeks before the subsequent Congress scheduled to follow in Geneva: *The Alliance for Socialist Democracy and the IWA* edited by Engels and Lafargue, with some contributions from Marx. The document – a pamphlet – contained the substance of a dossier of accusations: Bakunin was accused, with the Alliance, of seeking to destroy the International. Mehring would write that the decline of the International was due to causes quite other than the existence of this secret Alliance, and in any case the pamphlet against the Alliance offered not even the least beginnings of proof that this Alliance ever really existed. Already, in this matter, the commission of enquiry named by the Congress of The Hague had had to content itself with approximations and hypotheses.[151]

The presence of the Alliance arose obsessively and turned to paranoia in the documents that Marx and Engels drew up to motivate Bakunin's expulsion from the International. Although, as Mehring had written, no serious document could to be produced for the veritable trial that indicted Bakunin and his entourage at the Congress of The Hague, nonetheless the Alliance had really existed, but it was not formed as Marx and Engels imagined it to be. It was simply a coherent group of activists and friends dedicated entirely to the promotion of the International. The example of Spain is particularly striking: the Bakuninist Fanelli, a member of the Alliance, travelled there in 1868 to promote the IWA's principles. By the time Bakunin was excluded in 1872 there were over 300 IWA sections with over 20,000 members in Spain. It cannot be said, as Marx and Engels had it, that Bakunin wanted to *destroy* the International.

In his *Rapport sur l'Alliance*[152] Bakunin explained that if there was any element of conspiracy about the activities of the Alliance then this was essentially due to the fact that Italian, French and Spanish activists might be put in danger in these countries: 'there they were far removed from the freedom and personal security that one was used to in Geneva.'

It was probably this half-secret that led Mssrs Duval and Guétat into the delusion that they had been members of a secret society. They were wrong. There had been private meetings – but not secret ones. For us discretion was a necessity – out of respect for men who risked imprisonment, in Italy as much as in France, whenever they worked on subversive propaganda. But there was no other organisation, other than that which had been established by the first Alliance rules, rules that were so little secret, that we published them ourselves.

Bakunin added: 'It was understood between all of us that correspondence from abroad should not be divulged if it might compromise friends carrying out propaganda work in foreign countries.' Later there would be some irony, when militants of a Leninist persuasion reproached Bakuninists for taking the same security measures that Bolsheviks took in their revolutionary activity in Russia.

Two Congresses in Saint-Imier, September 1872

Soon after the Congress of The Hague, the Jura Federation convened an extraordinary congress, which met on 15 September 1872. Adhémar Schwitzguébel who, unlike Bakunin and James Guillaume, had not been expelled reported on what he had seen and heard in The Hague. The Jura Congress voted first for a resolution denouncing the conduct of the General Council in The Hague, which had been 'so suspect that it in no way really represented opinion amongst all sections of the IWA'. In consequence the congress of the Jura Federation did not recognise 'the resolutions taken at the congress of The Hague, seeing them as unjust, inopportune and beyond the remit of a congress'.

A second resolution declared that the accusations made against Bakunin and James Guillaume, and their expulsion, were the product of 'intrigue and of a few spiteful personalities'. In consequence 'congress considers that is its duty to loudly proclaim that it continues to recognise comrades Bakunin and Guillaume, in their quality as members of the Jura Federation and the International'.

One hour later, James Guillaume and Adhémar Schwitzguébel joined the international congress of Saint-Imier – which came together in the same assembly hall, convened at the initiative of the Italian Federation. Although the international congress of Saint-Imier voted for a split from the General Council, its agenda was not limited to this point. Four other matters were on the agenda.[153] On the first point: 'the attitude of the assembled Federations meeting in congress in Saint-Imier in respect of the resolutions of the congress of The Hague and the General Council' congress resolved as follows:

> The congress of delegates of the American,[154] French, Italian, Jurassian and Spanish Federations meeting in Saint-Imier, declares their complete

rejection of every resolution of the Congress of The Hague, they in no way recognise the powers of the new General Council which it nominated; and, to defend their respective Federations against the governmental pretensions of the General Council, and to save and further fortify the unity of the IWA, delegates have agreed the basis for the project for a pact of solidarity between these Federations.

The second resolution denounced every 'centralising power'. The unity of the International rested 'on the one hand on the real commonality of aspirations and interests of the proletariat of all nations, and, on the other hand on the absolutely free and spontaneous federation of free sections and federations of every nation'. The majority at The Hague had sacrificed 'every one of the IWA's principles'. Further, the new General Council, taking advantage of its added powers, 'threatened to destroy the unity of the International through its attacks on its freedom'. For this reason, the delegates of the American, French, Italian, Jura and Spanish Federations and sections resolve on the constitution of a 'Pact of friendship, solidarity and mutual defence'. All who wished to might join and associate themselves with it. These Federations and sections would establish 'direct and regular correspondence and communication wholly independent of any governmental control of any sort'. Lastly, should one of the Federations or sections have its freedom assaulted, other Federations and sections would declare their solidarity.

Under the circumstances there was no surprise over the first two questions. As far as the International was concerned, they established the basis for a new departure. The third matter on the agenda had particular interest, dealing with the manner in which the International should address 'the question of politics'. The Saint-Imier congress developed what appeared as an anti-sectarian attitude. It rejected the imposition over the proletariat of a 'uniform line of conduct, or political programme, as a unique path that might lead to its social liberation'. That would be, it said, 'a pretension as absurd as it was reactionary'. *The principle of diverse paths to socialism* was thereby recognised. Federations and sections were seen to be asserting their incontestable right to determine for themselves their own political path and to follow the path that they thought best.

Nonetheless the congress did set out limits to this freedom. Congress assigned to the proletariat as its objective 'the establishment of an organisation and an economic federation – one absolutely free, based on work and the equality of all, absolutely independent of all political government'. It noted that 'this organisation and this federation can only be the consequence of spontaneous action by the proletariat itself, of trades organisations and autonomous communes'.

Furthermore, congress took a clear position against all political organisations, such political organisation could only constitute 'domination – to the benefit of one class and to the detriment of the masses'. In consequence, 'the proletariat, if it wished to take power, would itself become a dominating and exploiting class' – and the congress concluded with declarations:

1. That the destruction of all political power is the first duty of the proletariat;
2. That the organisation of any and every so-called provisional or revolutionary political power, working for this destruction, can be only another deceit and it would be as dangerous for the proletariat as every existing government today;
3. That rejecting all compromise to procure the achievement of social revolution, proletarians of every country should establish, beyond all forms of bourgeois politics, the solidarity of revolutionary activity.

So on the agenda there was an unambiguous opposition towards Marxist political strategy for the conquest of political power and for proletarian dictatorship as a period of transition. Interestingly, two essential points of Marxist politics are elided – through the politics of electoral alliances ('compromise') which they implied – with 'bourgeois politics'.

The final point addressed by the congress was more concrete. It outlined general lines for working-class activity, considering workers' organisation as a precondition for workers' liberation. Such organisation could develop only outside any top to bottom administration of the popular masses and beyond all government of any sort. What was being advanced and promoted was 'a Free Federation of all Producer Groups based on solidarity and equality'. Sadly, this 'Free Federation of all Producer Groups' was never properly elaborated. Perhaps for activists the phrase had a sense that was self-evident at the time. Curiously, one can find a meaning for it in Proudhon's writings. This is pretty much of a paradox as the collectivists of the International had opposed Proudhonists. The negation of politics and the state are a consequence of a completely different *logic* being taken up. This thinking is grasped only with difficulty today because we are conditioned to think of social organisation only through the state. This 'free Federation' entailed two things:

1. *Organisational mode.* Producers are organised as a function of their role in the production process – workplace, industrial sector, etc. They are also organised geographically through all-trades structures. There are producers but not 'citizens' in this sort of organisation; Bakunin described this perfectly.
2. *The flow of decisions.* Directions and major social and political choices are discussed and resolved in structures towards the lower side of an organisational chart and progressively passed on, through intermediary structures towards the top.

This organisation is destined to replace the state. Activists in these times were aware that everything had to be prepared anew. A debate was held shortly after the Saint-Imier congress, concerning what *name* should be given to this organisation. Was this still a state, should one continue to call it a 'state' or find some other term? However, in the end the 'Anti-Authoritarian' project was simply one of having working-class *social power* replace bourgeois *political power.*

The fourth item addressed the question of the balance between proletarian protests and demands, and the revolutionary project. These two were not incompatible. Since capitalism might immediately reduce or absorb any improvement in workers' conditions, repeated and ongoing struggles were inevitable. Such struggles helped the proletariat promote fraternity within its community of interests in preparation 'for the final struggle'. So 'our broad intent is to build solidarity and organisation' and therefore one should 'on a large scale, organise and build the solidarity of resistance.' Strikes are 'a precious means of struggle' but one should have no illusions about them. They are only 'a consequence of the antagonism between labour and capital'. However, they allow workers' organisations to be 'strengthened, and, through ordinary economic struggles, the proletariat is prepared for the great and final revolutionary struggle'.

One initial impression of the Saint-Imier international congress is that there was a contradiction between, on the one hand, the rejection of an imposition of 'one uniform political programme' as 'the unique path' that might lead to its social emancipation, and the affirmation that sections and federations should have an 'incontrovertible right to decide for themselves and follow the line of political conduct that they deem best' and, on the other hand, that which follows, i.e. the placing of limits and the reduction of the choices that member sections and federations might make, to those orientations set out in the 'Anti-Authoritarian' programme.

The contradiction did not appear insurmountable at that moment, but after a little while it allowed the 'sectarians' of the so-called 'Anti-

Authoritarian' International an entry point through which they might justify the transformation of the organisation into a specifically 'anarchist' International, which would lead to its disintegration – confirming the prediction that Bakunin made in his writings against Marx that a wish to impose any one programme (the 'anarchist' programme included) to the detriment of others, would create 'as many Internationals as there were different programmes'.

In texts of a Marxist persuasion the constitution of an 'Anti-Authoritarian' International on 15 September 1872 at Saint-Imier is described as a split. This is utterly false. In terms of statutes the so called 'Anti-Authoritarian' International was nothing other than a continuation of the IWA founded in 1864. Violating both rules and statutes James Guillaume and the absent Bakunin were excluded from the IWA at the congress of The Hague. That expulsion was followed by the equally officious expulsion of the Jura Federation, which refused to ratify the decisions made in The Hague. The Jura Federation would be supported by the almost every IWA federation,[155] and for this reason they too were expelled...

The sixth IWA congress, in continuity with preceding congresses, met in Geneva on 1 September 1873, with delegates from France and from the Belgian, Dutch, English, Italian, Spanish and Swiss (Jura) Federations. The congress declared itself in favour of autonomy for federations, and for the wholesale abolition of the General Council. In its place congresses would designate a particular federation to be responsible for co-ordinating activities – a measure designed to avoid the indefinite concentration of power in one single place.

The response of the General Council in New York

The General Council, transferred by the congress of The Hague to New York, declared the resolutions of Saint-Imier null and void and called on the Jura Federation to annul them, implying the need for the convening of an extraordinary congress. Sorge,[156] called on by Marx to head the General Council, gave the Jura members forty days grace, after which their Federation would be suspended. However the ultimatum did not impress other IWA Federations. The Spanish federal commission wrote to New York on 22 February 1873: 'The General Council may be assured that despite the decree of suspension inveighing against the Jura Federation it will continue to be recognised by the immense majority of Internationalists throughout the world.'[157]

One month before, on 26 January 1873, the General Council had voted for a resolution declaring that 'all persons and societies who refuse to recognise congress resolutions or who deliberately fail to fulfil duties imposed on them by general regulations and statutes place themselves outside the IWA and cease to belong to it'.[158] ('They have placed themselves outside the organisation' – those aware of the history of the communist movement know how widely this argument would be used in after years.) In other words, *Marx and Engels threatened with expulsion from the First International the organised labour movement of the times* – with the exception of the Germans who, according to August Bebel, *never paid dues to London!*[159]

THE COLLAPSE OF THE MARXIST INTERNATIONAL

For the Jura Federation work continued as normal. When a jewellers' strike broke out in Geneva, the Jura Federal Committee promised to support it. An appeal was launched amongst sections of the Romande Federation asserting that despite divisions over questions of organisation and political practice we are all 'brothers in economic servitude'. The Jurassians held their annual congress on 24 April. A call was sent to the Romande Federation and to German language sections to participate in this congress. It was clearly a call for reconciliation:

> Rather than continuing recriminations, and mutual accusations, it seems to us better to recognise diversity – in philosophical and political ideas, in temperament... In the subjection of labour to capital we all suffer equally; our economic miseries are identical. It should thus be possible for the three groupings of Internationalists in Switzerland, whilst preserving their particular autonomy and their own forms of activity, to come to an understanding on everything concerning the economic struggle of labour against capital... Come to our congress as brothers and you will be received as brothers; ... we will give you sincere explanations, we will discuss things in a fraternal manner, as men do who search only for truth ... We dare hope that our call might be considered and that delegations from Romande and German Swiss sections will bring to our congress good news – that in your heart there is the same desire for peace as in ours.

Not many responded to this appeal: the jewellers of Geneva, who had received support from the Jurassians, sent telegraphic greetings. Guillaume says that the Geneva tailors, in reply to the conciliatory call from the Jura federal committee wrote expressing the 'regret that on this occasion they were unable to have a representative at the congress'. One representative from Geneva, Rossetti, arrived after the congress commenced, but the section that he represented was not a member of the Romande Federation, and this representative had received no mandate to offer his good services to bring about reconciliation. Rossetti did not understand why these two Federations, the Jura and the Romande, should not unite into one. An amazing fact was revealed in the discussions, as we shall see.

Adhémar Schwitzguébel replied that the past could be forgotten, but that reunification was not on the cards and that the three components[160] could continue separately while working together in the field of economic solidarity. Rossetti could not understand this attitude. James Guillaume explained that what separated the two federations was the congress of The Hague and the General Council in New York. The Romande Federation had approved the congress of The Hague and had recognised the General Council of New York, which had excluded the Jura Federation:

> Rossetti declared that he had never heard talk of this suspension of the Jura Federation and that he had no knowledge of what it meant; that in Geneva, amongst his acquaintance, there was no knowledge of this. His opinion was that a conflict that benefited only the bourgeoisie should not be prolonged and that it was better to hold out the hand [of friendship].

James Guillaume added for Rossetti's benefit that most IWA Federations had expressed their solidarity with the Jurassians and had been expelled on that account. *Rossetti had never heard about this*!!! In conclusion the congress voted this resolution:

> The Jura Congress thanks those sections of Geneva which responded to its call with expressions of good will, and hopes to see in the near future all bodies of Swiss Internationalists uniting in the field of economic solidarity, whilst preserving their autonomy, and without sacrificing their respective principles.

The Jura Congress voted for a resolution in favour of a revision of the International's statutes, which is discussed below. It also tackled the crucial question of creation regional trades federations and unions.

In fact the Romande Federation, the traditional support for 'Marxists' in Geneva, had disappeared into thin air. James Guillaume says their journal, *L'Egalité*, had neither editors nor readers and was no longer published. Sordid disagreements had broken out between its leaders. A general assembly that took place on 11 January 1873 revealed that there were only thirteen members in the Geneva central section.

Although the Saint-Imier congress has often been portrayed as marking the secession of an Anti-Authoritarian or anarchist network (sometimes by anarchists themselves), the International Congress of Saint-Imier was not the occasion for secession, and the so called Anti-Authoritarian IWA was not a new organisation! It was simply an Extraordinary Congress of the IWA which decided that the IWA of 1864 would continue, and decided new conditions for its continuation. The numbering of the congresses, from the following ordinary congress, held in Geneva in 1873, naturally followed on from preceding ones. In the month of September, 1873, two congresses were held in Geneva: one took place from the first to the sixth – what we might call the historic or continuity International and after that a congress of the Marxist International secessionists.[161] We speak of the 'continuity' International because, by this date, all IWA Federations had disavowed the decisions made in The Hague. So we have the same International continuing its legitimate existence. In fact it was the Marxist International that seceded, making decisions which violated the norms of the IWA, and which were challenged and rejected by every IWA Federation.

The International in Germany

The initial development of the IWA in Germany had been essentially the achievement of Johann Philip Becker, an old revolutionary of 1848 and also for a time a member of the Bakuninist Alliance. In 1865 he had organised a congress of dissident bodies in the associations created by Lassalle[162] and denounced Lassalle's organisation for its policy of support for the Prussian military state. The IWA would evolve from the most active elements of this nucleus, and this at a time when Bebel and Liebknecht were busy organising an anti-Prussian movement in southern Germany. Becker was able to create IWA sections in circles opposed to Schweitzer, who succeeded to the leadership of Lassalle's organisation on the death of the latter. At the time Bebel and Liebknecht were attempting to create a legal national party with bourgeois democrats. From afar Marx encouraged them to build their party whilst at the same time reproaching them for failing to work for the development of the IWA. Although generally in agreement with Marx, Becker distanced himself from him insofar as he sanctioned the organisation of IWA federations by language rather than by nation-state as Marx preferred. Further Becker preferred organisational forms based on the workplace, concepts that were very suspect and anarchistic. Marx wrote to Engels about this:

> You will note that old Becker cannot stop himself doing what really matters. His system of organisation by linguistic groups demolishes the

spirit and the letter of every statute of ours, transforming our very natural and rational system into a wicked artificial construction, founded on linguistic links instead of the real links formed by nations and states.[163]

This text written a month before the Basel IWA congress, exposes clearly and concisely Marx and Engels' project, revealing their thinking concerning the International. What was on their agenda was the construction of national parties that were destined to participate in parliamentary institutions, spreading the illusion that they might come to power – something that Bakunin had shown was in fact a practical impossibility because the proletariat was not necessarily in the majority and because socialist parties would have to make alliances which would adulterate their programmes.

If linguistic criteria were applied when an organisation was founded, there would certainly be some mismatch when it came to intervention against a state within the law, and parliamentary strategies would become somewhat inappropriate. The fact that men – in struggle, speaking the same language – might communicate and organise irrespective of national frontiers was thus termed an 'artificial construction' whilst bonds formed by the state were real ones. The problem Marx addressed concerned the end-goals of an organisation: Becker's conceptions contradicted participation by the proletariat in state parliamentary institutions.[164]

Vorbote (*The Herald*), the central organ of the IWA's German language sections, was published in Geneva and through it Becker was able to have an influence over sections in Germany, Switzerland and the USA. In Germany the IWA remained a clandestine body but helped ferment and distribute socialist ideas – a great contrast with the activity of strictly 'political' organisations. Leaders of the latter became compromised in all sorts of efforts to build up electoral forces. The German section was represented at the Geneva IWA congress in 1866. Despite its small numbers news of the development of the International in other countries spurred interest amongst workers, so much so that Liebknecht and Schweitzer made public their sympathies for the IWA. Liebknecht and friends announced their support for the principles of the IWA at the Nuremberg labour congress [1868]. In August 1869 at Eisenach, the new Social-Democratic party affiliated *theoretically* to the IWA, declaring itself as its German section, 'as far as is permitted by the law of associations' – German law forbade any affiliation to a foreign body. The Eisenacher party recommended individual membership of the International. This first great electoralist workers' party – the Social-Democratic Workers' party – would enjoy considerable development in Germany whilst older IWA organisations declined. The sections created by Becker lost their substance. Engels would say [later] that the German party had only a purely platonic relationship with the International. 'There was never a genuine membership, even of isolated individuals' he admitted, in a letter to Theodore Cuno (7 May 1872).[165] The labour movement, he noted, 'under the leadership of Bebel and Liebknecht, is *in principle* for the International'.

An echo of the debate with Becker is to be found in Engels' correspondence in 1872. Becker scarcely escapes being termed as an old rambler 'one who keeps in his head old fashioned ideas about organisation, belonging to 1848'. This letter from Engels to T. Cuno is astonishing. The author rails at Becker and his mania for things conspiratorial, as if this was only an old habit formed in the past: 'little societies, with leaders keeping contacts more or less systematically in their own hands, setting a common direction for all; on occasion a little conspiracy...' Becker is attacked above all because he thought it best that the location of the central IWA authority for Germany should be outside the country, which was not illogical, insofar as the IWA in Germany was prohibited and amounted to nothing.[166] But the International had an organisation, said Engels, far too vast to continue with the habits that Becker preferred, it was 'too powerful and too important in itself to allow itself to recognise the mother section in Geneva as its leading body; German workers hold their congresses and elect their own leaderships'.

In other words Engels counter-posed legal party activities to Becker's 'conspiratorial' methods. Carefully he refrained from saying that conspiratorial methods were justified only *because the IWA was prohibited in Germany*. He did not consider if the development of the IWA in Germany might represent a much greater danger for the authorities than the Social-Democratic party – it was not his concern. It is interesting that in other countries where the IWA was also forbidden it still managed to develop, but in those countries there was no representative system. At IWA congresses the German section would be represented only by the Social-Democratic party. The party's leaders, preoccupied exclusively with internal politics, would take no interest in what might be done irrespective of legal constraints. German Social-Democracy as a national political party, built on the same national mould as bourgeois parties and playing the game of institutions would no longer concern itself with obligations that, for it, had become matters with only theoretical interest. Roger Dangeville attempts, without conviction, to rehabilitate German socialists suggesting that they were 'less concerned with the formal membership of militants with the International because the party organisation was functioning correctly in Germany, and did so in line with the principles and statutes of the International' (sic).[167]

Dangeville nevertheless suggests that German leaders 'should have ... offered more resistance to Bismarck's government and its laws prohibiting international affiliations'.

A constant theme, in the literature of collectivists, was the idea that workers' international solidarity was the basis for the IWA's existence. Bakunin insisted on the incompatibility of international solidarity with a politics of participation in elections within the remit of a national state. Events would bear out his fears. Franz Mehring, Marx's biographer, saw it perfectly, noting that wherever Marx's strategy was applied, the IWA disappeared: '*Wherever national workers party formed the International began to break up.*'[168] This was *particularly* true of Germany.

One might have cause to consider what all this meant: a section of an international organisation was functioning 'correctly', in line with its principles, while taking little or no interest in international questions, and making little or no effort to demand its right to affiliate to the International. One might recall that active French IWA sections subsisted under the Second Empire despite repression,[169] that the Belgian government exerted ferocious repression against the labour movement, etc. Thus one can read a message of support sent on 26 April, from the Romande sections to the Belgian sections, after the repression of strikes in the Borinage: 'We fulfil a duty in expressing all our indignation against the massacres organised by your bourgeoisie, and the persecutions which you have been subjected to ... We warmly approve the firm and intelligent conduct of your General Council.' This address was signed by the committee of the Romande Federation. *L'Egalité* published this correspondence:

> Killings have ceased in Seraing and in the Borinage; but strikes continue, calmly and peaceably, ... the reasons for the strikes are: the poor wages of the miners ... the most horrible and dangerous of all jobs ... At every moment we expect to hear of the arrest of one of our own, after the arbitrary imprisonment of Hins, Croisier, etc., nothing would surprise us.[170]

Unless it was thought that one should of necessity obey every iniquitous law, the argument advanced by Marx and his friends over the legal prohibition of memberships of the International in Germany was invalid. Vigorous agitation for the legalisation of membership of the IWA would obviously have terrified the middle-class layers which the party hoped to influence. Had not Bakunin said that a parliamentary strategy was the negation of international labour solidarity?

It is not unreasonable to think that Marx and Engels' stance after 1849 helps throw light on their position after 1871,[171] when they felt control of the IWA escape them. Marxist commentators would explain that class struggle is shaped by cycles – something that Bakunin did not deny – and that periods of ebb, fall and defeat for the labour movement worker should be used to save from defeat whatever can be saved of forces remaining, whilst waiting for a rise in the cycle of revolution. Marx and Engels' attitude after 1848 is thus to be explained by the fact that in order to elaborate their directives they have 'applied the method of scientific analysis to the course of the revolution'; thus Dangeville wrote that they had taken note of the immensity of the crisis and 'the extent of the labour movement's reverse',[172] so attempting to reassure readers concerning sentences in which Engels violently disassociated himself from the party. One should not infer, he says, 'that at this point or from then onwards, Engels had rejected the idea of belonging to a party'. So are we reassured?

One gets the impression that for Dangeville it is enough to have said that 'the method of scientific analysis' has been applied 'to the course of the revolution', however anachronistic or improbable things may appear. That Engels had 'rejected the idea of belonging to a party' is something that one can hardly contest if one reads his correspondence. Dangeville can scarcely have imagined that Engels had simply not known in 1848 what a 'Workers' party' would be, because previously one had never truly existed; its role, function and objectives had – through a period of trial and error – not yet been properly staked out. The eagerness to affirm that Engels – or Marx – would never have rejected the idea of belonging to a party is an anachronism because what is implied is that they had then a complete theory of what a party should be, and this is not so. For them, in 1848 it was either an organisation of conspirators or an organisation for making propaganda; they do not appear to have considered the party an organiser of the labour movement. When the Communist League was dissolved there was no 'betrayal' on their part – they simply imagined that they would have no need for it. At most this amounted to an absence of good sense.

After 1871, as after 1848, the isolation in which Marx and Engels' found themselves was attributed, by them, to the 'period', not to their own errors. Neither the generality of the international labour movement after 1872 nor the German exiles in London after 1849 had properly understood their theories. On both occasions insults rained down on those who opposed them. There was almost pathological resentment, there was withdrawal into the shell, but never did they even consider that they might have made mistakes.

In the years that followed, from the crushing of the Commune up to the transfer of the seat of the IWA to New York, a pattern that had occurred in 1850 was renewed on a much larger scale. The isolation of the two men was now even greater – to the extent that they had been disavowed by practically the entire international labour movement. In this way these frustrated generals tried to save face and attempted to present humiliating defeat as strategic retreat; Dangeville explains all this as something that Marx chose, that he wished to organise the retreat and above all to save the honour and principles of the International; and then to rise again with historically validated theory, at a time when material conditions had become more favourable. Sometimes those who most often talk of scientific method are those who apply it least; Dangeville was concerned not so much with historical facts gathered from verifiable witnesses but rather with a self-validating commentary, elaborated from one text – given by Marx. He is engaged not in historical reflection, but in scholasticism.

The IWA Congress in Geneva, 1 September 1873

After the manipulations used by the General Council at Marx's behest at The Hague, the Congress of the Anti-Authoritarian International decided it should modify the IWA's statutes.[173] Article 3 was the principal new article: it set out that sections and federations forming the IWA preserved complete autonomy, that is to say the right to organise themselves as they saw fit, to administer their own affairs without any outside interference, determining for themselves the path they intended to follow to achieve the liberation of labour. Another important point – article 6 – followed on from article 3: the role of the IWA congress was to bring together the aspirations of workers from various countries and to bring them into harmony through discussion. The viewpoint represented here was much more open that that defended by the secessionist IWA, whose intent was to highhandedly impose article 7a into IWA statutes: once the conquest of political power had become 'the chief duty of the proletariat' no further discussion was possible. The attitude of the Marxists who took part in the congress at The Hague left little room for doubt. According to James Guillaume, Vaillant declared that 'those who did not think as he did were intriguers or were bourgeois; and that once this proposition was voted and inserted as an article of faith in the *Bible of the International* (sic), every member of the International would be obliged to conform to the political programme it outlined, on pain of expulsion'.[174] Expulsion became a veritable mania among Marxists. Allowing each federation the choice of its own strategy, the viewpoint of the Anti-Authoritarian International did not in any way exclude the possibility that a federation might involve itself in 'political' activity (politics understood in the sense of electoral propaganda – as in truth this was what was on the agenda).

There is obviously some misunderstanding in the view that asserts that anarchism was founded at the Saint-Imier congress, insofar as the resolutions put in place recognised in principle that federations had a right to engage in electoral work. The Jura Federation would not have had the support of other excluded federations, such as the English Federation, had this not been the case, and the latter asserted its right to engage in political work whilst also recognising that federations had a right to be autonomous. [The congress had asserted that no IWA congress majority should impose resolutions on a minority; and that there should be freedom for local bodies to choose their own line of political conduct; Resolutions of the congress are set out in an appendix.]

Reactions from the General Council in New York

The secessionist's congress was held on 8 September 1873. Fearing that autonomists might attend in numbers Engels had sent his instructions to Sorge in New York, to prevent the participation of too many delegates in this Congress. However those who opposed the Marxist General Council were not at all interested in the business of the 'authoritarian' congress, and had no intention of taking any part in it. Engels included a list of those he wanted Sorge to declare as having 'departed' from the International.[175] He went so far as to give him a list of those who should form the commission to check on delegates' mandates. Sorge carried out his orders scrupulously. The General Council in New York voted for a resolution declaring that all local and regional federations that had rejected the decisions of the congress of The Hague 'had placed themselves outside the IWA and no longer formed a part of it'.

For the secessionist organisation the transfer of the IWA's centre to New York, inaccessible from Europe, was a coup de grace. Marx justified this transfer citing that every year hundreds of thousands made the journey to America – driven by want or banished from their country – an argument it should be noted that has nothing to do with his earlier concern for powerful centralisation. Thus the transfer of the centre of gravity of the labour movement from France to Germany, which Marx had hoped for at the time of the Franco-Prussian war was to be matched by the transfer of the central body of the IWA to America and into the hands of German émigrés in the United States. In fact the new General Council would be Marx's creature; it would demand the names and addresses of all IWA bodies, but no one would reply. Former members of the General Council in London were given complete power to deal with European affairs. For a time the correspondence of Marx and his allies revolved largely around the distribution of responsibilities – giving one or another person full powers in respect of this or that country: Engels for Italy, Wroblewski for Poland, Lafargue for Spain, etc. Bakunin named such persons Marx's 'secret agents'; whilst James Guillaume called them his 'proconsuls'.

One of the first acts of the IWA's new organ was to suspend on 5 January 1873 the Jura Federation, which had been the first to announce its solidarity with Bakunin and James Guillaume. Marx and Engels expressed their regrets that the General Council in New York rather than expelling that federation had at first only suspended it. Marx justified his opinion using the argument – much used hereafter – that malefactors had 'placed themselves outside the organisation', thus neatly avoiding the pain of having to enact the formal expulsion of individuals or groups. One only had to 'note' that an awkward customer had left and record their departure.[176] Marx comments:

> So if the New York General Council does not alter its procedure, what will be the consequences? The Council will follow up its suspension of the Jura by also suspending secessionist federations in Spain, Italy, Belgium and England. Result: all this rubbish will turn up again in Geneva and paralyse all serious work there, just as they did in The Hague, and once again they will compromise the entire work of the Congress for the greater good of the bourgeoisie. The great achievement of the congress at The Hague was to induce the rotten elements to exclude themselves, i.e. to leave. The procedure of the General Council now threatens to invalidate that result.[177]

Following Engels' suggestions, the General Council voted on 30 May 1873 to exclude all those sections and federations which declared their rejection of the congress of The Hague. Thus was division consummated. Marx and Engels with around them a small clique of the faithful, excluded from the IWA the bulk of the international labour movement of their times. Bakunin was right when he said that the IWA had divided into two camps: 'on the one hand there was properly speaking only Germany, on the other – varying by degrees: Italy, Spain, the Swiss Jura, a large part of France, Belgium and the Netherlands, and in the very near future the Slav peoples'.[178] Bakunin reaffirmed that it was inappropriate to make one [electoral-party] politics compulsory for the International; solidarity, he said – on the terrain of struggle – unites us, whilst political questions divide us.

The 'Anti-Authoritarian' response

Anti-Authoritarians had some reason for satisfaction in September 1873. The International was rid of Marx and of German socialists – the latter did not feel themselves involved in the IWA. In no way was there a break-away by the Anti-Authoritarians – rather it was the General Council that was repudiated by every IWA Federation. Without doubt this was a moment of crushing victory for the 'Anti-Authoritarians'. This explains the sentiments of a letter from Bakunin addressed to his correspondent, Zamfirij Konstantinovitch Ralli-Arbore: 'We have demolished the authoritarians' mansion, our programme is anarchism, it follows that there is no reason to retreat.' Bakunin had every reason to be satisfied, though he was not unaware that the transfer of the General Council to New York in no way removed the control exercised by Marx and Engels over 'their' IWA. Bakunin notes that the facade of 'official government' in New York only concealed the real and secret power of Marx and his own. Referring to an article in *Volksstaat* on 28 September 1872, he noted the reasons that impelled Marx to arrange this transfer: firstly the impossibility of coming to an understanding with the Blanquist émigrés in London; secondly the defection of the English Federation from Marx.[179]

Many witnesses testified that the last months of the Marxified IWA's life were vexatious and incoherent. Johannard, one of the members of the General Council present at The Hague wrote to Jung on 9 September 1872, regarding the transfer to New York:

> Imagine the Council sending communications or instructions to members in Paris, to the Germans, or the Spaniards? I promise you that people would have a good laugh if they heard of such things ... M[arx] and E[ngels] are just so unbelievably inane, they have unequalled passion in whatever they do and even their friends are revolted by their disloyal games.[180]

Marx had strongly opposed any change in the location of the IWA General Council in the period running up to the congress of The Hague, so it came as some surprise when he proposed its relocation to New York. The report of the second congress of the English Federation explained that the motive for this fickle policy was that they had been assured of the votes of the Blanquist members of the council so long as Marx and Engels supported keeping the seat of the General Council where it was, since these Blanquists wished to keep the General Council in London. So the Blanquists were first flattered, then betrayed. When they were no longer needed they were thrown overboard and they then resigned their membership of the International.[181] This analysis corroborated that of Bakunin himself:

> Mr Marx, warier and niftier than his Blanquist allies, played with them. These Blanquists came to the congress in The Hague with the hope, no doubt incited by Mr Marx himself that through the General Council, they would be able to take for themselves the leadership of the socialist movement in France, and they gave their unqualified promise that they would remain very influential members of that council. (...) But it is more likely that he [Marx] had made positive promises to his French colleagues, without whose support he would have failed to obtain a majority at the congress in The Hague. So, once having used them, he gave them a polite refusal, and, in conformity with a plan he had made with his true intimates, Germans in America and Germany, he relocated the General Council to New York, leaving yesterday's friends – these Blanquists – in the very disagreeable position of having been conspirators, and now victims, of their own conspiracy.[182]

The choice of New York was obviously not an accident. In reality while Marx was manoeuvring for the expulsion of Guillaume and Bakunin from the IWA, there had developed amongst key IWA militants of diverse nationalities a desire to change the location of the seat of the IWA – to allow it to escape from the control of Marx. Marx himself proposed New York only when he realised that this tendency could not be reversed. There were a number of Germans exiles there, in particular Sorge, a very trustworthy partisan of Marx, but says Jung, one who made himself so unpleasant that nobody would vote for him. Marx promised that Sorge would not be a member of the Council but, Jung added, 'the first act of the new council was to call on Sorge to join them and become its general secretary'.

Matters became even more incoherent when two internationalists rejected their nomination for the General Council issued by the congress of The Hague. The first of them, Edward David, wrote in the New York *Socialist*, on 20 October 1872:

> I refuse to take a place on the General Council resulting from this congress... Whatever his genius [Marx], I can have no respect for him after the acts he committed before and during the congress of The Hague. I can no longer walk side by side with men who consent to serve as his dupes in the pitiable comedy that he played at this time, to the detriment of the International and of the universal socialist movement.[183]

The second, Osborn Ward, learnt of his nomination in the press. Writing to the same journal on preparations for the congress of The Hague:

> I tried to find an excuse for all this in my desire to see some rapprochement come about between us all. But when the proposition was made to elect delegates at the congress of The Hague, when I saw the same coterie, with very many of its members as delegates of inner sections, had prepared its list, chosen a propitious moment, massed its votes, elected its president for the session, all to expedite matters with calculated arrangements, the result was known beforehand.

Such indications show that Anti-Authoritarians were not the only ones to accuse Marx and his entourage of intrigue and bureaucratic machinations. Many shared such feelings at the time. Marxist discourse – which has prevailed for many years – gives credit to the idea that an ample organisational centralisation was indispensable to ensure IWA effectiveness, and that Marx was the one who promoted this idea. In reality there was no such thing. Everyone, or nearly everyone, had had enough of Marx. The organisation of a labour international had become too complex to function in one centralised fashion. It was no longer the case of a few small groups of artisans and workers but of federations having, as in Spain, several tens of thousands of members. In a society becoming ever more complex and with class confrontation, a good knowledge of local conditions was needed, as was rapid decision-making; it was absurd to imagine that a small group of London based intellectuals could govern everything.

The Congress of the Marxist secessionists in Geneva

The Marxist-enacted secession was ratified by the congress convened in Geneva in September 1873, one week after the Sixth congress of the 'continuity' International. It was a phantom congress convened by what had become a phantom General Council. Very few members participated in this secessionist congress. Almost all those on whom Marx relied politely refused him. This 'Marxist' congress, if one can call it so, was characterised by the same fakery and falsification of credentials as had been seen at the London conference of 1871 and at the congress of The Hague of 1872.

Much was at stake: firstly some internationalists in Geneva, who had previously worked constantly against the 'Anti-Authoritarians' and the Jura Federation appear to have thought that the congress of The Hague had gone too far, and were talking of conciliation. Swiss members in Geneva, who thus far had supported the General Council, seemed ready to defect – to move closer to the Anti-Authoritarian International, placing the Marxists in the minority; secondly they intended to transfer the seat of the General Council to Geneva, something that threatened to upset the work of Marx and Engels.

The international labour movement needed to be presented with a live body, but encountered a *complete fiasco*.[184] In the absence of Marx, who prudently stayed away, Becker was the master of ceremonies for the congress. Becker wrote to Sorge a month later (2 November 1873):

> We had expected a greater number of delegates from Austria and Germany and I had written beforehand to America and Germany stressing the urgency of the matter. When these hopes were disappointed, we had two reasons to recruit the greatest number of delegates possible: both to ensure that the congress would be held and to ensure an effective majority.

The General Council had been transferred to New York (as Marx had wished). Bureaucratic manoeuvres had placed it under the leadership of Sorge, Marx's fervent disciple. Being cut off from the living force of the European Labour movement its health was endangered. For some time it continued to register decisions taken by Marx in London, but to no effect. Active and living federations, which had been distanced from the General Council by Marx and Engels' manoeuvres did not return to the fold, and had ever less reason to once they had been formally expelled. Almost no one took Marx's side. Hereafter it is not really appropriate to think of an International under Germanic influence. The most one can say is that there were some Germans in a directing apparatus – the General Council – but that it had no troops behind it. German Social-Democracy there was, but none of its structures belonged to the International. The end of the Marxified International was pathetic. Its congress was for the most part composed only of German Swiss. Marx had with him only Austrian, German-Swiss and German socialists. The microscopic USA section was itself formed almost exclusively of German immigrants. Already, at the congress of The Hague, Engels had had to scrape the barrel to obtain some representation there. The Bolshevik historian, Steklov, acknowledges that 'in reality no national federation lined up behind the General Council'.[185] The rats had truly left the sinking ship.

The General Council had no funds

No American took part in this Geneva congress because 'the purse of the General Council was empty', (letter of Sorge to Engels). Even Engels refused to represent Sorge, not wanting to compromise himself in a congress in which everyone felt that he would make a bad impression. Sorge, having no funds to travel to Geneva, sent money to Serraillier to have him attend. An Italian, Enrico Bignami, also politely withdrew. Serraillier then announced he would not go, and so too did the pro-Marx English federal council. Only the members in Geneva remained. It was obvious that few would attend other than the Swiss. But it was equally vital to prevent opposition to the Marx-Engels-Sorge & Co project. Becker played the role of producer in the comedy about to take place and managed things so that there were a few delegates there and so that these delegates voted correctly. Becker was saved by the arrival of an Austrian, Heinrich Oberwinder, (alias Schwarz) a right-wing supporter of the Austrian socialist movement.[186] Oberwinder came to an understanding with Becker and gave him a dozen Austrian credentials, from places unknown, and these were passed on to Germans in Geneva. Becker found himself able to defeat a proposition from members in Geneva to transfer the seat of the General Council by 11 votes to 7.

Becker, undertaking Marx's underhand work, proudly declared in a letter to Sorge on 22 September 1873:

> Even before the bad news arrived concerning the abstention of Serraillier and of the English Federal Council, I had to give the congress somewhat greater prestige by an increase in the number of its members, and in order to ensure a majority for our good cause, more or less arranged the fabrication of thirteen delegates made all at once out of thin air, and the result at the end of the day greatly surpassed my expectations. You will have learnt through Serraillier and through the English Federal Council – who should never excuse their absence, or even justify it – the particularly difficult circumstances resulting from a certain dislocation of the Romande Federation. The Geneva members did their best to have the General Council transferred here [to Geneva] but the solid unity of German and German-Swiss delegates managed to prevent such an eventuality, which in these circumstances, would have produced a very unhappy outcome.[187]

This specialist of *Delegiertenmacherei* (fabricating delegates) had other things to celebrate: in a letter of 2 November he confessed to having manipulated the composition of the committee for verifying credentials, thereby obtaining approval of twelve delegates he had fabricated. Becker noted:

> If this fabrication of delegates had not succeeded we would naturally, through a retreat easy to justify, have made it impossible for the congress to take place. But, given the previous congress had impressed the entire world so much, it would have appeared as a terrible moral defeat, as the triumph of these dissidents.[188]

Despite this, the credentials committee refused to recognise certain delegates whose credentials were judged to be truly *too* fantastic. Nonetheless Becker's enthusiasm was barely scratched. He was not impressed by leaders who failed to go into battle to support their rather (in the circumstances) meagre forces. In his letter of 2 November, he wrote to Sorge:

> What has happened to that much vaunted and so richly praised solidarity if one stays at home when one sees the carriage of society stuck in the mud, leaving to just a few comrades the chore of pulling things out of the rut, so as to be able to say, if things turn out badly, we were not involved, thereby failing to take any responsibility, whilst properly speaking the entire fault for failure should fall on those who failed to act? Devil take those who don't care, those who shudder to lose their fame as big men! If danger was about they were doubly bound to come.[189]

So lamentable was this congress that its resolutions were not even published. The following year it was decided not to convene a congress but to wait for two years and hold one in New York. For Marx this was a resounding setback, and he himself recognised that the congress had been a 'fiasco'.[190] But the end of the 'Marxist' International was not particularly painful for Marx. What mattered was to prevent the General Council falling into the hands of persons that Marx and his close allies did not control – as is shown in the letter from Marx to Engels of 27 September 1873:

> As I view European conditions it is quite useful to let the formal organisation of the International recede into the background for the time being, but if possible not to relinquish control of the central point in New York to stop idiots like Perret or adventurers like Cluseret seizing control and discrediting the cause...[191]

But matters would escape his control even in New York:

> In New York, the shitheads and back-seat drivers on the General Council have obtained a majority and Sorge has resigned and retired. It means that now we no longer have any responsibility at all for all their business. How fortunate we are to have possession of all the records![192]

Marx was already busy trying to prepare what would follow. He noted: 'The events of the inevitable involution and the evolution of things will of themselves attend to the resurrection of the International in an improved form.'[193] What was essential, he said was not to let slip entirely from our hands a liaison with the best elements of the various countries'. Bakunin summed up the results of the 'Anti-Authoritarian' congress in a letter written in the first fortnight of October 1873, addressed to his comrades of the Jura Federation.

> Against the ambitious intrigue of the Marxists, you won today a complete victory, for the future of the International and for the benefit of the proletariat and its freedom. With the powerful support of your brothers in Italy, Spain, France, Belgium, the Netherlands, England and America you have put the great International Workers' Association back onto its [proper] course; Marx and his dictatorial machinations have failed in their attempt to make it turn away from its proper course.[194]

Bakunin commented on these two congresses in a letter to the comrades of the Jura Federation published in their *Bulletin* on 12 October:

> The two congresses that have just taken place in Geneva have demonstrated our decisive triumph, and the justice and strength of your cause. Your congress, respecting freedom, has brought together delegates from all the principal European federations with the exception of Germany; it has loudly and widely proclaimed and established – or rather confirmed, the autonomy and the fraternal solidarity of international labour. The authoritarian or Marxist congress, bringing together only Swiss and German workers, having no respect at all for freedom, has vainly attempted to patch up the ridiculed and broken dictatorship of Mr Marx.

Bakunin's thinking corresponded exactly with the reality of the moment – the burial of the Marxian tendency and the startling success of the federalist current. The same International Workers' Association lived on but the

Marxists had excluded themselves, revealing themselves as secessionists. Bakunin ended his letter affirming that the centre of reaction was now in Germany, represented 'as much by the socialism of Mr Marx as by the diplomacy of Herr von Bismarck'.[195] This reactionary force saw its objective as the 'pan-Germanisation' of Europe:

> It has declared a war to the death on the International, which today is represented only by free, autonomous federations. Though you may be a part of a republic that is still free, you have no choice but to combat it, as do proletarians of all other countries, because this reaction has placed itself between you and your final goal, the emancipation of the proletariat throughout the world.[196]

The international congress of Saint-Imier was a startling political success for the IWA federalists against the centralist bureaucrats, a success that other federations ratified as they came out for the idea that each one had the right to decide its course for itself without being constrained to adopt one uniform programme. However one has to say that this success was short-lived, since this experience ended six years later. The Jura Federation decided at its congress 3-5 August 1878, held in Fribourg (Switzerland), not to convene any further international congresses. So one needs to ask: what were the causes of this retreat within the 'Anti-Authoritarian' labour movement; and above all what were the causes inside the movement which brought about this situation?

The bureaucratic manoeuvres of Marx and his entourage discouraged an exceptionally valuable generation of organisers and militants. But one might ask, if Marx had so few aces in his hand, and if the 'anti-authoritarians' were so strong, why did they lose? The question is biased. Militants like those of the Borinage who risked their lives when confronting a charge of Belgian troops when they went on strike, and were sometimes killed, could not imagine that the very leadership of their International was plotting behind their backs. Such practices were quite simply *inconceivable*.

This is what was expressed by the Spanish delegates concerning the Marxists' manipulations at the congress of The Hague. In a letter to the editors of *La Liberté*, dated 18 September 1872, they wrote: 'we never suspected that even in the midst of the International adversaries would stoop to dishonesty, and because we preserved some portion of confidence in the loyalty of partisans of dictatorship in the International we could not have imagined that there would be such mystification.'[197]

In France the ferocious repression of the Paris Commune would greatly affect militants. 25,000 killed on the barricades, over 13,000 men, women and children shot or deported. And to this should be added the climate of repression and everyday terror that prevailed.[198] Pierre Monatte declared at the International Anarchist Congress in Amsterdam in 1907:

> The defeat of the Commune unleashed vicious repression in France. The labour movement came to an abrupt halt, its militants having been assassinated or compelled to go abroad. It was reconstituted, however, when some years had passed, weakened and timid at first, growing more hardy later.

Fernand Pelloutier in his *Histoire des Bourses du Travail* says much the same:

> The French section of the International was dissolved, revolutionaries were shot, sent to prison or condemned to exile; clubs were dispersed, meetings banned; terror tucked away in the deepest shelters those few men who had escaped the massacre – such was the situation of the proletariat in the period that followed the Commune.

One can understand the deep despair that seized many militants, a despair that led some to acts of individual and brutal violence and terrorism, justified by the idea that 'no one is innocent'. The French proletariat paid dearly for the terror that it inflicted on the bourgeoisie whilst the Commune lasted. Nevertheless the terror was not in itself a sufficient explanation for the melting away of French labour movement. During the same period the Spanish labour movement also experienced a tragic period of violent events but it did not cease to grow as a mass organisation.

The French libertarian movement, affected by some sort of inferiority complex in relation to Marxism, is perhaps a victim of 'martyr syndrome' and as regards the history of the IWA, it reacted as if the Anti-Authoritarians were the victims. *Exactly the opposite was the case.* Marx fell into the trap that he himself had erected, his feet were caught in his own net. Wanting to exclude *two men* who vexed him, he was in the end constrained to exclude firstly the federation that supported them, and then the *entirety of the labour movement*, since every federation rejected these expulsions. He ended up with a phantom General Council in New York, which in the end dissolved itself.

The pseudo-congress of the secessionists organised by the General Council in Geneva in 1873 was devoid of substance, and was a shocking setback, a 'fiasco' to use Marx's own words; while the congress organised in the same city at almost the same moment brought together almost all of those whom Marx and Engels has expelled. Marx and Engels' bureaucratic manoeuvres were transformed into a crushing defeat for the 'Marxists' and a spectacular victory for the collectivists – a victory which did not last for long.

But some terrible trauma was left behind, in that two men, Marx and Engels, because they controlled the apparatus of the IWA, were able succeed in excluding the totality of the labour movement of these times...

The departure of the Belgian Federation would be the prelude to disorganisation. The Anti-Authoritarian International, which for some years survived Marx and Engels's sabotage of the IWA, disappeared in 1878: it was simply decided that another congress should not be organised. The International Worker's Association – called Anti-Authoritarian – already greatly weakened, survived by only two years the 'Marxist' General Council of New York which was itself in total decay. Almost as if the two currents of the labour movement needed the other to survive.[199]

The dissolution of the General Council

In August 1874, Sorge proposed the dissolution of the New York General Council; he was replaced by another German, Speyer, and the General Council continued to stutter on for two more years; Speyer grew tired of presiding over a fictional organisation and convened a conference for July 1876 to declare that the International had ceased to exist. It was therefore 'suspended indefinitely'.[200] In his letter of 12 September 1873, Engels had written to Sorge: 'The old International is completely finished and has ceased to exist.' He was happy: he accused the Belgian followers of Proudhon of being jealous of German communists and of having thrown themselves into the arms Bakuninist adventurers. He had been happy with the transfer of the leading body of the IWA to New York but at the same time he noted that there everything was finished. He predicted that the next International, when Marx's writings had made their impact, would be overtly communist and would 'implant our principles'. Once again, the question was posed in terms of the hegemony of one doctrine above another.

Engels wrote to Sorge once again a little later, on 27 September that 'the congress was a fiasco'. On 15 July 1876, the General Council dissolved itself. Marx and Engels found themselves totally isolated. Apart from the Germans and the Swiss in Geneva, every federation had disavowed the decisions made in The Hague. Bakunin had commented in October 1873:

> Having cast many insults right and left, having carefully counted their majority of Genevans and Germans, they ended up with a hybrid which

possessed no integral authority, as Mr Marx dreamt might be created, and which had even less freedom; they left in profound discouragement; unhappy in themselves, unhappy with others. This Congress was a burial rite.[201]

Engels had been wrong to say that the 'old International' had ceased to exist. It was an IWA shell, transferred at Marx's instigation to New York which had died peacefully, while the federations that had thrown off Marx's yoke continued to develop and hold congresses. Kropotkin wrote later:

At the Hague Congress of the International Association, which was held in 1872, the London General Council, by means of an invented majority, excluded Bakunin, his friend Guillaume, and even the Jura Federation from the International. But as it was certain that most of what remained then of the International – that is, the Spanish, the Italian, and the Belgian Federations – would side with the Jurassians, the congress tried to dissolve the Association. A new General Council, composed of a few Social-Democrats, was nominated in New York, where there were no workmen's organisations belonging to the Association to control it, and where it has never been heard of since. In the meantime, the Spanish, the Italian, the Belgian, and the Jura Federations of the International continued to exist, and to meet as usual, for the next five or six years, in annual international congresses.[202]

Marxists believed that they needed an International that was really their own, even if the IWA had escaped from their hands. So just as the General Council in New York was being dissolved Marx was preparing the ground for the reconstitution of the organisation – one that would suit him and one in which 'anarchists' would be non-citizens.

THE ANTI-AUTHORITARIAN INTERNATIONAL AND ATTEMPTED CONCILIATION

The Seventh Congress of the International, Brussels, September 1874

The seventh congress of the International was held in Brussels from 7-13 September 1874. There was no 'anarchist' International. Federations that had denounced expulsions at the congress of The Hague did not necessarily approve the political choices of Bakunin or James Guillaume. They had expressed their opposition to the bureaucratic centralisation put in place by Marx and Engels but in no way did this imply support for 'anarchism'. They approved Bakunin's idea that the central body of the IWA had no right to impose one unique programme, strategy or doctrine on the all federations. But that was as far as things went. Hales, the new secretary of the British Federation, sent letters to the Jurassians in which he gave them his support but noted that he and his English comrades favoured the use of the universal suffrage and of electoral politics.

Given the real disparity in conditions that existed in each country, a desire to define one single politics for the International implied the imposition of the political programme of just one country on [all] the organisations of the IWA. In such a way one would arrive at 'dissolving the international by dividing it into many parties each of which would follow its own political programme' and would end up with a situation in which 'there would be as many Internationals as there were different programmes',[203] while what gave substance to organisation was the necessity of putting solidarity into practice.

The Brussels congress voted unanimously for a resolution on political action – which it understood in terms of participation in elections:

> On the question of determining as to whether or to what extent the political activities of the working classes might be useful or necessary in the development of social revolution, congress declares that it is for each federation or democratic socialist party, in each country, to decide for itself on whatever line of political conduct it should follow.

Two observations: 1. As can be seen, among the federalist current of the labour movement, there was no categorical anti-electoral position: the autonomy claimed for the constituent federations of the International went so far as to allow each to choose their own field of intervention. 2. The Marxist current would conduct a determined struggle against any attempt to guarantee the freedom of federations to choose their own orientation. Social-Democrats would struggle to impose their own orientation and would end up by once again excluding from the Second International those who opposed them.

The Eighth Congress of the International, Bern, October 1876

Two years passed before the eighth congress of the International was convened in Bern. Considering the subjects on the agenda it was not the least important congress, and it was notable above all in respect of hopes for reconciliation between the two currents of the labour movement. Militants of the Jura Federation – the true inspiration of the federalist current – spared no effort to promote reconciliation, in contrast to Marx and Engels, who always did their best to pour oil on the fire, to widen the division between the 'Anti-Authoritarians' and the 'State-socialists'.

It was for this reason that the Jura Federation, and then the Anti-Authoritarian International, at the Bern congress of 1876, proposed the calling of a further congress to bring together all currents of the labour movement and to seek out means for reconciliation. This was far from being the first such initiative attempted by the federalists.

Earlier attempts at reconciliation

The Jura Anti-Authoritarians never adopted towards the state-socialist current the sectarian attitude that the latter adopted towards them. While socialists were, by and large, in a state of total incomprehension in respect of federalist thinking,[204] the Jura internationalists continually attempted to promote dialogue. Thus towards the end of 1869, when a group of Zurich socialists founded a newspaper *Tagwacht*, with a programme that was not at all similar to that of the Jura Federation *Le Progrès* of Le Locle announced on 25 December 1869 the appearance of the new paper and wished it well. It published its programme and concluded:

> The editors of *Tagwacht* are our friends ... Being united on the terrain of fundamental principles, is it not regrettable that no thought was given to come to an understanding for some action in common? ... What has

so far not been done may yet be arranged ... It behoves the committee of the Romande Federation to take the initiative and call for a delegate meeting from all over Switzerland, which would no doubt bring about only a good outcome.[205]

In 1870, *Tagwacht* published an article which said notably: 'Would it not be good work for the Jura internationalists to become the link between the German-speaking trades' bodies and those that are French-speaking?' *Solidarité* replied: 'Five months ago *Progrès* proposed a meeting between delegates from French and German-speaking Switzerland, aimed at bringing us closer together, in a closer union. Nothing resulted from that proposal. We think that now the moment has come to seriously consider an assembly of this sort, one that would bring only good results, since both sides are ready for common action.'[206]

Labour candidates – a question of circumstance

Jura militants even considered the question of labour parliamentary candidates in a wholly non-sectarian manner. The question had divided the socialist movement in francophone Switzerland, and had spread to the international socialist movement. Yet *Solidarité*, which defended the viewpoint of the Jurassians, considered that in this there was a question of tactics 'which might be resolved in different ways, country by country, depending on circumstances,' said James Guillaume. *Solidarité* of 4 June 1870 noted, in an article entitled 'The International and labour candidates':

> If the English, Germans, and Americans ... believe through the means of labour candidates they serve the cause of labour, we cannot say that they are acting in bad faith ... After all, they are more competent than us to judge their own situation ... But we ask that they allow us the same latitude and tolerance. We ask that we should be allowed to pass judgment on what tactics best serve our position, without any scornful conclusions being drawn over our intellectual inferiority.[207]

So, the position of the Jura activists[208] was extremely pragmatic and conciliatory, '*we have to relate to facts as they are*' (author's emphasis) as this article says

> ... what suits a certain group of men may not be appropriate for others, and let us leave each group to choose in complete freedom the doctrine, tactics and organisation, as may arise in their judgement out of the force of circumstances.[209]

From the beginning of this dispute over the question of labour candidacies, the Jura Federation addressed the matter without any form of dogma – a contrast, moreover, with what would later become the anarchist position. The federation was never chary when it came to attempting some reconciliation with Social-Democrats, notwithstanding having suffered expulsion from the Marxified IWA.

The Congress of Olten, June 1873 – dialogue with little rancour

James Guillaume's *L'internationale, documents et souvenirs*, is a monumental and irreplaceable work – a hive of information for the history of the IWA. As well as pages relating to events in the year 1873, one can read a report on the Congress of Olten of 1 June 1873.

This congress was a striking event for the Swiss socialist movement, but what is of particular interest for our work is not so much these dates or the historic aspect but rather the fact that it produced a rare event, somewhat surrealist and almost non-rancorous, in any case without invective, – a dialogue between two representatives of the Jura Federation and representatives of German and Swiss-German Social-Democrats. At the same time one has to note the amazing level of disinformation that state-socialists disseminated about the IWA's situation.

James Guillaume and Jean Louis Pindy had been given a mandate to represent the Jurassians. The congress was looking to create a 'central organisation for the working class in Switzerland' – a Labour Union (Arbeiterbund/Union ouvrière). The two men attended with few illusions, intending to defend their viewpoint and to listen to that of other delegates. To recall the context in the months prior to the congress, the Jura Federation had been excluded from the Marxified IWA along with every other IWA federation. James Guillaume and Pindy met and exchanged ideas with German Swiss militants. The account of their discussions gives some extraordinary insights into the attitude that German Social-Democrats – or those they influenced – might adopt towards 'Anti-Authoritarians'. In his report, James Guillaume recognises that state-socialists had a right to defend their choices; he says, they had their legitimate ideals:

> But the vexing side of things was that in their camp, there was no equal tolerance: there was a belief that they were in possession of the true *scientific doctrine*, and dissidents were looked on with pity; furthermore not content with pity, there was a belief that they had been given the mission to extinguish heresy and it was their duty to implant everywhere one wholesome eternal doctrine. Nothing was so amusing as discussing

with one of these citizens and to see them smiling with condescension as they heard one's arguments; nothing then or in the future would ever trouble the serenity of their convictions; he was conscious that he was superior and you inferior, as far as he was concerned that was enough.

Guillaume appears to be extremely irritated by the self-satisfaction and arrogance of those who defended 'scientific' socialism, some of them going so far as to accuse the Jurassians of being 'enemies of the workers', 'traitors paid by the bourgeoisie to preach false doctrine'.

Thus one is made aware that dialogue was impossible, because the mind-set of Social-Democrat militants made any mutual comprehension impossible; because the meaning of words was not the same, and so too were certain concepts that 'Anti-Authoritarians' used, [allegedly] having no simple equivalent in German. Thus, in congress sessions the Jurassians explications of federalist organisation, in opposition to centralist organisation, was translated systematically into German expressions that conveyed that 'the Jura delegates wished every organisation to remain isolated, with no union one with another.' The Jurassians reported that their protests against these translations was met with the response that 'this is what we understand from your speeches, and since we do not desire *centralisation*, we are necessarily demanding *isolation*, with *all looking out for themselves.*' 'Every attempt to get a better translation was frustrated. Not out of ill will, but rather, they said, because it was impossible to translate us more clearly.'[210]

Here we have a perfect illustration of the total impossibility of a dialogue between representatives of the two currents of the labour movement because Social-Democrats were simply incapable of understanding basic Anti-Authoritarian concepts. Federalism was neither centralisation, nor fragmentation. James Guillaume's and Pindy's conversations revealed that their interlocutors had no information on the state of the International. At the time this congress was taking place – in Olten on 1 June 1873– they were unaware that every IWA Federation had disavowed the decisions of the congress of The Hague, and had disavowed the General Council; and that for this Marx and his friends had simply excluded the totality of the organised labour movement of these times from the IWA – the Germans could not be excluded because no German section or federation had ever [officially] joined!!! When James Guillaume and Pindy tried to explain this the Social-Democrats simply did not wish to believe them!

On Bakunin's tomb

On 3 July 1876, at Bakunin's tomb, a call was issued 'to forget discord and to unite all fractions of the socialist party from the old and new worlds on the terrain of freedom'.[211] After the burial of the Russian revolutionary a meeting took place ending with a vote and a resolution calling for unity:

> Workers of five different nations, meeting in Bern on the occasion of the death of Michael Bakunin, some partisans of a Worker's State, other partisans of the Free Federation of Producer Groups, believe that a reconciliation is not only very useful and very desirable, but also very easy, on the terrain of IWA principles as these were formulated in article 3[212] of the revised general statutes [adopted] at the congress of Geneva of 1873. In consequence, this assembly meeting in Bern proposes to workers that they should forget vain and vexatious past dissension, and should come together in closer unity on the basis of a recognition of the principles announced in article 3 of the statutes mentioned above.

Article 3 stipulated that sections and federations should preserve their autonomy, that is to say their right to organise themselves as they thought best, to administer their own affairs without any outside interference and to choose for themselves the path that they intended to follow to bring about labour's emancipation. Unity, from the viewpoint of the International, did not signify lining up behind one single position. It was not incompatible with different approaches for labour emancipation; it was revealed in the reality of concrete solidarity whenever there was conflict with capital and with the state. Evidently this was a viewpoint that the Marxist current could not accept.

Initiatives for reconciliation appear to gain ground

Initiatives aiming at reconciliation were proposed by the International and in 1876 it appeared that these were becoming ever more concrete. An article in the *Bulletin de la Federation jurassienne* of 3 September 1876, recalled that this wasn't a new idea and that since 1869 it had not stopped advocating 'peace and unity':

> Reconciliation – so much desired between socialists of various nuances, and especially between those of the fraction that is called anarchist[213] and those whose ideal is a popular state (Volksstaat) – seems to be the best way forward. We joyously salute this important development which will result in a considerable increase in the forces of the revolutionary party;

dissipating much misunderstanding, and providing, for men who may have judged each other on hearsay, an opportunity to learn to know and value each other. This reconciliation is something we have desired and demanded even at those times when struggle between the two fractions of the International was at its sharpest. It would be no waste of effort, to make plain, through some quotations from the various papers that have served successively as the organ of the Jura socialists, that we have always sought peace and unity, and that the conciliation that is being accomplished now is nothing but the realisation of desires that we expressed time and time again over the last eight years.

Indeed, precisely at this moment, as most German language papers – *Volksstaat* and *Tagwacht* especially – were waging a most lively polemic against the Jurassians, *Solidarité* of 25 June 1870 had encouraged Jura sections to subscribe to socialist papers without distinction. Among the German papers it recommended *Volksstaat*. 'So then', comments James Guillaume, 'amidst the sharpest struggle between Bakuninists and Marxists, the organ of the Jura socialists recommended the reading of *Volksstaat*. So foreign was all spirit of sectarianism to the Jurassians, so great was their desire for solidarity and peace!'[214]

Was this just the mood of one moment, driven by a perspective for reconciliation between the two opposed currents of the labour movement? James Guillaume commented on an article in *National suisse*, a radical journal of La Chaux-de-Fonds, praising German socialists. The journal congratulated Social-Democrats for being practical people, because 'abstention, is an empty dream, is not for them'. For James Guillaume this came as 'a brick tossed into our garden': it was indirectly an attack on the Jura socialists. Yet, James Guillaume goes to the trouble to remark, once again, that he does not condemn 'the tactics followed by our friends from Germany in their own backyard. We go as far as to add *that in their situation, it is very probable that we might act exactly like them.*' (My emphasis.) And inversely 'it is no less probable that, if they found themselves in the same situation as us, they might do as we do'. James Guillaume sees proof of the latter in the fact that German socialists, forced to live in Switzerland, 'give their approval to the line of conduct that we have chosen, as soon as our politics are explained to them'. Bakunin's comrade made this comment with some real exaggeration, as by no means all Germans living in Switzerland came close to being in agreement with the Jura Federation.

Somewhat maliciously, James Guillaume provides another 'proof'. The Gotha Social-Democratic congress had decided that 'in the constituencies of Alsace-Lorraine[215] where local socialists decided on abstention, we will respect that decision.' German socialists who recognised this choice for one region could not deny it for another, could they? 'If they allow it for the workers of Alsace-Lorraine quite obviously they cannot view what the Jura socialists choose as a bad choice.' James Guillaume went further. While the *National suisse* affirmed that, according to the Gotha congress, only a socialist government could 'assure freedom and material well-being for the masses', he wrote that the resolution had been badly translated: 'the original text does not speak at all of a socialist government; it declares that "freedom and well-being can exist only in a socialist society" (nur in der sozialistischen Gesellschaft), which is a very different matter.'[216]

Lastly, although the German Socialist party since its formation twelve years earlier, had been involved in electoral struggle, 'it neither has, nor ever will engage in parliamentary politics'. German socialists knew well that electoral politics would not lead anywhere. If they take advantage of the tribune in the Reichstag to shout out their slogans, 'this is in perfect awareness of their cause, knowing full well that legal means will always be powerless to accomplish their programme'. This is a constant for all socialist parties attempting parliamentary adventures – they declare that they want simply to carry out agitation, political propaganda.

James Guillaume, it is clear, made *great efforts* to show that the positions of German socialists were not so far removed from those of the Jura Federation. The Gotha resolution clearly established, he said, that socialists did not send deputies to Parliament 'to fashion' laws, that it never imagined that it would have a majority, but rather that it 'used elections as a means of agitation, that the politics they engage in, in the Reichstag was completely negative, consisting of ceaselessly denouncing the vices of bourgeois society amongst the people, divulging socialist principles from the height of the [parliamentary] tribune'. This may have been the attitude of Social-Democracy in 1876; it would be far from being the case after the foundation of the Second International.

German socialists oppose rapprochement

Nonetheless this attempted reconciliation was not approved by all German or German-speaking socialists. On many occasions the Jurassians had attempted to maintain cordial relations with *Tagwacht*, but when Bakunin died, it published an article that was absolutely scandalous, among other things reiterating the accusation of him being a 'Russian agent' while pretending that it did not believe it. The manager of a Peoples' bookshop in Zurich – in a clear attempt to stoke up the fires – put back on sale a

Marxist pamphlet of 1873, 'The Alliance of the Socialist democracy and the International Workingmen's Association'. From the start the Zurich *Tagwacht* had shown itself ferociously antagonistic to the Jura Federation.[217] On 17 October 1876 it published a text signed by Greulich and four others, on behalf of a 'central committee of the association of German language international sections', which was a violent attack on the International. One could read among its kind words:

> In all the mumbling of conciliation and unity, designed to betray sentimentality and mislead hearts, we see simply, and once again, *the Bakuninists at work*,[218] as always seeking in all places, consciously and unconsciously, to provoke discord and disorganisation, instead of unity and organisation, bringing to the labour movement contention and division instead of peace and conciliation.

The obvious intent of this letter, which was published in two instalments, was to demonstrate that no understanding was possible between the two currents of the labour movement, 'between the representatives of scientific socialism, as the authors of this letter modestly signed themselves, and the flaky heads of the Bakuninist International'.[219] For James Guillaume, the intent of these authors was to:

> ... preach the prolongation of eternal discord, to ridicule attempts to reconcile the various fractions of the party of labour, to cast these attempts as a perfidious 'Bakuninist' manoeuvre; and this at a time when, from Germany, the best known of Socialist-democrats of that country applaud the idea of a reconciliation.[220]

One of the signatories of the letter was Becker, one of the most violently anti-Bakuninist members of the General-Council of the IWA, a man close to Marx (and a former member of the Alliance). It was he who had been the organiser of the lamentable Marxist congress of 1873. In a further letter from Becker – published at a later date – one could read:

> How could we, having such profound differences of opinion, allow ourselves to be made into the laughing stock of the world, through an attempt to reconcile fire and water; how could we fetter our path by introducing into our midst mendacious spirits, capable of introducing amongst us confusion and error! ... In consequence an end needs to be made as soon as possible of any sentimental desire for reconciliation.

As with the fiasco of September 1873, and on many other occasions, it was, without doubt, Marx who sent Becker into battle, on this occasion to try to sabotage the tentative reunification of the labour movement. In Becker's polemic, beyond the explicit reference to Engels' anti-Bakuninist pamphlet, there were two of Marx's favourite themes: a rabid anti-Bakuninism; and, above all his intention to construct *another International* more in keeping with his own opinions. A reconciliation between the two currents of the labour movement would greatly obstruct such a project. The consequences of *Tagwacht*'s attitude appear to have been marginal, however. On 11 October 1876, *Vorwärts*, the central organ of the socialist party in Germany announced: 'The international labour congress convened by the Jura Federation will meet on the 26 October.'

Debates at the Bern Congress

It had been agreed that congresses should not be convened by a General Council – which had been suppressed – but in accordance with the will of all IWA federations. The notification and agenda for the congress in Bern emanated from La Chaux-de-Fonds because the Jura Federation had taken on that responsibility that year. César De Paepe and the Belgian section presented to the congress a project for convening an international socialist congress to bring together representatives of organisations from the two currents of the labour movement; but Social-Democrat opponents of reconciliation did not give up.

The letter of Greulich and his four friends published in October 1876 in the Zurich *Tagwacht* ferociously opposing the Jura Federation was republished in *Vorwärts* on 13 October. Those who signed were men linked to the former General Council of New York. The letter demanded that the Bern congress should abandon the current statutes of the International, statutes that had been revised by the Geneva congress of 1873, and should return to the older statutes – those of 1866, so that a General Council should be re-established. However, the revised statutes of 1873 were perfectly suited to facilitate reconciliation between the two currents of the international labour movement:

> We proposed, to those former members of the International who had separated themselves from us at The Hague congress (1872), reconciliation 'on the basis of the principles of the International, as these were formulated by article 3 of the general statutes revised at the congress of Geneva of 1873' i.e. on the basis of the autonomy of its constituent parts. Such a basis seemed to us wide enough to satisfy everyone. We

did not seek thereby to impose an obligation on dissidents to enter into the organisation that was voted at the congress of Geneva, to accept for their own the every article of the 1873 statutes. We wanted to say that the International, reconstituted on the basis of the statutes of 1873, desired an end to quarrels between socialists, and proposed, to those who have remained outside our organisation, not *fusion*, but a friendly *reconciliation*.

It should be noted that in the eyes of 'Anti-Authoritarians', it was the Marxists who had separated themselves from the International and were 'dissidents' and that this corresponded wholly with reality.

German socialists accepted the invitation to participate in the international congress in Bern, but there was some misunderstanding. The Jurassians specified that German socialist representatives were there as observers, not only because German law forbade affiliation to an international organisation, but also, as was clearly said, because the latter were not members and they could not come as delegates with a decision-making vote:

German socialists, coming to Bern, come as guests, as invitees, as friends: they come to meet representatives of those Anti-Authoritarian federations which have for some time have been the butt of attack by friends of Karl Marx. What will be the outcome of such reconciliation? Understanding, we hope.[221]

As for the reconstitution of the International on the basis of the statutes of 1866, there was no question of that: 'Indeed, that would be to propose to the eight regional Federations which had agreed the statutes of 1873, to change their minds, to return to the old rut from which they had definitively broken.' Scalded by earlier experiences, the Jurassians were not seeking to rush things.

On 29 October *Vorwärts* acknowledged the receipt of this clarification, but contested the right of internationalists to designate the Bern congress as the eighth congress of the international, because, said the Social-Democrat journal, 'the IWA can obtain absolutely nothing from such a congress, with precisely a mission to seek out means of reconstituting this Association, or reconciliation.' Of course, the *Bulletin* of the Jura Federation contested this interpretation and on 5 November, when its own congress was concluded, replied that the General Council of New York had held no further congresses since the setback of its last in September 1873; and given the information that it had, one could conclude that only the 'Anti-Authoritarian' part still existed, and that:

> [F]ar from being on the way out, it manifested energy and vitality; it could show ground gained and progress made. Since the Anti-Authoritarian half of the International alone still existed, since it alone constituted all that remained of the International, it evidently had the right to call itself the International, since no other body could contest that title.[222]

As if to confirm the viewpoint of the editors of the *Bulletin de la Federation jurassienne*, the General Council of New York decided to dissolve itself in July 1876.

Some of the debates at the Bern Congress were more noteworthy than others. The agenda was perfectly in tune with problems of the moment:

1. A report from the Belgian representative on the situation there, revealing profound social change and warning of profound crisis for the International if the latter was unable to confront things.
2. The underpinnings of an anarchist drift in a debate over forms of representation;
3. War in the Balkans;
4. Perspectives on reconciliation with German Social-Democracy.

The report of the Belgian Federation

César De Paepe's congress report to the Bern congress for the Belgian and Dutch IWA was particularly enlightening. It showed that changes at work there had greatly affected the international's federations. In many of the sections of the International older members and original sections had almost all disappeared. The Federation of Charleroi, which had comprised numerous sections had vanished and so too had the IWA in Liège. In the Borinage district only one section remained. A new generation had appeared, 'men who were only children at the time of the first IWA congresses', said De Paepe. There was also a geographical shift in the organisation: many sections had vanished, or had declined, from Walloon districts, while there was progress and activity in Flemish areas. De Paepe spoke of a 'new line of conduct' adopted by a new generation. Moreover a serious problem – child labour – was attracting attention and the way in which it was to be tackled would greatly affect the future of the IWA. Sections in Antwerp and Gent as well as Brussels intended 'to make overtures to parliament to obtain a law on child labour.' This was, said the Belgian representative, 'a first step on the political terrain', one which would probably be followed by others. Child labour also incited the activity of Swiss socialists and it would be the results obtained through political action over this which would encourage many militants to pass over to the side of Social-Democracy. One can also put things another way: it was perhaps the inability of the Anti-Authoritarian current to find a means of political intervention on the question of child labour – and on many other questions – that was partially responsible for its decline.

Questions of representation

The Bern congress had to decide on the status of three delegates representing isolated sections who were not members of their regional federations. Here, perhaps, there appeared, clearly and for the first time, a line that would separate 'syndicalists' from 'anarchists'. The Belgian delegate, De Paepe, believed that these delegates should be refused the right to vote on decisions. The Italian delegates, Cafiero and Malatesta, thought on the contrary that votes had a value only as 'statistics of opinion' and representatives of isolated sections should be allowed the right to vote. The majority agreed with De Paepe. Put another way, should sections that were not members of the IWA be allowed to express opinions? The 'syndicalists' said they are not members, so they cannot take a part in decisions. 'Anarchists' said they can contribute to debate, since votes have no value and decisions are not being made.

Here were the premises for a debate that would preoccupy the anarchist movement on the question of representation and on the function of general assemblies and congresses. It is significant that this issue brought out the opposition between the Belgian and Italian delegations. The first was a federation that for some considerable time had been characterised by positions of a syndicalist type, close to those of Bakunin, and the second a more recent federation which would play a decisive role in the formation of what might be called proper 'anarchism'.

Representation, in terms of a 'delegation of power', would be considered by anarchists as 'authoritarian' since it deprived individuals of their autonomy. A congress was only a meeting in which opinions confronted each other, but in which no decisions would be taken. Thus an organisation could not define and put into operation one globalised activity, it had only a technical function: circulating mail, etc. So Malatesta would say, in 1907, to the international congress of Amsterdam that these congresses are 'exempt from any authoritarianism because they make no laws'; they do not impose their own deliberations on others.' They serve only to

[D]evelop and maintain personal relations between those comrades who are most active, to provoke the study and to sum up programmes – forward paths and means of action. They make known to all the circumstances and the activities that are most pressing in diverse regions; they serve to draw out diverse opinions current among anarchists, and allow some form of soundings (statistique). Their decisions are not obligations and rules, but suggestions, advice, propositions – to be submitted to all interested parties; these become obligations and directives only for those who accept them, only insofar as they do accept these.

Administrative organs, nominated by congresses, have:

[N]o power to issue orders, they take initiatives only on behalf of those who solicit and approve such initiatives, they have no authority to impose their own views, Of course they – as a group of comrades – can support and propagate these views, but they cannot present them as the organisation's official opinion ...[223]

For the Italians, the fact that three delegates – not members of any federation, and in consequence not members of the International – might vote was not important because it was not essential that they should represent something. What mattered were their opinions, and it was not decisive if their opinion might go one way or another, since in no way did congress debates lead to the making of decisions. Such practices – perceived as introducing specifically anarchist practices to class organisation, but totally absent from the Spanish anarcho-syndicalist movement for example – no doubt incited a number of militants, like those of the Belgian Federation, to leave the Anti-Authoritarian current and to re-join Social-Democracy – even though that federation had been one of the pillars in the struggle against Marx's centralism.

The Balkans War

In 1875, the Austrian emperor made a tour along the frontier with the Ottoman Empire, in Dalmatia and Croatia. The Christian population – peasantry for the most part – in Bosnia-Herzegovina interpreted the journey as an invitation to rise against the Turks. The uprising would be repressed with great brutality by the Turks, strongly supported by local Muslims – Serbian notables and converts to Islam from previous centuries.[224] This repression provided the pretext for Austria-Hungary to occupy the province three years later to 'protect' Christians, an occupation that would be made permanent by annexation in 1908. The uprising grew, spread throughout the entire province, to Bulgaria, and then throughout the Balkans. Serbia and Montenegro, desiring the partition of Bosnia-Herzegovina and wanting at the same time to contain Bulgarian attempts to expand westwards, took part in the movement in July 1876. 15,000 Bulgarians were massacred by the Turks, and there were disturbances in Russia and Europe. Serbia then declared war on Turkey but was defeated. Russia finally declared war on Turkey in April 1877. Matters were brought to a conclusion by the Treaty of San Stephano, of 3 March 1878, recognising the supremacy of Russia in areas with a Slav or Orthodox majority. The Treaty was unwelcome in Britain – it saw its strategic interests threatened by the rise Russian power in the region. A chain of local conflicts was now in place, and these conflicts would culminate in the butchery of 1914-1918.

Hopes for reconciliation

One of the principal arguments advanced by the Jurassians, and by James Guillaume in particular, justifying getting closer to German Social-Democracy – and this is what was on the agenda – was that differences between the two currents were not of such great importance and the Jurassians were not opposed in principle to the electoral tactics, since the very resolutions of the congress of Saint-Imier had left to each member federation the right to choose its own path. In the conclusion to the report of the Jura Federation, James Guillaume declared: we ourselves are agreed, to combat the bourgeoisie step by step, 'to defeat it bit by bit', to tear away from it every element of its influence' – or to put it another way, to engage in struggles for particular demands. On this point the Jurassians were in agreement with the Belgians and the Swiss Labour Union (Arbeiterbund):

> Those who represent the Jurassians as theoreticians, disdaining everyday struggles, living in the clouds and passively waiting for the day of the great revolution, such people are conjuring up malevolently inspired fantasies.[225]

The Jurassians became involved in all the controversies of the day, but could not adopt the same methods as Flemish or German Swiss socialists. In his attempts to explain why Jura workers could not adopt these methods – using reasoning predicated on the local context – James Guillaume departed from the terrain of anti-electoralism-on-principle and made the question of participation in elections a question of simple expediency and context. Where previously he had said: 'our task, is quite the opposite, one of separating workers from all bourgeois political parties, which in our eyes form just one reactionary mass,' then he stood on the domain of principle, since such an analysis remained valid in all circumstances. James Guillaume proposed, for the Swiss Jura, an alternative method of opposing recruitment by the 'electoral agents' of the bourgeoisie: 'Organise yourselves firstly on the economic terrain, through trades' organisations. On that terrain, you will perceive very quickly that the bourgeois, who as members of the Radical Party appear as co-religionists and allies, are in reality your enemies...' and this, implicitly, did not appear to be the case *elsewhere*. The report of the Jura Federation specified that in order to get themselves elected – so there was no opposition in principle – labour candidates would be constrained to contract alliances with the radical bourgeoisie,[226] so in Switzerland a labour and socialist candidacy 'was not a *practical* possibility'. Did similar risks exist elsewhere?

The Jura Federation report, without doubt edited by James Guillaume, continues:

> One should not believe that the Jurassians have, in respect of labour candidacies envisaged as a means of agitation and propaganda, the insurmountable repugnance that is attributed to them. On the contrary, they might not be so far from giving them a trial, if only to demonstrate experimentally – to those who believe in the possibility of transforming society by the way of simple legislative reforms – that they have illusions.[227]

Bakunin and parliamentary institutions

Bakunin's opposition to the participation of the labour movement in parliamentary institutions was based on what he saw as the class character of the latter; their role in modern capitalist society; the deviation from labour's programme that became inevitable along with participation in unnatural [cross-class] alliances; the distance dividing electors from the elected; and finally the negation of international solidarity that inevitably resulted. Bakunin was not content to say that parliamentary institutions were imposing a dicey game on the proletariat. His principal objection arose because the ruling class would itself not hesitate to sabotage parliamentary democracy when its interests were endangered; the bourgeoisie only played the game of democracy when it suited them. Put another way, democracy was just one potential system among others, easily giving way to dictatorship whenever that would be necessary. Such – in summary – was Bakunin's theoretical schema.

Most authors, often including anarchists, have gone no further than this incomplete vision of the Bakuninist critique of the representative system and of universal suffrage, without taking note of the positive elements admitted by the Russian revolutionary. In fact Bakunin does not contest *universal suffrage as such*, as a means to designate electoral responsibilities – he contests the illusion that universal suffrage might achieve socialism and suppress private property in the means of production. All this, he said, was impossible because the bourgeoisie would never respect a majority vote which might harm their interests and moreover there would never be a majority vote for such things. Furthermore, even before recourse to the more violent methods that would guarantee its privileges, the bourgeoisie had other very powerful weapons: the control of opinion and keeping the mass of the population at a level of knowledge of economic and political mechanisms such that the system could not be really threatened. He also commented:

> Is this to say that we revolutionary socialists do not want universal suffrage, and that we prefer either a limited suffrage or the despotism of one person alone? Not at all. What we affirm, is that universal suffrage, on its own, and working in a society founded on social and economic inequality, will never be anything other than a trap; that on the part of bourgeois democrats, it will never be anything other than an odious deception, the surest means to consolidate, with a façade of justice and liberalism the eternal domination of the owning and exploiting classes, to the detriment of popular liberties and interests.[228]

In a document dated 1866, in which Bakunin expounded the programme of the 'International Revolutionary Society', point *F* read:

> Immediate and direct election by the people of all civic, legal and public officials, as well as all village, provincial or national representatives or councillors, that is to say by universal suffrage, by all individuals, adult men and women.

So there was no ambiguity. Note also that women were to have the right to vote. Further, point *N* read:

> As soon as the established government is overturned, communes should reorganise in a revolutionary fashion, providing themselves with leaders, an administration and revolutionary tribunals, founded on universal suffrage and on the real accountability of all officials before the people.[229]

Thus universal suffrage was set out as the technique to select responsible persons. As for its application in the political reality of the moment, Bakunin was also not so categorical. He recognised that there was a certain amount of validity in village and local elections. In a letter to Gambuzzi he even counselled intervention in parliament in particular circumstances. So electoral abstentionism was not raised to the level of a metaphysical principle. Likewise, the parties of the different fractions of the bourgeoisie were not lumped together indiscriminately. In the course of the cantonal insurrection[230] of 1873 in Spain, libertarians, a well organised minority, allied themselves in action with bourgeois radicals. Bakunin wrote:

> Letters that I have received from various parts of that country tell me, indeed, that the socialist workers in Spain are very well organised, and not only workers but also the peasants of Andalusia, amongst whom socialist ideas have been propagated most happily, and they are ready to take a very active part in the revolution that is being prepared, for the moment working with political parties, without however confusing themselves with them, and with a well-considered intention to impose a frankly socialist character on this revolution.[231]

Bakunin did not hesitate to advise Italian Internationalists to collaborate with persons close to Mazzini and Bertani to obtain particular political objectives. However, he never went so far as to advocate electoral alliances in which labour's socialist programme might be adulterated and absorbed into the programme of radical bourgeois parties.

Bakunin's politics did not begin with some abstract concept of relations between classes, established once and for all and immutable. At times when the proletariat was in a position of weakness, he did not look to fight indiscriminately against all fractions of the bourgeoisie. The various political forms through which capitalist rule was established were not all seen as identical; for workers it was not a matter of indifference whether they were confronted by parliamentary, Tsarist or Bismarck-type regimes. In 1870, Bakunin recommended working on the French proletariat's patriotic reaction and converting it towards revolutionary war. In *Lettres à un Français*,[232] he made a remarkable analysis of relations between the various fractions of the proletariat and bourgeoisie and, some months in advance of events, in a prophetic manner, he developed thinking as to what might become of Paris and the communes in other parts of France.

The fact that the proletariat (and with it the small peasantry) might be in the majority or not had little importance; what counted, was the idea of the productive class. This idea, of the social function of the productive class is essential. It is perfectly summarised in *Integral education*, a text written by Bakunin in 1869.[233] In this text he argued that in particular conditions, the question of a numerical majority hardly mattered. In the middle ages productive forces were little developed and the productivity of labour was very weak: to sustain a small number of privileged people a large mass of productive workers were needed. One could easily conceive of a more developed system in which layers of non-productive persons (not necessarily exploitative persons, one should note, but often developing the ideology of exploiters) and parasitic layers, are in a majority simply because the productivity of work is such that that a relatively small number of producers suffices to generate necessary social surplus-value. It is enough to look around oneself to imagine all those trades which might go on unlimited general strike, without our everyday existence being fundamentally changed: the military, contractors, debts collectors, notaries, etc. In contrast a strike of rail workers, of garbage collectors has immediate repercussions.

Bakunin is indebted to Proudhon for his sociology of social classes. In his *De la Capacité politique des classes ouvrières*,[234] Proudhon wrote his political testament, an astonishing account of the situation of the labour movement of his times. He shows under what conditions the proletariat might acquire political capacity and concludes that for the moment such conditions are not fully available:

1. The working class has come to an awareness of itself 'considering its relations with society and the state', he says: 'it distinguishes itself from the bourgeois class as a collective entity, with liberty and morality';
2. It owns an 'idea' a notion 'of its own constitution' it knows 'the formulae of its existence, conditions and laws';
3. But Proudhon asks if 'the working class is in a position to come up with its own practical conclusions as to the organisation of society'. He answers in the negative: it is as yet not ready to create organisations that would facilitate its emancipation.

It is significant that Proudhon's work, written in 1864, appeared a few weeks after his death in 1865. Proudhon affirmed that workers' democracy should be radically separated from the bourgeoisie. Such an act of separation 'would indicate that the working class had decided to make a radical break with those who had been the ruling classes hitherto, with the practice of subordination and with all systems of alienation.'[235] The working class should act 'spontaneously through and for itself, not hoping for anything from either other classes or from existing political parties'.[236] 1864 was also the year the IWA was formed – it would seek practical responses for the problems highlighted by Proudhon.

So one cannot conclude from the Bakuninist critique of the representative system that there was an apologia for a political 'void', for 'nothingness', for a transcendental spontaneity – out of which the 'masses' might discover immanently new political and radically different forms. The Bakuninist critique of representative democracy is not a critique of the principle of democracy (and of its more or less immutable techniques) but rather a critique of the capitalist context in which it is applied. What a distance the anarchist movement has travelled since the end of nineteenth century.

Activity in parliamentary institutions is often designated as 'legal action'; and revolutionary propaganda is contrasted with 'legal agitation'. Parliamentary action is itself conceived of in two ways: it is a part of 'legal action' where it is permitted, but some believe in it and some do not. German Social-Democrats who took up legal action thought, or pretended that they thought, that this was temporary, and eventually revolution would be necessary. Right to the end German Social-Democracy would attach itself to an illusory, revolutionary vocabulary, even when it was completely mired in thoroughgoing reformism.

The German Social-Democratic position was well described by Brousse[237] and Pindy,[238] French delegates to the Bern Congress:

> There is no workers' party in France like the one in Germany that, whilst it adopts legal agitation as a means of propaganda, nevertheless proclaims the necessity of a social revolution. Those amongst French workers who carry through legal activity are not people who clothe themselves in this legality as a disguise, whilst at heart they look for revolutionary goals; no, they desire really nothing more than what they say in public. So for example, speakers at a recent workers' congress in Paris were men who never thought in any way of quitting the terrain of legality; every measure that they seek is exclusively a legal reform. But members of the clandestine sections of the International in France have another programme, and they situate themselves on another terrain; their principal activity continues beyond what is sanctioned by law, and aims towards organising workers for revolution. This does not stop them, however, besides their secret activities, being involved publicly in peaceful organisations. In addition to working in secret for their own organisation they join in every public association, and they bring their revolutionary socialist propaganda to these.[239]

In Germany, the Social-Democratic party carried on 'legal agitation' but recognised the necessity of a social revolution. The German party, even when its practice wholly contradicted that objective, never ceased to consider itself as revolutionary. German socialists took as their foundation the idea of the imminence of the 'collapse of bourgeois society' that they drew from a mechanical reading of Marx. In the 1890s, Eduard Bernstein, struck by the widening divide between the theory and practice of German socialism, and concerned at the sight of the party adapting its practice and fitting in with the institutions of the Reich, proposed a revision of Marxism attempting to spread the assumption that violent revolution would never happen and that a transition to socialism might be accomplished bit by bit through pacific and gradual reforms. In 1912 he wrote a letter to the Stuttgart congress in which he rejected the idea that Social-Democracy must 'allow its tactics to be guided in the light of the great catastrophe'. 'Partisans of this theory of grand catastrophe invoke the support of *The Communist Manifesto* – as they interpret it; wrongly on all counts.' Bernstein's ideas would be vigorously fought against in the party – which refused to abandon its revolutionary rhetoric.

Julius Vahlteich

Julius Vahlteich, a German Social-Democratic, was invited as an observer to the Bern congress. It is necessary to consider who he was and what he represented, because, perhaps involuntarily, he had a hand in convincing the Jurassians that reconciliation with Social-Democrats might be possible. Was he sent to manipulate Anti-Authoritarians?

A shoe maker, born in 1839, he had been one of the founders of the General Association of German Workers (*Allgemeine Deutsche Arbeitervereine*, ADAV) led by the charismatic Lassalle. But he had broken with Lassalle in 1864. Vahlteich had been active since 1862 in an organisation in Leipzig, the Industrial Workers Educational Association (*Gewerbliche Bildungsverein*) alongside August Bebel and Friedrich Fritzsche. In that body he had defended the idea that workers should be involved in political action. The three men came into conflict with liberal partisans who thought that workers needed educating first. Their group left the organisation to create an association named 'Vorwärts' (Forwards). Vahlteich and his two allies were chosen by workers in Leipzig to be part of a preparatory committee looking to constitute a workers' organisation. A congress took place in Leipzig between 18 and 25 November 1862. Early in 1863, the Leipzig committee called on Lassalle to be the spokesman for its demands, and to take the lead in the movement. Lassalle replied in an open letter of 3 March 1863. On 23

May 1863 the ADAV was founded. Julius Vahlteich was one of its founders and became the organisation's secretary. Lassalle was elected president, accepting the position on the condition that he should be given complete powers. On his death in 1864, the ADAV had only 4,500 members, but it had become the kernel from which a mass organisation would develop. A veritable cult of personality developed around Ferdinand Lassalle. Vahlteich ended up by resigning – as a protest against his dictatorial behaviour. Vahlteich became a member of the IWA in 1866.[240] Between 1867 and 1869 he was president of the Dresden Workers' Educational Association. In 1869 he took part in the foundation of the Social-Democratic Workers' Party (*Sozialdemokratische Arbeiterpartei, SDAP*) in Eisenach. From 1874 to 1877 he was elected to the Reichstag for Saxony, and he was elected again between 1878 and 1881. He was also a contributor or an editor-in-chief of various Social-Democrat journals. In this capacity he was condemned to 22 months imprisonment for press offences. In 1875-6 he was a member of the party's central committee. In 1881, after the enactment of the anti-socialist laws, he emigrated from Germany to the United States. So Vahlteich was a central personality in the German socialist movement. Having seen the personality cult for Lassalle up close, he had both experience of militant activity and moral and intellectual stature enough to avoid being unduly impressed by the personality of Marx or Engels.

His name achieved some prominence in 1878 when Engels' *Anti-Dühring* was published. He protested against the polemical tone of that work, declaring that both Engels and Dühring had a place in the party and that the serial publication of this text in *Vorwärts* had been an error. A resolution condemning Engels came very close to being voted through at the Gotha congress of 1875. It was Bebel's last minute compromise that saved Engels, and many of those who supported him did so, not on the basis of his theoretical arguments, but rather because Dühring had 'insulted' Marx.[241]

So, contrary to what has been said, this German observer of the Bern congress of the IWA was no 'creature' of Marx infiltrated into the Anti-Authoritarian International. He presented the opinions of his party, although he declared that he was not its official representative. He made a remarkable declaration that if particular attacks had been made against socialist federations of other countries by such and such a person, the mass of workers was indifferent. Amongst us, he said, there are 'neither Marxists nor Dühringians'. 'No antipathy exists in Germany against persons or against the tendencies of other country's socialists.'[242] Vahlteich expressed the feelings of those at the base of socialist organisations who were not interested in conflicts between party intellectuals, and who without doubt had a better sense of theoretical divergences between currents in the labour movement. There was a clear declaration here of being open-minded.

Vahlteich's perspective infuriated Engels. Some months after the Bern congress, he wrote to Liebknecht (31 July 1877):

> Vahlteich has nicely affirmed that socialists are neither Marxists nor Dühringians (?!?!): all the papers noted this formula when, after the congress, they published the speech he perpetrated in a public meeting. I do not believe that he will want to recant. Just because he is in prison that is no reason for me to consider him any better than he really is.

When he declared at the Bern congress that there were 'Neither Marxists, nor Dühringians', Vahlteich was trying to say that there was no question of reference being made to some omniscient or providential theoretician. Experience with Lassalle had vaccinated him against personality cults. Evidently this did not please the headmen of the party, particularly Engels. All evidence seemed to suggest that it was the party caciques who adopted sectarian attitudes and attempted to discredit anything that was not of Marxist persuasion, opposing any form of convergence with the Anti-Authoritarian International.

The Gotha Congress

The Bern congress had voted unanimously for a resolution reaffirming the necessity for 'reciprocal respect concerning what means should be employed by socialists in various countries to achieve the emancipation of the proletariat':

> Congress declares that the workers of every country are best placed to judge what means should be most conveniently used for socialist propaganda. In every case the International sympathises with workers, so long as they are not attached to bourgeois parties of any sort.[243]

It should be noted:
a) One can see that among those internationalist wrongly called 'anarchists' there was no anti-electoral obsession.
b) There was no desire to exclude workers who chose other paths towards socialism.
c) Class criteria were given priority, through a rejection of all attachment to *bourgeois* parties.[244]

In its congress meeting of 1 October, the Belgian Federation had agreed to propose to the Bern congress, the convening of a 'Universal Socialist Congress', admitting delegates of all socialist organisations whatever their tendency, to meet in Belgium in 1877. We shall return to this point.

The initiative taken by the International to convene an international congress of all socialist tendencies did nothing more than give a form to desires expressed on the occasion of Bakunin's burial for reconciliation between the two currents of the labour movement. At the congress of the Jura Federation (6-7 August 1876) held three months before the Bern international congress, a vote had been taken in this spirit, to send an Address to the Gotha German socialists' congress, which was to meet on 19-23 August.[245]

At its congress of August 6-7, the Jura Federation based at La Chaux-de-Fonds, bringing together representative of French, German and Italian language sections, resolved to send fraternal greetings to the congress of German socialists meeting in Gotha.

We are aware the current legislation does not permit workers in Germany to be a part of one International organisation with their comrades in other countries; but we know that amongst German workers the feelings of solidarity that should exist between proletarians of every region are as strong as they are anywhere else. If then we cannot be linked together in a formal organisation, we can nevertheless exchange expressions of our sympathy and commitment to achieve common goals.

In recent years there have been differences of opinion, which too often degenerated into regrettable quarrels, not only between the socialist groups of various countries, but also between socialist groups in one country. Such divisions have greatly harmed the development of our propaganda. Brothers of Germany you have set a great example: socialists of the Allgemeine Deutscher Arbeiterverein and of the party of Eisenach have foresworn their past enmities, have shaken hands with each other. The work of conciliation which you have so happily inaugurated at home through this reconciliation of two fractions that yesterday were enemies can and must be continued elsewhere. This need is keenly felt amongst all the groups that we represent, and on 3 July 1876 in Bern, on the tomb of Michel Bakunin socialists of many nations expressed our dearest wish – urged that irksome and vain past dissensions should be forgotten. Yes, we believe that, while keeping their own particular programme and organisation, the diverse fractions of the socialist party should establish friendly understanding between themselves, permitting all to contribute more efficaciously to the achievement of our common goal – the emancipation of workers by the workers themselves. Comrades, we are persuaded that you will receive this present address with the same feelings of sincere fraternity with which it was written, and we offer our best wishes for the success of the work of your congress. Greetings and solidarity; in the name of the Jura congress, the bureau: *Ali Eberhardt, Voges, R. Kahn, H. Ferré.*

These proposals show that there was a real desire for closer relations with German Social-Democracy. The so called 'Anti-Authoritarian' International did not seek to impose one strategy; it was aware that situations might differ from one country to another. The Gotha congress report acknowledged this message:

It noted the Address voted by the Jura congress held in La Chaux-de-Fonds on 7 August. The congress had expressed regrets for past divisions that had reigned between workers of various countries; satisfaction felt for the happy success of the union of German workers, and the need to forget past discord and to bring together all forces to accomplish common goals. Bebel then spoke in the following terms:

To see workers of all civilised countries taking advantage of the opportunity of our congress to affirm their solidarity with German workers is a matter for celebration. In an assembly in which the speaker took part lately in Bern, the question arose of closer relations with socialists from France, Russia, etc. It had to take note, it is true, that in the current situation in Germany, an International organisation is not possible. But what can be done – and should be – is to start a friendly correspondence between representatives of various socialist organisations, and to take advantage of opportunities arising in meetings to exchange views so that a moral link between ourselves and our brothers in other countries is created. The speaker proposed that a reply in such terms be made to the Address just read out.[246]

Bebel's comments reverberated with some irony – albeit irony offered unintentionally. When Marx and Engels controlled the General Council of the IWA, they had demanded the 'strong centralisation' of the International, a centralisation in parenthesis that could not be applied to German Social-Democracy, since the law did not give it the right to join to an international organisation. (This was also the case for French, Italian and Spanish workers, but nevertheless they did join.)[247] One might ask how this 'strong centralised' international could exist with an organisation that did not affiliate. But at least Bebel acknowledged the fact – and there was obviously no question of German workers breaking the law of the land. Also what was proposed was to 'create a friendly correspondence between the representatives of various socialist organisations'. Interestingly, those federations that had been excluded by Marx and Engels – which had opposed the bureaucratic centralisation that the latter had introduced – wanted precisely to suppress the General Council in order to establish direct relations between them. This was exactly what Bebel was proposing! – Although not expressed in so many words.

Liebknecht replied on behalf of the Gotha congress and expressed 'his joy that the congress of the Jura Federation should have declared itself in favour of the unity of all socialists'. He underlined that the 'discord in the ranks of the proletariat itself was the only enemy that we should fear' and that all would be done to put an end to past discord. The *Bulletin* of the Jura Federation commented:

> As was proved by the feelings expressed in this letter, the work of seeking peace begun on the tomb of our dear departed friend Michel Bakunin[248] is well on the way to being accomplished; and we hope that the general congress of the International, which will take place this autumn in a Swiss city, will contribute towards making the various fractions of the great socialist party take a new step on the path to unity.[249]

There had always been cordial relations between the Jura Internationalists, and those who followed Lassalle – with their paper *Neuer Sozial-Demokrat*, and an exchange of papers had been introduced; but the Marxist socialists never hid their hostility to the ongoing IWA. *Volksstaat*, says James Guillaume, 'portrayed us as enemies, and on more than one occasion showed no restraint in its outrageous libels against our militants'. The exchange of letters at the time of the Gotha congress might give the impression that things were getting better: certainly an exchange of publications was agreed. The manner in which the Bern congress was announced in the papers of the two German socialists organisations was, all the same, of significance. *Volksstaat* announced it very curtly in a sentence: 'This congress will discuss closer relations between fractions that today are divided, and efforts will be made to accomplish the unity of the whole international labour party.' *Neuer Sozial-Demokrat* (of the Lassalle tendency) was warmer and published the programme of the congress in-extenso, from the circular sent out by the International's Federal Bureau. Later, James Guillaume would come to think that the idea of an expanded international congress was a part of a plan directed against the Anti-Authoritarian International:

> Later I understood – several months after the Bern congress – that something else was happening: the attitude of the leaders of the Flemish socialist party, which was set up in 1877 opened my eyes. There were people there who wanted to destroy the organisation of the International: and it was these people who put forward the idea of a 'Universal Socialist Congress', to use it as a weapon against the International.[250]

In fact, after the dissolution of the 'Marxist' International, Marx and Engels had in mind nothing other than the founding of a new ideologically homogenous International, one which would exclude 'anarchists'.

TOWARDS THE END OF THE 'ANTI-AUTHORITARIAN' IWA

The Ninth Congress of the International, Verviers, September 1877

The ninth congress of the IWA held in Verviers from 6-8 September 1877 would be the last congress of the Anti-Authoritarian International. It brought together eleven delegations adhering to new radical ideas, i.e. separation from the remainder of the socialist movement. Representatives of the participating federations agreed only to oppose a tendency in favour of a rapprochement with Social-Democracy: 'All parties are part of one reactionary mass ... all must be fought against.'[251] So, no entente was possible with the 35 'authoritarian socialist' and 'Marxist' delegates – who would be present some days later in Ghent at the Universal Socialist Congress. The delegates from the Verviers congress would be in the minority in Ghent. Moreover, the Verviers congress had expressly chosen to transform what remained of their International into an anarchist affinity organisation (with common ideas as the criteria for recruitment). The Belgian Federation and the Flemish sections left the International – which they considered as having been annexed by anarchists – and chose to support the socialists. 'The Ghent congress', wrote Marx, 'had at least this good, that Guillaume and his comrades were abandoned completely by the old allies.'[252] Marx might well rejoice at the situation after the departure of the Belgians, but circumstances for his friends in France were much worse. Of the three representatives of the General Council on whom he had relied, one had been revealed as a police-spy, another, when arrested, reneged on the International, and a third was in flight. Once again the schism was obvious and the divorce was plain. But on this occasion the advantage was with the 'Marxists'. The malaise amongst the Anti-Authoritarians would increase, and they would represent ever less of a real force.

In Verviers, at the last IWA congress, measures were put in place that would lead to its disappearance as a mass organisation. Delegates came from Belgium, Egypt, France, Germany, Greece, Italy, Spain, Russia and Switzerland. As in previous congress, delegates of organisations which were not members of the International, but which had adopted its programme, were given consultative rights and allowed to speak. Congress reaffirmed the necessity of 'real solidarity in socialist revolutionary activity', and defined this as being 'not just the most practical means, but also one that was indispensable in securing the triumph of the social revolution'. A resolution proposed by Costa and Brousse was voted on and, it should be noted, the delegate of the Jura Federation – James Guillaume – was the only one *to vote against*:

> Considering that if the social revolution is, by its very nature, international; and if, for its success it is necessary that it should spread to every land, nevertheless there are certain lands more than others which, because of their social and economic condition, find themselves more ready for a revolutionary movement,
>
> Congress declares: That it is the duty of every revolutionary to give material and moral support to every country in revolution, as it is the duty to help make it spread,[253] because only through such means is it possible to ensure the success of the revolution in those countries where it breaks out.[254]

We have no explanation for the Jurassians' opposition. One might see in such things some, almost imperceptible, evidence, revealing that some important differences had appeared within the Jura Federation, which James Guillaume does not elucidate. There was nothing new in the observation that the social revolution should not be confined to one country alone, and it was not this that would have motivated James Guillaume to vote against the motion of Costa and Brousse. Perhaps it appeared to him as somewhat demagogic. It is possible that the Jurassians understood better than others the reasoning behind the resolution, which arose from a need to legitimise after the event the action that had taken place in Benevento, in southern Italy, five months earlier, and in which Costa had taken part, rather than with a general preoccupation with principles. Interpreting in a very partial and restricted manner certain of Bakunin suggestions, internationalist militants in Italy had decide to make a start with 'propaganda by the deed'. In January 1874, they had a created an 'Italian Committee for Social Revolution' which attempted to organise several popular uprisings, amongst them the one of Benevento. On the occasion of the congress of the Italian IWA Federation held in Florence in 1876, Costa, Malatesta, Cafiero and Covelli had proclaimed anarchist communism – a doctrine and a *political* programme – which put them in opposition to the viewpoint, hitherto accepted by the

International, in favour of collectivism as a principle of *social and economic* organisation. Without doubt this was a step in the transformation of the International as a class organisation into an affinity group, a political organisation. The idea of 'propaganda by the deed' began to spread with a meaning that was completely different to that which the International had initially adopted. 'Propaganda by the deed' had at first had a constructive meaning: the creation of aid and welfare funds, of cooperatives, workplace unions, libraries, etc. Later the phrase would be interpreted differently.[255]

Costa, who would be one of the founders of the Socialist party, gave a presentation on this theme on 9 June 1877, and Paul Brousse would write an article on propaganda by the deed in the *Bulletin* of the Jura Federation. It was, he said, 'a powerful means of awakening popular awareness'. A discourse of 'revolt', illegality, and violent action became ever more virulent as the International splintered. One might even say that it was a symptom of its disorganisation. The disappearance of a mass movement went hand in hand with a breakdown in the theoretical level of the movement. So in 1880 anarchist activities would be defined as 'Permanent revolt in word, in print, with the dagger, the gun or with dynamite ... in our view, whatever is not legal, is good'.[256] Jean Maitron describes very well a crumbling away of the theoretical sophistication of the anarchist movement:

> If, on an international plane, almost nothing remained of the old IWA, in the name of the same principle of autonomy, there also disappeared all links between groups on a regional and national plane. The principle of organisation – or of lack of organisation – accepted in these times is well defined in a few lines of *Révolté*:
>
> We do not believe ... in associations, federations, etc. in the long term. For us, a grouping ... should not be established except in immediate fashion on a narrowly defined basis; once an action is accomplished, the group should re-form on new basis, either with the same elements or with new ones.[257]

One can try to imagine the state of James Guillaume's spirits in 1877. He can see that the International is beginning to break up. He must think that the lesser evil would be a rapprochement with Social-Democracy, whilst preserving the specific identity of the Jura Federation. The Italians, who now openly proclaimed themselves as 'anarchists', seemed to want to engage in rash and irresponsible adventurist activities – which James Guillaume believed would lead nowhere. Significantly James Guillaume moved to Paris and would work very closely with revolutionary syndicalists. Brousse and Costa would become parliamentary socialists. By the time of the Verviers congress, the Anti-Authoritarian International was only a shadow of its former self.[258] Few delegates came. The Belgian Federation which had been one of the pillars of the International, was not represented and after the congress other defections followed. Curiously the Federal Bureau of the IWA, which had been located in La Chaux-de-Fonds from 1875 to 1877, was transferred to Belgium, whose federation was not represented at the congress! Some collectivist sections were still active. The federation of the Vesdre valley was made responsible for the functioning of the Federal Bureau for the coming year but was unable to immediately accept the mandate because the Belgian Federation was unrepresented at the congress! In the end the congress of the Belgian Federation decided to transfer the Federal Bureau to Brussels, which implied that it should be placed in the hands of Social-Democracy!

Paul Brousse and Andrea Costa

After his medical studies, Paul Brousse (1844-1912) joined the IWA, worked with the Jura Federation and participated in the Geneva congress of 1873. 'Brousse was an active participant and defended ideas of what – from this point on – might be called anarchism', writes Marc Vuilleumier, 'Brousse was developing in an ever more extremist direction; within the Jura Federation, he was opposing James Guillaume ever more clearly.'[259] On 18 March 1877, against James Guillaume's advice, he drew key militants of the Jura Federation into a demonstration in Bern, in memory of the Commune. After a confrontation with the police, he was sentenced to one month's imprisonment. In June he created, with Jean-Louis Pindy, the journal *L'Avant-Garde*, which declared itself to be the 'Organ of the French Federation of the IWA'. From April 1878 *L'Avant-Garde* became 'An anarchist and collectivist organ'. Paul Brousse attempted to revive the French IWA Federation, which met in congress on 19-20 August 1877, in La Chaux-de-Fonds, in Switzerland. After an apologia appeared in its columns for the attacks of Emil Heinrich Hödel and Karl Eduard Nobiling – attempted assassinations of German Emperor Wilhelm I – *L'Avant-Garde* was banned in December 1878 and Paul Brousse arrested.[260] On 15 April 1879, he was sentenced to two months prison and ten years banishment from Switzerland. From June to August 1879 he lived in Brussels, and he was then in London where he contributed to the launching of *Révolté*. But his political positions were changing: he now wanted to be closer to a variety of socialist currents. He created *Le Travail*, a monthly bulletin of the London international club for social studies. After returning to France in 1880, Brousse distanced himself from anarchist ideas and from 1880-1900 became the leader of one of the major socialist parties, the Federation of Socialist Workers of France (FTSF). He then opposed Jules Guesde, an orthodox Marxist, believing that it was possible to come to socialism through progressive reforms. In 1902 the FTSF would fuse with the French Socialist Party of Jean Jaurès. He then resumed his medical work and was appointed in 1911 as director of the Ville-Evrard mental hospital. Paul Brousse was the very model of the young bourgeois who for a time supports 'anarchism' – sowing confusion in the movement through their ultra-radical positions then withdrawing and taking up for themselves everything that they had condemned in their brief 'extremist' period.

Andrea Costa (1851-1910) was similar to Brousse. He held an arts diploma from the University of Bologna. In reference books he is best known as one of the founders of the Italian Socialist Party. But he too had been an anarchist militant, a comrade of Errico Malatesta and Carlo Cafiero in the Jura Federation. James Guillaume wrote that he was the author of the phrase 'propaganda by the deed' popularised by Paul Brousse. On 9 June, 1877, Costa gave a lecture in Geneva in which he defined a principle of political activity that was founded on violence, and that aimed to develop popular awareness.[261] 'Propaganda by the deed' would be adopted by the London anarchist congress of 1881.

Costa was converted to parliamentarianism in 1879, influenced by his partner, Anna Kuliscioff.[262] In his memoirs, Bernstein refers to the manner in which an acquaintance, an Italian anarchist, Marzotti, reacted to the news of Costa's conversion in 1879: 'When he heard the news that Costa was lost to the cause of anarchism, he raised his hands above his head in excitement and cried repeatedly, almost in desperation: 'Anna! Anna! Anna!' In 1881 Costa founded the Partito Socialista Rivoluzionario Italiano, precurser of the Partito Socialista Italiano.

The debate about the Ghent Universal Socialist Congress, September 1877

Belgian delegates had proposed the idea of a Universal Socialist Congress to the Bern IWA congress of 26-29 October 1876. The idea had aroused opposition, particularly from within the current which now explicitly identified itself as anarchistic, which had no wish to hear talk of rapprochement. A commission responsible for drafting a resolution was unable to prepare a text, 'given the different views within it', writes James Guillaume, and nothing more is known. However, the sequence of events allows one to deduce what these differences may have been. Obviously two currents were in opposition within this commission: those who favoured a rapprochement with German Social-Democracy, who defended the idea of an International in which member federations could each define their own strategy, be it parliamentary or not – a view that corresponded completely with the perspectives of the Saint-Imier congress, a congress wrongly presented as founding 'anarchism'; and those who were opposed to this rapprochement, who looked for an International especially defined by its anti-parliamentary activity, in reality something of an affinity International which would be opposed to a Social-Democratic International, which was also an affinity organisation, but one with another direction. It was the 'anarchists' who ended up imposing their viewpoint, by putting to the Universal Socialist Congress of Ghent conditions that would be unacceptable for Social-Democrats. Two currents were emerging and appearing from the 'Anti-Authoritarian' IWA: one the embryo of revolutionary syndicalism, the other the embryo of a 'specific' anarchism.

The consequences flowing from the predominance of the radical position after the Verviers congress are plain: the Anti-Authoritarian IWA disappeared very quickly. One can only guess what the result might have been if those in favour of a rapprochement had been more influential and one would need to reason counterfactually, disregarding what actually happened. Until 1896 many anarchists having no International simply continued to take part in Universal Socialist Congresses, at which date German Social-Democrat manoeuvres succeeded in making their exclusion permanent. They were, after a fashion, 'squatters' in a Social-Democratic International. It would have been preferable that they participated in congresses in a regular fashion; their position would have been more solid and perhaps they would have been able to maintain themselves in the organisation, avoiding expulsion. The continuance, in the Second International, of a more radical current might perhaps have modified appreciably its attitude towards the dangers of war, and might perhaps have incited it to consider seriously the possibility of a general strike. As things turned out the Social-Democratic leaders systematically nullified every discussion of the matter. Of course such thoughts are just speculation.

Since, at the Bern congress, the commission had been unable to propose a resolution about the Ghent congress, César De Paepe, being charged with preparing a draft, read the mandate that he had received from the Belgian regional Federation. What was proposed was the 'the organisation of a Universal Socialist Congress, to be held in 1877, admitting delegates of various socialist organisations, whether the latter were branches of the International, or existed outside that association'. The objective of the congress would be to 'cement, as closely as possible, a rapprochement between diverse socialist organisations, and discuss questions of general interest for the emancipation of the proletariat'. It was to be convened by the International, and also by other socialist organisations that had come to support the idea of the congress.

James Guillaume asserted that he had no information on the origins of this Belgian proposition. In it he saw at first 'only a praiseworthy attempt to draw together all who were in favour of labour emancipation', an attempt inspired, he thinks, 'by the same conciliatory spirit that had driven the Jurassians to hold out their hands to the Social-Democratic party of Germany'.[263] The substance of the debate within the commission charged with drafting this proposal is unknown. In the public discussion, some Spanish delegates opposed the idea of a Universal Socialist Congress. As for the rest, the only reservations specified in the debate on the project concerned the preservation of the autonomy and independent principles of the International. James Guillaume emphasised that what was on the agenda was not the *reconstitution* of the International, since one existed already.

As usual, César De Paepe saw much further forward. He thought that 'the extension of freedom of association in certain countries' might lead to new organisations joining. De Paepe did not expect miracles from this first congress, but other miracles might follow, and these might lead to the reconstitution of a new International bringing together socialists from all countries, with the Socialist parties of Germany, Denmark, Portugal, the Netherlands and the Swiss Labour Union [*Arbeiterbund*]. De Paepe was not unaware that such organisations were not working particularly along the lines of the 'Anti-Authoritarian' International. Perhaps he had some intuition of the rift which would divide the labour movement, and for this reason perhaps he envisaged, for a time, the possibility of two Internationals: one for the Latin countries, the other for the countries of the North. These two Internationals, diverging on questions of tactics, would not, he thought, be hostile, because they would be 'united by aims and principles in common'.

> Today perhaps, personal bitterness and enmity are too vivid to allow any of this to come about immediately; well, then the Universal Socialist Congress of 1877 will be at least a trial run and challenge, which should lead us to an Association that is really International and for all Socialist workers.[264]

For the most part, the viewpoint that prevailed amongst the Jurassians was that it was not useful to create a new organisation while one already existed, offering every guarantee of freedom for different opinions and ways of action. This was the position of Guillaume, Perron, Joukovsky and Gutsmann.[265] The viewpoint of De Paepe was somewhat ambiguous: he was thinking of 'the reconstruction of a new International' and specified that it would bring together socialists from every land 'as was the case before in 1866'. One might think that a new International, one like that of 1866, is precisely not *new*.

The objections that were spelt out did not challenge the continuation of the current organisation but did touch on its role and function. They came from, on the one hand, certain men who in the past had appeared as opponents of the 'Anti-Authoritarian' International and, on the other hand, from the anarchist Errico Malatesta. Greulich and Franz had asked to be admitted to the congress on the same terms as Gutsmann and Vahlteich, and this was agreed.

Greulich had published an article in *Tagwacht* after the death of Bakunin that had scandalised the Jura Internationalists. The *Bulletin* of the Jura Federation replied that this article was not 'written to facilitate a rapprochement between the Socialists of various nations, something which both friends and opponents of Bakunin had hoped to see accomplished'. Greulich had joined the IWA in 1867 and helped create its section in Zurich. He edited *Tagwacht* from 1869 to 1880. The main elements of his campaigning were social progress, the creation of unions, women's emancipation and a struggle against child labour. In 1873 he was one of the founders of the Swiss Labour Union. A pragmatic reformist, he believed that problems should be negotiated between equal partners within the framework of the current political and social order. Hermann Greulich was a German immigrant and a naturalised Swiss. The Labour Union which he helped create was a motley assembly of IWA sections, of *Grütli*[266] organisations, of unions and of educational associations of German worker immigrants, with *Tagwacht* as its journal. In the years 1875 to 1878 the organisation had some 5,000 members.

The Labour Union confined its activity to the economic and professional domain and sought to develop unions. In 1877 it played a key role in the decisive vote (only passed narrowly, however) for a national factory law reducing the work day to 11 hours, prohibiting child labour, night work, imposing health and safety norms on management, making the latter responsible in cases of workplace illnesses or of accidents at work, and introducing a body of national factory inspectors responsible for watching over the observance of legal norms. Up to a point it implied an end to savage capitalism, obtained peacefully, by legal means.

The passing of this law produced a paradox: the management of Zurich metal-working businesses, 'taking into consideration the law on factory regulation, wanted a return to the eleven hour day, instead of the ten hour day that had been normal previously; workers resisted, and management sacked them'. The *Bulletin* of the Jura Federation of 4 February 1878 commented: 'So then, as we predicted, the factory law was used against workers, against the ten-hour day. Workers of German speaking Switzerland, thinking that they were voting for a progressive change, gave a stick to their bosses and they used it to give them a beating.'[267] These words place readers in the middle of a debate opposing partisans of 'political action' and those favouring revolutionary action. The satisfaction of these demands gave grist to the mill for partisans of action within the law, even though the implementation of this law, in particular its articles on the length of the working day, was long and difficult. Without doubt the achievement of one part of the programme of the democratic movement put a spoke in the wheel of those wanting more – those in Switzerland looking for more radical options.

As for Franz, he had been the editor of the Augsburg paper *Proletarier* and had been a manager of a Zurich bookshop. At precisely the point when the Jurassians were talking of reconciliation, his bookshop distributed the old stock of an anti-Bakuninist pamphlet by Marx and Engels, 'The Alliance for Socialist Democracy and the IWA'. It is difficult to believe that this was accidental. The *Bulletin* of 6 August responded: 'While socialists of diverse nuances (including the Labour Union), meeting in Bern, on 3 July declared unanimously that one should "forget past vexatious and vain dissension" citizen Franz on the contrary believed that now was the opportune moment to stir up old hatred and to bring up again lies and insults that we did not wish to remember.'[268] Facing a general hostile reception and outcry, Franz had to back pedal. So, one might expect that when these two men intervened, they would not do so by going along with the drift of the majority of congress delegates. The fact that they were given the opportunity to participate in the congress shows that at that moment there were hopes for a new beginning.

Franz was in favour of the reconstruction of the International, for him it should be 'some sort of vanguard for the labouring masses, an organisation of conscious Socialists, of agitators'. Greulich opposed Franz, believing that there should not be any sort of aristocracy in the International: there was a place for English trade unions.

As for Malatesta, speaking in the name of the Italians, he thought that the International should not be an association that was 'exclusively of workers' since the social revolution should emancipate not only workers, but also 'humanity in general'. Consequently the International should organise all revolutionaries, without class distinctions. For Malatesta, the International should be a political organisation (or a 'specific' organisation to adopt anarchist phraseology). To sum up, Franz wanted to create a political party, Greulich appeared to have a balanced perspective of social relations and Malatesta looked to create affinity groups – class considerations notwithstanding. We shall see that it was this latter viewpoint that came to dominate, and this precipitated the end of the 'Anti-Authoritarian' International.

The Ghent Congress, 9 September 1877

The congress in Ghent was dominated by a very numerous group of Flemish representatives – 27 delegates – but at least half of them took very little or no part in congress sessions. The delegates of the International, coming on from their congress in Verviers, were eleven in number. A German group had three delegates, one of whom, Wilhelm Liebknecht, did not attend the whole congress. There were two English representatives. According to James Guillaume there was a fifth, heterogeneous group, 'difficult to define'.[269] James Guillaume comments that there was a 'confused mass' in these groups, but this impression dissipated as soon as basic questions were addressed: two camps formed, one of 'authoritarian communists' and one of collectivists – delegates of the federalist International. Each person had a vote. Voting had the form of an 'opinion poll'. A lively discussion began as to whether debates should be public or not. César De Paepe's view, in favour of public sessions prevailed but, comments James Guillaume, 'beyond three or four journalists, *not a single visitor attended the congress debates*, and this was one of the unusual things which most astonished the International's delegates'. Guillaume asked if this was the result of Ghent workers indifference, or of 'an order issued by some unknown authority'. In retrospect the strange impression given as the congress went on seems to be that its organisers were not very convinced of its usefulness.

James Guillaume would come to say that they had fallen into a trap. Such disagreeable impressions amongst delegates of the International were reinforced one evening when they were asked not to speak in a meeting held in a theatre hall, so as not to strike a 'discordant note'!!! The behaviour of the congress organisers seemed to imply that their intention was to put on a demonstration of strength for their own troops but not engage in any real debate with the federalists. One thing however was certain: German Social-Democrat policy-makers, at whatever cost, wanted nothing to do with an International in which there were 'anarchists'. One event confirmed James Guillaume's view that the congress organisers themselves were not serious about things. In Bern the year before a discussion of 'property and prospects concerning modern production' had been proposed for the Ghent agenda. One might have expected that representatives from every labour organisation in Europe might have been attracted, including those who were partisans of individual property. But, notes Guillaume:

> The only persons who replied to the call of the Belgian socialists were men known to be in favour of collective property; organisations whose views on this point was doubtful or hostile had sent no delegates to the congress: such that the latter formed, not a meeting that really represented the whole of the labour movement worker in all its diversity in respect of principles and tendencies, but only a meeting of partisans of collective property, one that nevertheless was divided amongst itself on an important point: some being authoritarians, or one might say statist communists, others being Anti-Authoritarians, or one might say collectivists, or put another way anarchist communists (federalists).

The discussion on property no longer attracted any great interest – since already, in earlier IWA congresses, everything had already been said, but there was an exchange of views in Ghent between collectivists and communists as to 'how collective or communal property might be organised'. In a morning session, Greulich and De Paepe on the one hand, and Guillaume and Brousse on the other, presented their views of the subject. The exchange was quite academic and brought nothing new to the debate between collectivists and communists, or federalists and state-communists. For the communists 'property as a whole should return to the hands of the state'; but such a transformation might be carried through slowly, 'after one or more centuries'. De Paepe considered that the worker might even take 'a share of wealth', but on condition that this was practiced 'with integrity', and that there was a general participation. Responding to this Brousse and Guillaume argued that if property was simply transferred from the hands of capitalists into the hands of the state, then waged-work would truly be transformed, but not abolished; workers would become employees of the state.[270] After a fashion, Brousse and Guillaume were more 'Marxist' then the communist speakers ... Following this debate, two resolutions were proposed summing up both viewpoints.

It was the debate of Wednesday morning, concerning 'the attitude of the proletariat in respect of various political parties' which was the most significant one in the congress. All were agreed that nothing could be expected from bourgeois parties:

> Immediately thereafter differences appeared – some said: to combat bourgeois parties, the proletariat must constitute itself as a political party, and should aim to take over the state; others said, on the contrary: to combat bourgeois parties, the proletariat must look towards the destruction of the state through a social revolution, and should abstain from participation in parliamentary politics, there it would always be forced to play the role of the dupe and victim.[271]

From James Guillaume's account, the debate dragged on, and was repetitious, with some arguing for parliamentary politics (Hales, Anseele, Greulich, Brismée), and others against it (Montels,[272] Brousse, Costa). The former saw in 'political action' only a means 'to agitate amongst the people, to interest them in their own affairs, to organise them as a force capable of fighting against their enemies', said James Guillaume.

The fourth question on the agenda was the one that in large part had motivated the convening of the Ghent congress: the inauguration of a *Pact for solidarity to be agreed between the various labour and Socialist organisations*. For Bakunin, it was this that gave legitimacy to *the very existence of the International*. Different orientations – political, ideological, religious and philosophical – should not be allowed to take precedence over international labour solidarity. The congress ended with recognition of a setback. Greulich and Fränkel thought that it was impossible to bring together two tendencies – such opposed bodies as those that confronting each other at this Ghent congress – into the same organisation

Concerned about unity, De Paepe thought that despite differences sufficient common ground remained between the two currents of the labour movement to establish a Pact of Solidarity. Costa, Brousse[273] and some others observed that a rapprochement was no longer possible; it would be worse if the two tendencies were constrained to fight each other. James Guillaume proposed a motion with two points, which were voted on separately:

> Congress recognises that a pact of solidarity, which of necessity implies an identity in general principles and in the choice of means, cannot be agreed between tendencies with different means and principles.
>
> Congress expresses the wish that within the Socialist party of every nuance, one should avoid falling back into injurious insinuations and attacks which have unhappily been forthcoming on one side or another; and whilst recognising the right of each fraction to a reasoned critique of

other fractions, it recommends mutual respect to socialists, which is due to men with a feeling for their dignity and out of the conviction of each other's sincerity.

A majority, including James Guillaume himself, as well as Costa, Brousse and Montels, was of the opinion that a Pact of Solidarity was impossible. The second point was adopted unanimously, but on reflection, it reveals a setback, insofar as delegates of a labour congress worker were committing themselves to refrain from insulting each other ... On the margins of the congress, a private meeting brought together by the English, Flemish and Germans delegates, 'with two or three others', says James Guillaume, to conclude a special pact, with a federal bureau federal based in Ghent.

> Thus was constituted, facing the ongoing IWA a new grouping, which is not an association, as this grouping has no statutes, but which nevertheless constitutes, as some sort of special party, the diverse organisations whose programme is analogous to that of the German socialists.[274]

Indubitably what was coming together was the embryo of the Second International. And equally, perhaps, this was the unstated initial objective of the congress in Ghent.

Many resolutions on political action were put to the vote, among them two eccentric ones which obtained only, or almost only, the votes of their authors. The resolution of the International concluded that it was necessary to 'combat all political parties, whether they be called socialist or not, hoping that workers who for the time being join the ranks of such diverse parties, should be enlightened by experience, opening their eyes, abandoning the ways of politics so as to adopt the path of *anti-governmental* socialism'. Evidently this was a declaration of war. The Social-Democratic resolution was curiously less categorical than that of the federalists:

> Considering that social emancipation is inseparable from political emancipation, congress declares that the proletariat, organised as a distinct party, opposed to all other parties formed by the wealthy classes, must use all political means that work for the social emancipation of all its members.

Finally, congress concluded with an appeal, adopted by all except Costa, for the constitution of an international federation of trades bodies and the creation of a 'Central Bureau for correspondence and workers' statistics' which was to bring together and publish information on the price of labour, foodstuffs, working hours, factory regulations, etc.' Supporting it, César De Paepe declared that it 'would not have a great practical value', and 'its activity might be almost nothing', but it would be, vis-à-vis the enemy bourgeoisie, 'the exterior sign of socialist unity, a sign comparable to the Red Flag, which despite our divisions, nevertheless remains the emblem of us all' – a somewhat downbeat comment.

James Guillaume was equally disappointed. The men who had organised the Ghent congress were certainly not enemies, but 'men who given the path they had adopted, have become somewhat more distant from us'. Some of them, in 1873, had helped federalists 'to reorganise the International on the basis of autonomy' and, they had worked together since The Hague congress. Such feelings and emotions 'were common amongst the greater part of the delegates of the International, and I had the satisfaction of seeing almost all my comrades adopt the same attitude as me,' declared James Guillaume. As to the atmosphere of the congress, it is indicative that the latter decided to publish no official report of its deliberations.

Marx, having been informed on the Ghent congress by Maltman Barry,[275] wrote to Sorge on 27 September 1877. His comments were much in character:

> Whilst the congress in Ghent left much to be desired on other points, it was good in this at least: Guillaume and Co. were completely abandoned by their former allies. It was with difficulty that the Flemish workers were prevented from doing as they desired, thrashing Guillaume.[276] That pretentious chatterer De Paepe insulted them,[277] as also did Brismée.[278] Mr John Hales ditto.[279] The latter placed himself under the orders of – [Maltman] Barry whom I had had attend in part as a member of the congress in Ghent (as a delegate of some society, which one I do not know),[280] and in part as a correspondent of the London *Standard*. For my part, I personally want nothing more to do with Jung and Hales, but, vis-à-vis the Jurassians their second apostasy is useful.[281] Here Barry is my factotum; he also directed the reporter of *The Times* (that newspaper has ceased to employ Mr Eccarius).[282]

James Guillaume commented that this letter, published by Sorge, did little to add to the reputation of his master.

Was the convening of a reunification congress part of some Machiavellian plan targeting the International? It is impossible to answer this question. One can only say that within the European proletariat there was a real desire for unity and that, among some Social-Democratic leaders this desire for unity was not without ulterior motives. It is equally obvious that the chief leaders of German Socialism – Marx, Engels and the Social-Democrat leaders – wished at any price to prevent a unification of the European labour movement in which anarchists might have been an active element. Their persistent efforts, between 1889 and 1896, to exclude them from the Second International, prove as much. It is also true that the IWA current – which might now be termed as 'anarchist' – greatly helped the German Social-Democratic leaders by choosing to present to a congress aimed at rapprochement a motion so restrictive it would have been impossible for the other side to accept it.

James Guillaume's feeling that the International had fallen into a trap would be expressed retrospectively, after he had become aware of subsequent events. Bakunin's comrade obviously lacked sufficient distance to be able to analyse the circumstances which had led to this 'trap' and, above all, he was not ready to take into account that there were certain elements of the 'Anti-Authoritarian' International itself which had helped to bring an end to the International.

The results achieved by the Social-Democratic model produced an irresistible force of attraction. The German party grew from day to day and its organisation grew stronger. It obtained 340,000 votes in the 1874 elections, in January 1877 it had 490,000. 'This could not fail to make an impression on all Socialists, and greatly impacted on those that were hesitant,' writes Yurri Steklov in his history of the First International.[283] The ways and means used by the 'Anti-Authoritarian' International appeared to have hit a buffer, one which they could not get over; many workers were looking for something else. The Belgians were not slow in moving on. In Ghent and Antwerp the Social-Democratic programme was adopted, and most Brussels workers followed suit. Only a few French-speaking Belgians resisted and remained in the International, opposing the use of universal suffrage and 'political action'. Lastly, César De Paepe, one of the pillars of the Anti-Authoritarian International, also turned towards Social-Democracy, recognising the importance of political reforms and rejecting abstentionism.

However one should be careful not to fall into simplistic explanations of these developments towards action within the law, or towards parliamentary action, either accusing workers of wanting to join the system at all costs, or, following De Paepe, and also Bakunin, dividing the working class into 'Northerners' who favoured legal action, and 'Latins' who opposed to it.

The Congress of Fribourg, 1878. The end of the Jura Federation and the evaporation of the 'anti- authoritarian' International.

After Verviers and Ghent, some sections and federations still struggled along in the Jura, but they ended up moving towards a closer relationship with parliamentary socialism. The Jura Federation survived the evaporation of the 'Anti-Authoritarian' International by only a few years. The decay of the organisation which had beaten the London bureaucracy so spectacularly in September 1872 was such that after Verviers and Ghent many Jura anarchist delegates – Costa, Montels, Werner, Rinke and Kropotkin – simply did not return to Switzerland. Kropotkin, however, returned to Geneva a little later. Then James Guillaume and Paul Brousse left. This haemorrhage of key persons left a gap which was not filled. Adhémar Schwitzguébel turned little by little towards parliamentary Socialism. As for Auguste Spichiger, Jean Louis Pindy and their friends, they remained loyal to 'Bakuninist' ideas and soon would form a small group with no real influence.[284]

A congress of the Jura Federation was held from 3-5 August 1878 in Fribourg, with representatives from sections from La Chaux-de-Fonds, Bern, Zurich, Boncourt, Vevey, Fribourg and from the Courtelary district Labour Federation. The Le Locle section had ceased to exist some years before and the Neuchâtel section had declined since James Guillaume's departure. The weakness of some sections was induced by economic crisis, but changing ideas and support for political, i.e. parliamentary, action also caused a decline that affected many sections.

A period now began, lasting some twenty years, in which two main labour strategies would coexist: a revolutionary strategy for labour action and another for electoral and political action, which would be termed 'reformist'. This was a reformism that did not abandon a project for a global transformation of the system, but kept in mind that it should be accomplished through successive stages. Thus, it is important to distinguish it from what is often called 'reformism' today, which has in mind only some partial rearrangement of the capitalist system, and which does not deserve to be called 'reformist'. So, this period is characterised by the coexistence of these two strategies and this is shown by the movements of activists, changing sides back and forth from time to time, as circumstances dictated. As yet nothing was fixed. Within the Social-Democratic current some activist groups supported revolutionary action, while not in principle excluding recourse to elections, or ready to return to revolutionary action whenever electoral experience produced only disappointment. On the other hand within the revolutionary movement (and in these times the only revolutionary movement was anarchist), certain activists ended up supporting 'political' action. So there was no rigid division between these two options. The dividing walls would be progressively built up by the most intransigent activists of each camp: those who may be termed 'anarchists' and who would reject any recourse to 'legal' action, that is to say using the recourse of the law to have demands implemented; and those – German Social-Democrats above all – who would do their utmost to impose a single, legal and parliamentary path, excluding all others, and who would go on to expel 'anarchists' from Socialist internationalist congresses from 1896 onwards.

Unsuccessful attempts were made to bring together anarchists and revolutionary Social-Democrats. It is true that on the whole, revolutionary Social-Democrats tottering towards anarchism had a tendency, after a short while, to return to the mainstream. Such a tendency to retreat should not necessarily be analysed as a symptom of the intrinsic reformist roots of these activists. It might also be explained by the disappointing observations made relative to their cohabitation with the anarchist movement. In 1891, Malatesta took part in the congress of Capolago which hoped to constitute a 'revolutionary anarchist socialist party' with anti-parliamentary Socialists and anarchists.[285]

The Fribourg congress is quite revealing as to the evolution of the Jura Federation. In the main it had been a labour organisation, one of a workplace union type, but, bit by bit it became an affinity organisation. The congress delegates included Schwitzguébel, Spichiger,[286] Kahn,[287] Kropotkin, (who had returned to Switzerland) and Brousse. The congress agenda featured a reading by Rodolphe Kahn of a work of Élisée Reclus, who was unable to attend, on the subject: 'Why are we revolutionaries? Why are we anarchists? Why are we collectivists?' Kropotkin and Brousse also made contributions. Kropotkin elaborated a programme founded on four points:

- Negation of the state.
- Free Federations of Communes and Associations of Autonomous Producers.
- Spontaneous popular uprisings, social revolution, expropriation of owners of capital, wealth being shared out among communes or producer groups.
- Propaganda by the deed, to awaken in the people a spirit of initiative, looking forward to the disorganisation of the state and the preparation of a 'final liquidation'.

Brousse defended the principle of propaganda by the deed. In his view it should facilitate some immediate improvements in social conditions. Congress expressed its approval for a collective appropriation of social wealth, for the abolition of the state, and for insurrectionary action; but beyond the congresses lining up with the radical discourse of particular personalities, the congress report takes note of interesting reservations on the electoral question:

> But, although all congress delegates unanimously expressed the same thinking – against voting that helps constitute the regular functioning of the workings of the state – yet, considering a vote that was revolutionary and anarchist, a vote that would be destructive of such workings, they also accepted that this question should be studied further.[288]

Kropotkin, in a letter to Paul Robin, indicated that only eight congress delegates were present, but nonetheless there was a discussion of what today might be termed libertarian municipalism:[289]

> Paul Brousse, who in a short while would go over to the camp of reformist Social-Democracy, began by vigorously defending the principle of autonomy, 'to discourage, the use of the vote, as much as possible'. Adhémar Schwitzguébel underlined that communal autonomy 'might, for us, become a starting point for general popular agitation and might open up a practical path, helping us to put our principles into practice'. According to him, it would be a very favourable ground for experimentation. Kropotkin went much further: 'States are fatally destined to fail and in their stead will come free communes, freely federated amongst themselves ... In a commune, where there are innumerable questions of communal interest, we will find places more conducive to our theoretical propaganda, and to the insurrectional achievement of anarchist and collectivist ideas.' Additionally, he emphasised that: 'a clear distinction has to be drawn between, on the one hand a preoccupation with the details of communal life, that help legally achieve some fragile improvements, and on the other hand seizing opportunities to incite the spirit of revolutionary socialism'.

An article of Marianne Enckell notes that Brousse had defended the principle of voting in certain circumstances, on occasions when a protest vote sought to obtain an amnesty, but he also thought that elections might serve provisionally at least on a communal level. 'When it is not yet possible to overthrow a state in its entirety, if for a certain time conditions do not allow one's own forces to be put to the test, it is better with the vote to spoil its spiralling tentacles, seeking to block things rather than sitting back watching it carry out its work in peace.'[290] Rodolphe Kahn did not share this opinion: for him a vote in a commune had no use. Either there wasn't a revolutionary majority or there was, in which case it could do whatever it was elected to do. Ten years earlier, James Guillaume had observed from experience and from the participation of IWA sections in local elections: 'The cap of a councillor – for a commune, state [canton] or [national] confederation – once it tops the head of even the most sincere, or most intelligent socialist, immediately becomes something that extinguishes the flame of revolution.' But the alternative proposed by the comrade of Bakunin was to promote the mass action of the working class on the class terrain. The problem in 1878, and doubtless for some years previously, was that the Jura Federation was no longer in a fit state to act on this terrain. For activists, being attracted to the electoral path, even at times when it was dressed up with subversive intentions, as Brousse suggested, was perhaps a symptom of the loss of an active revolutionary perspective. In fact, shortly afterwards Brousse would move to support Social-Democracy.

The administration of the *Bulletin* of the Jura Federation had been transferred, for the year 1878, from Sonvilier to La Chaux-de-Fonds. The organ of the Jura Federation had declined in the face of a growing Social-Democratic movement in the Jura and its circulation had been going down for some years. Towards the end of 1877 a number of readers stopped subscribing because economic crisis left them unable to keep up payments. The departure of James Guillaume to Paris in 1878 also had a fatal impact on the *Bulletin*. The last issue of the organ of the Jura Federation appeared on 25 March 1878:

> As we retire from the arena, we are conscious that we have not worked in vain over six years to agitate for socialist ideas. At the time of the conflict between Anti-Authoritarians and authoritarians in the International, our modest newssheet was one of the first to champion federalist principles; as far as its strength permitted it contributed to the defeat of the General Council, and those principles which it defended are now accepted even by our former adversaries: no international organisation will be possible hereafter except on the basis of federation and the autonomy of each grouping. As for our political and economic programme – Collectivism and Anarchism and, one might say 'freedom in a community '– this has become better and better understood, and every day, the number of

serious minded persons who support it is becoming ever larger.

Circumstances became more complicated for the Jurassians because Paul Brousse, who was prone to verbal extremism, took up a position in favour of regicide in a dozen issues of *L'Avant-Garde*, and this had led to its disappearance at the end of 1878.[291] In April 1879, Brousse was sentenced to two months imprisonment and ten years exclusion from the country. *L'Avant-Garde* vanished. Kropotkin in Geneva then took up the challenge and published, almost single-handed, *Le Révolté*.

So it came about that I, a foreigner, had to undertake the editing of the organ for the federation. I hesitated, of course, but there was nothing else to be done, and with two friends, Dumartheray and Herzig, I started a new fortnightly paper in Geneva, in February 1879, entitled *Le Révolté*. I had to write most of it myself.[292]

The thoughts of Kropotkin are revealing about the circumstances facing the Jura Federation: it no longer had a capacity to publish a journal and it had to be taken in hand by a foreigner, one who recognised that he had to act almost alone. The downwards trend was confirmed in the decision taken by the Congress of Fribourg that: '[given] the crisis that now exists in all countries and with uncertainty as to [prospects for] a good attendance at such a congress, or conference, there are no grounds for the federation to organise an annual congress of the International, nor a conference that might serve to replace it.'[293] In reality the disappearance of the Anti-Authoritarian International resulted from this decision, its existence, having become thoroughly theoretical, was quite dependent on the survival of the Jura Federation. The latter would only survive for a little longer before it too disappeared.

The last Congress of the Jura Federation was held in La Chaux-de-Fonds on 9-10 October 1880. All the big names of anarchism were there, beginning with Kropotkin who made a speech on reformist socialism and anarchist socialism; also Élisée Reclus, and Carlo Cafiero, who came specially. The Congress proclaimed anarchist communism as the 'necessary and inevitable consequence of social revolution'. Kropotkin proposed communism as a goal and presented a report on the subject of 'the anarchist idea and practical means of achieving it'. 'The economic revolution takes in the direct expropriation by workers of the owners of capital through communes. Social reorganisation will be based on groupings of independent communes and federations of communes.'

Thereafter only isolated traces of anarchism can be found in the Jura. The future destiny of the Jura Federation is illustrated by the choices made by the two men who were closest to Bakunin. James Guillaume became closer to activists, who were beginning to build revolutionary syndicalism in the French CGT (General Labour Confederation). Adhémar Schwitzguébel moved over to Social-Democracy.

THE BIRTH OF ANARCHISM

Collectivists and Communist Anarchists

Collectivists had focused on the collective ownership of *the means of production*. From 1876 onwards, in response to initiatives coming from Italian groups, the Jura Federation developed ideas about collective property *over the products of labour*, as a necessary complement to the collectivist programme. At the Jura Federation's congress in La Chaux-de-Fonds on 12 October 1879, Kropotkin proposed the adoption of communism as a goal with collectivism as a transitional form.

From the viewpoint of the Russian revolutionary, and for IWA collectivists, the notion of 'to each according to their work' sought to separate out those who did no work, social parasites, but not in any way those who were incapable of working. So one might say that the dictum proposed by 'anarchist communists', 'to each according to their needs,' only served to make more precise that which was already self-evident. But, at the same time, this approach also introduced some ambiguity (each persons' needs are subjective) and some perverse aspects. Whereas the basis for the collectivists' comparative analysis derived from the idea that rights, which may be claimed from society, result from duties that one has towards it, the position of the Kropotkinite communist-anarchists suggests that all have rights without it being clear that duties go hand in hand.[294] One might deduce that these two systems are not variations on the same trains of thought, but two different doctrines. This change perhaps explains the transition from an ideology based on work, to an ideology based on consumption (not necessarily linked to work or, in general terms to a concern that favoured collectivism).

But it would be a great error to reiterate word for word the problematic posed by Bakuninists and Kropotkinians who, after a fashion, as far as matters of doctrine were concerned, were only trying to put things in their proper place. In reality, speaking of 'to each according to their work' or of 'to each according to their need' had little sense, any more than did 'returning to the worker the product of his labour'. Such notions should be understood as metaphors. It was not a question of giving to each person, one by one, in proportion to output. Nor was it a question of giving nothing to all those who did not work. Each person at work had around them a number of persons who are not working, or have ceased working: children, perhaps spouses, parents, the infirm, etc. Did communist-anarchists, partisans of 'to each according to their needs' really believe that collectivists would not allow such non-workers social support? In a text dating from 1866, before he joined the International, Bakunin wrote: 'The old, the disabled and the sick will be supported with care and respect, they will enjoy all their social or political rights and will be generously treated and supported by society.'[295]

Our descendants, when they come to build a libertarian society will confront the problem of putting in place overall arrangements that define peoples' social needs, and means that will facilitate the fulfilment of these objectives. The demands of schools, hospitals, crèches, etc. will need to be considered, and more besides: does the son of a neighbour 'need' a 'ghetto blaster'. On this point Bakunin and Kropotkin are quite in accord: the former said that a revolution that does not immediately improve peoples' lives is doomed not to progress. The entire thinking of the latter was built around the necessity of constructing an anarchist society for popular needs.

One might say that anarchism, in the contemporary meaning of the word, was born at this moment, at the end of the Anti-Authoritarian IWA, as the activists who were formerly in the Jura Federation abandoned collectivism and defined 'anarchist communism'. However what constituted anarchism as a movement was not so much this timely theoretical innovation, but rather the new ways and means that it would adopt in its activity. The Anti-Authoritarian current ceased to exist as a mass movement. It was atomised into groups based on the affinity of ideas, but lost its character and quality as a class structure. Edouard Dolleans, in his *History of the labour movement*, explains that towards the end of the Jura Federation: 'If the *Bulletin* of the Jura Federation informs us of the creation of new sections, these new sections are not workers' groupings, but rather purely revolutionary groups.'[296] Dolleans adds that within these revolutionary groups, various opinions were at odds, some would become followers of Guesde, others of anarchism.

The 'Anti-Authoritarian' concept

The libertarian movement's ability to critically analyse the bureaucracy that developed in the management of the IWA was doubtless ill-served by an error of interpretation in the concept of authority, or at least by a gradual adjustment in the meaning of the word. The 'Anti-Authoritarian' concept was derived from a concept of authority often found in Proudhon and Bakunin, but for these authors it was a concept applied to diverse forms of political power. 'Authoritarian communism' is state communism. The concept was created as a synonym for 'bureaucratic' to characterise Marx and his friends. 'Anti-Authoritarians' were opposed to the bureaucratic practice in the management of the International. Undeniably Marx and the General Council did behave in this fashion, but it was not this that was mostly targeted.

Being Anti-Authoritarian was not a moral attitude, a character trait, or a rejection of every form of authority, it was an alternative *political* attitude. Anti-Authoritarian signified 'democratic'. That word existed at this time, but it too had another meaning. Less than a century after the French revolution, it was something that characterised the political practice of the bourgeoisie. The democrats were all bourgeois. Only later were notions of democracy and the proletariat joined together in the expression 'workers' democracy'. The Anti-Authoritarian tendency of the IWA was thus in favour of workers' democracy, whereas the Marxist tendency was perceived as being in favour of bureaucratic centralisation.

The defeat of the collectivists at the congress of The Hague in 1872 would be placed on account against this 'authority', and then against the very principle of organisation, which had produced this 'authority'. The word came to be used more and more in a psychological and behaviourist sense. Thus there developed opposition to all forms of organisation as a reaction against the centralisation and bureaucratisation put in place by Marx. Engels made no mistake when he characterised Anti-Authoritarians through the term of 'autonomists'.[297] The very basis of the doctrine elaborated by Proudhon and Bakunin – with federalism as its centre of gravity – would be abandoned. What now appeared on the plane of doctrine, was a particular form of radicalised liberalism, whilst on the plane of organisation, there came something which today might be called horizontalism, which is in fact the negation of federalism.

Anti-Authoritarian activists wanted to draw lessons from history. They would argue that it was the centralisation of the organisation, the control of its apparatus by a small clique that was the cause of authoritarianism, i.e. the bureaucratic degeneration of the International. So all centralisation, whatever form it might take, should be prevented. In reaction they would turn to the defence of autonomy exclusively, becoming bitter opponents of all forms of organisation. Organisation was accused, it was the natural source engendering 'authority'. In this way they come out against the viewpoint defended by the great theoreticians of the libertarian movement, who advocated federalism, i.e. an equilibrium between on the one hand the autonomous action of basic structures, and on the other centralisation.[298] Now there was opposition to all forms of representation whereas previously delegates nominated by sections *had represented* the latter in congresses, but, little by little, the meaning contained in the term 'Anti-Authoritarian', which at first was equivalent to 'anti-bureaucratic', moved on. Hereafter authority was considered as form of behaviour and it was were opposed in whatever form it might take. A simple respect for guidelines that had been freely debated became 'authoritarianism'. The simple fact of taking on any elective function was termed as 'authoritarian', because voting to temporarily delegate power had become an intolerable abdication of one's individual liberty. Individual initiative alone became acceptable.[299]

Previously, then, the *political* concept of authority had been applied to something that related to the power of the state, or to relations of power within an organisation, now the term 'authority' ended up taking on a *psychological* connotation, something that Malatesta explained perfectly well:

> The fundamental error of anarchists who oppose organisation is the belief that there is no possibility of organisation without authority. And, once this hypothesis is accepted, they prefer renouncing all organisation, rather than accepting a minimum of authority. Now to us it is self-evident that organisation, that is to say association for a particular purpose and with necessary means and forms to achieve this goal, is a necessity in social life, ... But even so we would prefer some annoying authority which might make life somewhat less happy to a disorganisation that would render it impossible.[300]

Despite everything, this thinking remained within a behaviourialist Anti-Authoritarian perspective, organisation was inevitable, but it was intrinsically fated to produce 'authority': the simple fact of taking on responsibilities was 'authoritarian'. Nominating someone for responsibilities involved an abandonment of one's personal sovereignty. In the same article, Malatesta cited the example of an engineer and train chief who were 'natural authorities', but 'people prefer to submit themselves to their authority rather than to having to travel on foot ...' What was tragic in this business was that anarchists had come to consider as a relation of 'authority' the fact that an engineer might drive a train (or that a dentist might take care of a cavity, etc.), whereas these were only cases of a people doing their job – anyone could refuse by avoiding taking trains (or not going to the dentist).

Such thinking distorted any reflection on problems of 'authority' and made for much time-wasting over quibbles.

These new fashioned 'Anti-Authoritarians' defended total decentralisation as a method of avoiding the centralisation that they had encountered. In reaction to centralisation, complete autonomy was adopted by anarchists as their magic word, to the point where there was no real organisation but only structures at the base. If some instance of regulation was needed it would have no 'political' function but only a technical one: to distribute correspondence, etc. So, when anarchists put in place such structures – ones without any 'political' or decision-making function – the distribution of mail would never work, doubtless because to distribute mail money would be needed, and to have money it would be necessary to decide on raising subscriptions, which would be a proof of 'authority'.

Organisation of any sort would be seen as leading to authority, to centralisation and bureaucracy. The solution proposed would be to constitute autonomous structures, with only occasional links between them. All this would challenge one of the fundamental of anarchism, federalism. 'Federalism was a constitutive element of anarchism since the IWA period, since in this matter the anarchist current was asserted through its critique of centralism and its celebration of autonomy', says Marianne Enckell,[301] and she is perfectly right in noting that federalism 'is the antonym of centralisation, rather than decentralisation'.[302]

'Anti-Authoritarian' activists, observing what they considered as the harmful consequences of the *very principle of organisation* after the end of the IWA, emptied federalism of its content and advocated extreme decentralisation. They moved over to rely, firstly on small affinity groups supposedly guaranteeing the absence of bureaucratisation (of 'authority'), then to the individual, after which there was nothing more to decentralise. Organisation, limited to the affinity group, had no role analysing a situation or defining a common line of action, its function was to facilitate personal development.[303] When Kropotkin wrote in *La Science moderne et l'anarchie* that: 'we are looking for progress through the widest emancipation of individual initiative from the authority of the state; and in the limitation of governmental functions,' the reader has to conclude that organisation is not a place where a strategy for struggle against capital is worked out collectively but a place where individuals come to discuss their problems, to explore their individuality and develop their individual initiative. Rather than capital,[304] 'Authority' and by extension the state – concentrated Authority – ends up becoming the main enemy of the anarchist, and thereafter anarchism dissolves into individualism.

Affinity groups were to be set up in which individual revolutionary initiative and exemplary action would facilitate moving on to communist society without a period of transition. An anarchist theoretician expressing such views had no idea strictly speaking, of what unionism or syndicalism might be, or in more general terms of the organisation of groups of workers who defend themselves against capitalists. For some time the activity of such anarchists, notably in Spain and Italy, consisted of provoking or taking part in local insurrections, in the course of which a few dozen persons would take over the offices of a local mayor, burning administrative documents, proclaiming communism, most often in the face of general indifference, before being chased away by the merciless police . So people would be offered an example. Readers will find a very long and extremely revealing quotation from Malatesta in an end-note – probably the longest ever definition of a 'letterbox'.[305] Organisation in itself, as an element of authority, became an evil and autonomy a virtue. Group autonomy, however minimally organised, itself became a source of 'authority', and out of this there arose calls for the autonomy of the individual within the group. Indubitably, this reaction, which might be termed as centrifugal, was the spark of a current which would define itself as individualist anarchist. Max Stirner, a man totally unknown, who at this point had no influence, would be 'rediscovered' only ten years later.[306] Those who opposed organisation in principle would push their convictions a long way. Gaston Leval recalls that Malatesta was wounded by a shot from a revolver fired by an anarchist who considered organising a federal movement as treason, and that he would have been killed but for the intervention of other comrades.[307]

CONCLUSION

When the history of the IWA is examined with the benefit of hindsight one may see that there were two ways of approaching political questions – in their broadest sense. In his correspondence Marx was incapable of accepting disagreement without showing contempt and heaping insults on his opponents. Bakunin was able to disagree with someone without denying that he or she had the right to be respected. One might say that someone in disagreement with him, who expressed opinions resolutely and with conviction, was therefore worth that much more respect.

Despite disagreements, despite innumerable slurs spread by Marx and his entourage, Bakunin did not contest that Marx had his merits, both theoretical[308] and practical. So, in *Protestation de l'Alliance* (July 1871), the Russian revolutionary set out his opinion on the role of Marx in the International:

> We seize this opportunity to render homage to the illustrious chiefs of the German communist party, to citizens Marx and Engels …, and also citizen J. Philipp Becker, our one-time friend, and now our implacable enemy. They were – as far as it is possible for any individual to create something – the veritable creators of the International Association. We do this with as much pleasure and we will soon be compelled to combat them. Our esteem for them is sincere and profound, but does not go so far as idolatry and will never draw us to enslave ourselves to them. And, whilst continuing to recognise – in full justice – the immense services that they have given, and continue to give even today to the IWA, we will never cease to fight their false authoritarian theories, their dictatorial leanings, and that manner of subterranean intrigues, vain grudges, miserable personal animosities, dirty insults and infamous slurs, which moreover characterise political struggles of almost all Germans, and which they have sadly brought with them into the IWA.[309]

Such ideas, however surprising they may seem, were sincere; Bakunin reiterates them many times. He was of course in error in attributing to

Marx the 'creation' of the IWA, but he often repeated that the latter had preserved the International from bourgeois influence.

There was a group of men around Marx through whom he controlled the apparatus of the IWA, but he had few supporters – individuals, rather than structures. An examination of the minutes of the General Council and of Marx and Engels' correspondence with the two competing tendencies of German Socialists – Lassalians and Eisenachers – reveals three surprising facts:

a) German leaders displayed no particular enthusiasm for the IWA, and if they were interested for a short time, whilst the IWA was at its peak – barely over two years – they showed no interest later. A link to the IWA had interest only insofar as it aided them in respect of their internal politics.

b) Lassallians and Eisenachers called on Marx only in the course of the argument and competition between these two socialist groups; they took no notice of Marx whenever it might be inconvenient for them.

c) Above all Marx and Engels wanted German socialists to take part in the IWA in order to have some reinforcement for their own position in the IWA – all told a precarious position in the General Council; with this in mind their reports on the least event in Germany were very exaggerated and deceitful.[310] At the congress of The Hague their panic, in the face of a quasi-absence of dues from Germany, revealed just how little interest there was in the IWA among German activists. The complete absence of support from IWA federations for Marx and Engels explains why the founders of so-called 'scientific' socialism were completely isolated, once federations understood that they had been manipulated at the congress of The Hague, and the 'fiasco' – Marx's own expression– of the 'Marxist' congress of 1873.

In Bakunin's view the International should preserve its character as a mass organisation. Workers should join, not on the basis of ideas or a programme, but on the basis of reciprocal solidarity and for the defence of their material interest. Long years of internal debate would be needed to build homogeneity. Meanwhile debates were to be encouraged but above all the imposition of one single programme for the IWA – a project that Bakunin attributed to Marx – was to be resisted. But the working class had not achieved a state of sufficient maturity that might allow it to do without a revolutionary minority. In 1870 no exact model had been found as to how such a revolutionary minority should organise.

The history of the IWA was not confined to a confrontation between 'Anarchism' and 'Socialism' or between Bakunin and Marx. One might equally well say that it also revealed the embryo of a confrontation between Anarchism and Revolutionary Syndicalism. In this book I have wanted to show that many ideas firmly imbedded in people's minds did not match up to reality. Collective memory in relation to the First International has largely been monopolised by the Marxist current, producing a deformed history, one which even the Anarchist movement has ended up accepting. The idea – widely understood and accepted idea in the libertarian movement – that the Saint-Imier international congress was an 'anarchist' secession is a perfect example. One hundred and fifty years on, in relation to the history of the IWA, one has to take a step back to make some critical observations.

1. The libertarian movement has, it appears, never sought to explain why the Saint-Imier international congress, which Bakunin termed as a 'victory for freedom and for the International against authoritarian intrigue'[311] and which was an *immense success* for the federalist current of the International, led, six years later to the very real fading away of the IWA. Bakunin, when he resigned from the International in 1873, wrote to his friends a letter in which he declared that 'the time for great theoretical discussion – spoken or written – has passed. In the last nine years in the IWA more ideas have been developed than would be needed to save the world, if ideas were enough to save it, and I defy anyone to invent something new. The time is not for ideas but for acts. Today, what matters is the organisation of proletarian forces. But this organisation has to be the work of the proletariat itself.'[312] It was at this particular moment that Bakunin set out his appeal to organise 'solidarity that is ever more practical, militant, and international, amongst workers of all trades and all lands', and these words were deformed by Italian anarchists, who would launch themselves into attempted insurrections which would end lamentably and would precipitate the dissolution of the Anti-Authoritarian International.[313]

2. The disappearance of the IWA would be the event that would mark the separation of the two currents of the International, the Marxist, and the Federalist – not 'Anarchist'.[314] Thereafter these currents evolved in different directions. But this separation did not occur all at once. It is significant that the federalist current, with James Guillaume as its leading spirit, clearly attempted on several occasions to prevent this separation being made irreversible, and sought compromise – to allow a minimum of common action. It was the Marxists who systematically refused any rapprochement with 'Anarchists' a term that German Social-Democrats applied to all (Rosa Luxemburg included) who, if necessary, promoted class struggle and the

use of the general strike. One might say that the IWA was the place and the event which put in place a model of relations between Marxism and 'Anarchism', a model which excluded any possibility of coming together.

3. At a distance of 150 years, one might forget that between 1870 and 1900 not everything was fixed or clear, and that the separation between the Federalist-syndicalist current and the Social-Democratic current was not absolutely definite. For many years after the end of the Anti-Authoritarian IWA, activists of these traditions – Anti-Authoritarian and Bakuninist – obstinately took part in international Socialist congresses; and likewise from when the Second International was set up until 1896 they took part in its congresses. The opposite was equally true: within Social-Democracy there were opposition currents close to Anarchism. There was, as yet, no fixed model. There were a number of comings and goings between groups affiliated with a federalist and Anti-Authoritarian tradition and groups emanating from a Social-Democratic tradition. It would be tiresome to mention them all, but let us mention some of those from Social-Democracy: Johan Most, Gustav Landauer, and Domela Nieuwenhuis.

There was up to a point a 'transition period' in which workers' groups, trying out one or another strategy, might move from one current to another according to circumstance. The categorical refusal of Second International leaders to integrate in their ranks any group that would not accept parliamentary action may have contributed to the formation of a relatively homogenous façade on the side of the 'official' socialist movement, but it worked to the detriment of life and debate. The hard-heartedness of German Social-Democracy towards any discussion of a general strike in case of war was an obvious consequence of its dogmatic and sectarian approach to such problems.

However, the model of the Second International was not entirely rigid at first, because the latter accepted workplace/union organisations – on the condition that the latter were in favour of an electoral strategy (such a strategy was called 'political action'). French activists who had been expelled from one Socialist congress as anarchists reappeared at the next with a mandate from the CGT (General Labour Confederation). In the years leading up to 1900 there was a real convergence between Anarchism and left non-parliamentary Socialism. At this point socialist delegations in international congresses were not yet homogenous, insofar as the Social-Democratic model was thus far neither completely fixed nor wholly imposed. When in 1893 the German delegation to the Second International congress in Zurich had Gustav Landauer's Independents – a tendency opposed to parliamentarianism – expelled from the hall of the congress this act of intolerance sparked an outcry, and fifty delegates left the hall in solidarity. These congress dissidents held separate meetings: amongst them were Anarchists from Britain, France, Italy, most of the Dutch Socialists and French Socialists. It was in these meetings that Domela Nieuwenhuis declared that *'a fusion of all revolutionary elements is possible'*. [315] This convergence between anarchists and revolutionary socialists might have led to a congress in 1900, and might have resulted in the formation of an Anti-Authoritarian International. That congress was dispersed by the police, acting within the letter of anti-anarchist laws of 1894, and it never met.[316] But doubtless it would be wrong to attribute to the French police the entire responsibility for setbacks that impeded the creation of an Anti-Authoritarian International: internal factors played a considerable role. If, at the time, the initiative had encountered an overwhelming need it would have succeeded. But there was delay and, as had happened before, many anti-parliamentary Socialists ended up returning to the ranks of Social-Democracy.

4. When it became evident that there was a 'crisis' of Marxism, and also a 'crisis' of Anarchism, a certain number of activists pondered whether it was possible to found a 'Libertarian Marxism'.[317] Such new thinking emerged with an idea that Anarchism had some theoretical shortcomings and the remedy was to be sought in Marxism. There was talk of 'historical materialism' (an expression not to be found in Marx), even of a dictatorship of the proletariat with some anarchist sauce (although this was a concept that was entirely marginal in Marx).[318] Bakunin was presented as a disciple of Marx,[319] and Marx was even presented as a theorist of Anarchism.[320] Those Anarchist activists who devoted themselves to such work seemed to be ignorant of all, or almost all, Anarchist theory, and took on an excessively narrow vision of Marxist doctrine. Among those Marxists who wanted to draw an Anarchist covering over themselves, there was a turn to the texts of his youth, which presented 'humanist' characteristics – although these had been categorically rejected by Marx.[321] *Civil War in France*– an entirely opportunist work – was taken as a model, one which Bakunin termed a 'comic travesty' of Marx's real thinking.

Neither Anarchists nor Marxists appeared to be aware that on a theoretical plane the thinking of Bakunin and Marx were very close in reality, and if an assessment was to drawn up, critical analysis was needed on the plane of political practice and strategy. So if after all Anarchism and Marxism developed separately – on the level of doctrine and theory – this development emanated out of identical preoccupations but with the formulation of different conclusions. If a certain number of Anarchists refuse to consider that the birth of Anarchism and Marxism came out of identical conditions, this refusal both impedes a grasp of points on which they come close and equally impedes a true perspective and understanding of differences.

I have said that the end of the Anti-Authoritarian International was marked by a break with positions defended by Bakunin.[322] So the question is: should one return to Bakunin; would it be desirable? Of course, society has changed profoundly since the 1870s. Although the principles he elaborated remain completely valid, unless one takes into account and reflects upon new contexts and profound changes, these principles are inapplicable.

What can be learnt today from Bakunin? His philosophical thinking, his critique of bourgeois society, his analysis of the Socialist movement and of those 'exploiters of socialism' – bourgeois people who use the labour movement as a foot-stool for their ambition, and his critique of Marxism and state-Socialism: these fields of thinking remain relevant. So too are his reflections on the organisation of the labour movement and his description of class organisation. One cannot deny that Bakunin outlined the basis of revolutionary syndicalism.[323]

Of course, there should be no need to say that the Bakunin considered here is not the insurrectionary, revolutionary democrat of 1848. Today that insurrectionary practice is entirely outmoded. Bakunin himself expressed it so at the end of his life – after the crushing of the Paris Commune, and with the constitution of the German Empire political power had access to means of constraint that were infinitely superior to those that insurgent groups might use.

The last letter of the Russian revolutionary,[324] written to Élisée Reclus shortly before his death, is particularly significant: 'for the moment revolution has gone back to bed' he said, 'We are falling back into a time of evolution, that is to say of revolutions that are invisible, subterranean and often even imperceptible.' Bakunin had not suddenly become 'reformist' or a partisan of gradual reforms, he was only commenting on what for his friend was a favourite theme: evolution and revolution. For Élisée Reclus, there was no fundamental opposition between evolution and revolution.[325] One should remember that this was at a time shortly after the victory of Prussia over France, a time that saw the inauguration of German hegemony over Europe, the same hegemony that Marx and Engels had looked for. One should recall Marx's letter of 20 July 1870, in which he declared that a German victory would assure the preponderance of the German proletariat on the 'world stage' *(sic)* and at the same time 'the predominance of our theory over Proudhon's'.[326]

The changes perceived by Bakunin in the aftermath of the crushing of the Commune are 'the last incarnation of an exhausted class, playing its last card, protected by the military dictatorship of MacMahon-Bonapartism in France, or of Bismarck in the rest of Europe'. Bakunin had foreseen that a French defeat would lead to a long-lasting period of Prussian hegemony over Europe. It was this observation and fear which pushed men like Kropotkin and Cornelissen to line up in favour of the Entente against Germany in 1916, fear of German hegemony over Europe becoming ever stronger. When he declared that 'the hour of revolution has past', Bakunin intended to say that revolution was not necessarily always on the agenda *at all times*, that there are cycles. We are now in a period of downturn, in which 'revolutionary passion, hope and thinking are not to be found at all amongst the masses', and in such periods 'it is vain to complain, nothing can be done'. Bakunin admired the Jurassians and the Belgians,[327] who persevered and continued 'in the midst of general indifference' working away as they had done earlier 'when the general movement was on t8he rise, and when the least effort created a powerful effect'. They were the 'last Mohicans of the International … and despite every difficulty and every obstacle, in the midst of general indifference – they put up an obstinate front, they continue working'. We should note that one year after these words were written a majority of the Belgians joined the ranks of Social-Democracy.

To escape this 'cesspit' 'an immense social revolution' would be needed, but Bakunin notes that 'never has international reaction in Europe been so formidably armed against every popular movement. Repression has been made into a new science – one taught systematically to lieutenants in the military schools of every nation.' Put another way, the power to repress revolution then at the disposal of the state was infinitely superior to that available to the working class – insofar as there were [only] 'unorganised masses' to attack this 'impregnable fortress'. These masses 'lack even enough passion to save themselves…' as, 'they do not know what they should want' to save themselves. There is terrible final sentence in this unfinished letter – words that anticipate events forty years on: 'One other hope remains, universal war. These huge military states will surely destroy and devour each other sooner or later. But what a prospect!'

APPENDICES

In date order:

1. Preamble to the Statutes of the IWA, Geneva, First Congress of the IWA, September 1866.

Considering,

That workers' liberation should be brought about by workers themselves; that workers' struggles to win freedom should create the same rights and duties for all and should not allow the development of new privilege;

That workers' subjection to capital is the fount of all servitude – material, moral and political;

That for this reason the economic emancipation of workers is therefore the great goal to which every political movement ought to be subordinated;

That hitherto all struggles have failed for want of solidarity between workers of various professions and trades within each country, and for the lack of fraternal unity between the workers of different countries;

That the emancipation of labour is not a problem that is simply local or national, rather it concerns all civilised countries and its solution necessarily depends on their practical and theoretical cooperation;

That the movement now growing amongst the workers of the most industrialised countries, raises new hopes, calls for the combination of movements that are still isolated and, gives a solemn warning against falling back into old errors.

For these reasons:

The Congress of the International Worker's Association, held in Geneva on 3 September 1866, declares that this Association, and every individual or society joining it, will acknowledge *morality, justice,* and *truth* as the basis of their conduct toward to all men, without distinction of nationality, creed, or colour;

Congress considers that its duty is to demand the rights of citizens and men not only for members of the Association, but for whoever fulfils their duties. *No duties without rights; no rights without duties.*

Inspired by this spirit Congress has adopted definitely the following statutes of the International Worker's Association.

From: Jacques Freymond, *La première internationale*, Vol. 1, Geneva: Droz, 1971, p. 68-9.

2. Extract from the minutes of the Brussels IWA Congress, 13 September 1868

[*Murat read the conclusions on property in land, adopted in an administrative session. These had been agreed by only a small minority, and with many abstentions. In view of disquiet it was agreed that the matter of collective property should be discussed again, at a subsequent congress.* Trans]

1. *Relative to mines, coalfields and railways*

Considering – that these large-scale instruments of labour fixed to the ground, occupy an important part of land and that nature has provided humanity with this domain without cost; – that these instruments of labour necessarily call for the use of collective strength and machines; – that machines and collective strength which today exist for the sole benefit of capitalists should, in the future profit and benefit only labour, and that for this it is necessary that in every industry in which these two forces are indispensable should be driven by emancipated groupings of wage-labourers;

Congress is of the opinion:

a. That quarries, coalfields, and other mines, as well as railways should, in a sensible society, be allocated to the social collectivity, represented by the State, but a regenerated State subject to the laws of justice;

b. That quarries, coalfields, railways should be allocated not to capitalists, as they are today, but to labour organisations and that these should work within a two-fold contract: one giving title to the labour organisation and guaranteeing society a rational and scientific exploitation of the concession, with services at a price very close to the cost price, with the right to verify the accounts of the organisation, and in consequence making impossible any reconstitution of a monopoly; the other guaranteeing the mutual rights of every member of the labour organisation vis-à-vis his colleagues.

2. *Relative to agricultural property* ...

From: Jacques Freymond, *La première internationale*, Vol. 1, Geneva: Droz, 1971, p. 405.

3. Program of the International Alliance for Socialist Democracy, October 1868

1. The Alliance declares itself atheist; it seeks the abolition of cults and

the substitution of science for faith, and of human justice for divine.

2. It wants above all the political, economic, and social levelling of classes and individuals of both sexes, and to obtain this goal it demands above all the abolition of the right of inheritance, so that in future all should enjoy equally their productivity, and so that, in conformity with the decision taken at the last workers' [IWA] Congress in Brussels, land, instruments of labour, and all forms of capital, should become collective property of society as a whole, and should be used only by the workers, that is to say by agricultural and industrial associations.

3. It wants equal conditions for the development of all children of either sex from birth, i.e. nurturing, education, and training to the extent allowed by science, industry, and the arts, being convinced that this equality, if at first it is only economic and social, will result more and more in a greater natural equality of individuals, eliminating all sorts of artificial inequality that are the consequence of past history and a social organization that was as false as it was iniquitous.

4. Being the enemy of all despotism, recognizing as a political form only the republican form, and rejecting completely any reactionary alliance, it also rejects any political action which does not have as its immediate and direct aim the triumph of the workers' cause against Capital.

5. It recognizes that all actually existing political and authoritarian States, should be dissolved into a Universal Union of Free Associations – agricultural or industrial – and their activities should be reduced to simple administrative functions of public service in their respective countries.

6. Because the social question can be resolvable definitely and practically only on the basis of international and universal solidarity of workers of all countries, the Alliance rejects any politics founded on so-called patriotism and rivalry between nations.

7. It seeks a Universal Association of all local Associations working for freedom.

From: Mémoire présenté par la Fédération jurassienne de l'Association internationale des Travailleurs à toutes les Fédérations de l'Internationale, Sonvilier: Fédération jurassienne, 1873, pp. 39-40.

4. Resolutions at a meeting at Crêt-du-Locle, May 1869

1. The meeting, whilst recognising that co-operation is the social form of the future, declares that under existing economic conditions it is incapable of emancipating the proletariat and of resolving the social question. (Approved unanimously bar three votes).

2. The meeting requests the General Council of London to add to the

agenda of the Basel Congress the question of the more real and efficient organisation of the IWA, one with power and ability both to oppose the coalition of bourgeoisie and the state, and to triumph over it. (Approved unanimously bar two votes).

3. The meeting approves the manner in which *L'Egalité* and the *Progrès* have defended socialist principles and repudiates the line of conduct adopted by the *Montagne*. Furthermore, it declares that the IWA should totally abstain from participating in bourgeois politics. (Approved unanimously bar three votes).

4. The meeting requests that collective property, and the abolition of the right of inheritance, should be discussed in the journal *L'Egalité*. (Approved unanimously).

From: *Mémoire présenté par la Fédération jurassienne de l'Association Internationale des Travailleurs à toutes les Fédérations de l'Internationale*, Sonvilier: Fédération jurassienne, 1873, pp. 48-9.

[*L'Egalité* and *Progrès* were radical newspaper opposed to the *Montagne*, the latter being the journal of Dr Coullery. At the end of Napoleonic wars the King of Prussia had been installed as the Prince of Neuchâtel – although that canton had joined the Swiss confederation. Later the pro-Prussian administration had been overthrown and a republic declared. Dr Coullery had formed an electoral alliance with this party of royalists; it was this bourgeois politics that was condemned by this meeting.]

5. Key demands of the Social Democratic Workers' Party, August 1869

[*Founded in Eisenach; in Marx's opinion it embodied the leading principles of IWA Statutes,* Trans.][328]

1. The granting of universal, equal, direct, and secret suffrage to all men aged 20 and over for elections to the [North German] parliament, the parliaments [Landtage] of the German states, the provincial and municipal assemblies, and any other representational bodies. The elected parliamentary deputies are to be granted adequate per diem pay.

2. Introduction of direct legislation (i.e., the right to make and reject proposals) by the people.

3. Abolition of all privileges attached to class, property, birth, and religious faith.

4. Establishment of a people's militia in place of standing armies.

5. Separation of the church from the state and of schools from the church.

6. Obligatory classes in elementary schools and free instruction at all public educational institutes.

7. Independence of the courts; introduction of trial by jury and specific trades' courts; introduction of public and oral court proceedings, as well as the administration of justice at no cost.

8. Abolition of all laws aimed against the press, associations, and labour unions; introduction of a normal workday; restriction of female labour and a ban on child labour.

9. Abolition of all indirect taxes and introduction of one progressive income tax and inheritance tax.

10. State support of the co-operative system and state loans for free producers' co-operatives subject to democratic guarantees.

6. The Basel Congress of the International, September 1869
[Summary and extracts of the reports on the opening day, Trans.]

The fourth congress of the International took place over eight days from 5-12 September 1869, meeting in the 'Café National'. After an address from the leader of the local IWA the first session considered mandates and set up a bureau with Hermann Jung[329] as its president; two vice-presidents Bruhin[330] and Brismée,[331] and nine secretaries: three for the French language, three for German, two for Spanish and one for English. The second session ratified procedures: no one could speak more than twice on a subject – ten minutes at first, and five minutes in reply; sessions would run from 9 to 12 noon and from 2 to 6pm. The composition of commissions considering the points on the congress agenda was then agreed; there were nineteen names on the commission considering societies of resistance [unions], eighteen for education commission, fourteen members of the commission on property in land; eleven to consider rights of inheritance; and eight for the question of mutual credit. The Congress agreed a seventh point: that it would concern itself in the first instance with the above five points that had been set for the agenda by the General Council; and an eighth point: that following consideration of the first five points congress should consider popular direct legislation (This agenda, as proposed by Robert[332] and Goegg[333] was agreed after a discussion quoted below).

The first lively controversy concerned the introduction of a sixth point on the agenda. Goegg proposed that a question suggested by Bürkli[334] of Zurich, and supported by many Swiss and German sections, should be added to the agenda: popular direct legislation by the people (la législation dirècte du peuple et par le peuple) – a question that he considered highly important.

Robin: replied first, saying he had no prior knowledge of it, and, without discussing how opportune it might be, believed congress should consider the five questions placed on the agenda by the General Council; and should time permit, should then discuss the Bürkli's point as a personal, rather than as a general matter.

Schwitzguébel: commented that he was opposed to such ideas, but if there was a demand to consider the matter, such a demand should not be refused.

Bruhin: although papers in England and France had published five points only, in German and Swiss journals this sixth point had added:

We Swiss and Germans do not consider the matter in the same way as do the French and Belgians. For us this sixth question is the most important of all; the other five only come after this. Why? The state is not for us a bourgeois institution – it is the people – direct representation by the people. And if the state is the people, then it can decide whatever it wants, and so it may achieve the International's objectives. Representatives of other nations may reject discussion of this question, because, in their counties they do not now possess the means to accomplish this representation, but they should not refuse to the Swiss,[335] who have these means, the discussion of a matter so important to them.

Bakunin:[336] opposed this sixth point being added to the agenda:

We are an International Association, which through its resolutions declares that social and political questions are intimately related, but which, by its very name indicates that political questions must be international, not national.

Rittinghausen:[337] You are going to consider at length grand social reforms which you consider as being required to end the deplorable situation in the world of workers. Is it then [any] less necessary to consider the means of execution through which you might accomplish these reforms? I hear many amongst you say that you wish to achieve your objectives through *revolution*. Well citizens, revolution, as a material fact, accomplishes nothing. If, after the revolution, you do not manage to formulate your legitimate demands through legislation, the revolution, like that of 1848, will perish miserably; you will be the prey to a most violent reaction, and you will once again be subjected to years of shame and oppression. What then are the means of execution that democracy should employ to achieve its ideas? Legislation by a single person works only to the advantage of that man and his family; legislation by a group of bourgeois called representatives serves only the interests of that class; it is only in taking in hand its own interests through direct legislation, that the people can make them prevail and establish the reign of social justice. I therefore insist that you put on the agenda of this congress the question of direct legislation by the people …

Murat:[338] then demanded that the agenda be followed and that one should not enter into a discussion of the question.

Robert: protested against the assertions of Bruhin; all Swiss did not share the opinion that consideration of this question is opportune and many of them have only heard of them accidentally. From another viewpoint he did not believe that one could refuse to discuss this question, as with any other question that might be presented, so long as it was well understood that first of all one should address the five questions presented by the General Council, and then others afterwards.

Hins:[339] Since we are discussing now not just whether it is opportune to discuss the sixth point, but the question itself, I would like to add a few words to those of Bakunin. As to the part of sections of the International – I do not understand all this running after governments. One wants, they say, through representation or direct legislation to secure the transformation of current governments which have been the creation of our enemies the bourgeoisie. To this end, one wants to enter these governments and through persuasion, through numbers, through new laws establish a new state.

Comrades, let us not follow this course; because we could have followed it in Belgium and France, as in other places; rather, let us leave these governments to fall and rot; let us not, with our morality, support them. And this is why: the International must be a state amongst states, it should let them go on in their own fashion until our state is the stronger. Then, on their ruins, we will construct our own, all prepared, all ready, such as exists in each section ...

Liebknecht:[340] 'To refuse discussion of this question is reactionary; has not the International said in its first decisions that political questions are also in its domain. Why then should we not consider them? All German papers announced it, German programmes contained it, and German delegates ask that it should be discussed. If it was not important for Paris, Berlin or Brussels where social questions but not political questions may be discussed, it is even more [important] for other countries where this distinction does not exist.'

Murat and *Dereure*:[341] 'declare that they do not oppose the introduction of this sixth point onto the agenda, but it should come after the others.'

Starke:[342] 'supports the necessity of having this question discussed, he again stresses that German papers announced it and that the Swiss desire it.'

Schwitzguébel: 'declares that, as a delegate of a Swiss section, he does not want it at all, nor does his section either; even less so because the matter has not been put on to the agenda to study, as other questions.'

Robin: agrees that others who wish to meet to discuss this sixth question should do so.' And *Langlois*:[343] 'proposed, for example, an extraordinary evening session, which all should be free to attend. After Jung's reading, the seventh and eight point as proposed by Robert and Goegg, [see above] were unanimously accepted. The sitting adjourned at 6.15.' [344]

On Workplace Organisation

Pindy[345] read the Congress commission's report stressing the question had two facets:

In what fashion should resistance societies (trades/workplace organisations) be formed, in order, on the one hand to prepare for the future and – as far as possible – to take care of current needs; and on the other hand how should our ideas about the organisation of work in the future help us to establish resistance societies usefully in the present; these two aspects of the question reciprocally complement and reinforce each other. Indeed, we conceive of two types of organisation amongst workers: at first local organisation helping workers in one place to develop daily contact; then an organisation between various areas, localities, regions, etc. A first type. This sort of organisation corresponds to political relations of current society and advantageously replaces them: up to now this is the type of organisation typical of the IWA. This state of things implies that, as for resistance societies, local federations of these societies should help each other, through loaning funds, through the organisation of meetings to discuss social questions, through common decision-making on matters of collective interest.

But as industry grows larger, in addition to this first sort, and at the same time, another form of organisation [also] becomes necessary....

The organisation of various trades by town and district creates another advantage: each trade, when the occasion comes for it to go on strike, can be supported by others. It pursues its struggle up to the point that it has achieves pay parity, a prelude to functions being made equal [l'équivalence des fonctions].

Moreover, this type of organisation creates the commune of the future just as the other type forms the labour organisation of the future. The organisation is replaced by the united councils of trades' bodies, and by committees of their respective delegates, which will regulate the relations of work that will replace politics.

To conclude and because organisations in towns and districts already partially exist, we propose the following resolution:

Congress agrees that workers should actively work to create resistance funds in various trades. As such societies are formed, sections, federal groupings and central councils should be requested to advise societies of the same trade, in order to provoke the creation of organised national trades' bodies. These federations should be responsible for the collection of information relative to their particular industries, for shaping common measures that should be taken, for regulating strikes and for working to ensure their success, until the time comes for wage-labour to be replaced by a Federation of Free Producers. Congress invites the General Council to serve, in case of need, as an intermediary pending the unity of resistance societies of every country.

From: Jacques Freymond, *La première internationale*, Vol. 2, Geneva: Droz, 1962, pp. 108-9.

7. L'Egalité *criticises the General Council, 6 November 1869*

One reads in the Report (Compte-Rendu) of the Geneva congress of 1866, page 26: 'The General Council [of London] will publish insofar as means allow and as often as possible, a *Bulletin* which will consider everything of interest to the IWA and should concern itself above all with offers for work and demand for work, in various places, with co-operative societies, and the state of the labour classes in all countries. This *Bulletin* edited in many languages, should be sent gratis to the central sections which will distribute copies to every sections.' This article was never implemented.

The matter was taken up again by the Congress of Lausanne, (1867) and the following was resolved (page 37 of the official Report): 'If the General Council cannot publish a *Bulletin*, every quarter it will issue a communication to the central bureau of each country, which will be responsible for having them reproduced in local journals, and above all in the journals of sections.' This decision – like the previous one – was also never carried out.

[... *the matter was discussed again in Brussels... in Basel and it was agreed that the General Council should send a monthly official note to all IWA organs...*]

We hope that it will not tarry in fulfilling a desire expressed many times and we invite our counterparts, other journals of the IWA – which become more numerous by the day – to join us in reminding it of its responsibilities.

From: *Mémoire présenté*, pp. 88-9ff. [This article was written by Paul Robin. *L'Egalité* was published in Geneva and was the journal of the Franco-Swiss IWA. The criticism of the General Council's record pointed to its poor practice, its poor rapport with IWA bodies, most especially with its critics and its limited capacities. Marx viewed it as an attack by Bakunin. The General Council did not reply to the editors directly – it wrote privately to the Geneva IWA that the General Council had no obligation to reply a journal. *Trans*]

8. Minutes of a Committee Meeting, Geneva Alliance for Socialist Democracy Section, 14 January 1870

Under the presidency of cit[izen] Ch. Grange. Present: Grange, Poignet, Schindler, Guilmeaux, Desjacques, Lindegger, Robin and Becker. The meeting began at 8.30[pm].

A letter from cit[izen] Gonz. Morago of Madrid is communicated by the president. Cit. C. *Gomis* had been asked to participate in this session to give us explanations concerning the said letter. From these explications it emerges that cit. Gonz. Morago asks our opinion of the path he should take as a member of the International [and] of the Alliance, and that he might advise other members of the International and of the Alliance, concerning the question to which the two organisations named above should involve themselves in politics, or whether they should not involve themselves.

A rather [lively] discussion arose on the matter, with all members present participating, in quite different, or to put it better, opposing, senses.

On the proposition of cit. *Lindegger*, it was decided that the reply to cit. Morago should be made in the sense of the principles elaborated in the meeting by cit. *Robin*. That is to say that the reply should make cit. G Morago understand that working towards socialism should in no wise imply involvement in politics, and further, even if one did not reject or deny that the republican form of government might be more conducive to propagating and promoting our principles, it was noted that it was not worth getting involved in politics for the few advantages that the establishment of a bourgeois republic [might] offer us, and that in consequence the IWA and the Social and Democratic Alliance should be involved only in destructive politics, to put a new social order in place of the existing social order, one in which the worker would enjoy the full and complete fruits of their work, which would not be possible until current governmental constructs were replaced by another organisation based on absolute equality. The reply was to read out at the first meeting of the committee and communicated to the section at the first general assembly to be incorporated into the minutes. The committee decided to convene a general assembly session on Saturday 22 January at the *Croix Féderal*, 3 place St. Gervais, first floor with the notice below:

1. Roll Call. 2. Payment of dues. 3. Reading of minutes and important correspondence. 4. Admission of candidates [new members]. 5. Renewing the committee. 6. Minutes of the surveillance commission. 7. Individual propositions.

After cit. *Robin* informed us of his forthcoming departure from Geneva, the committee expressed its most great regrets concerning this and thanked him for the eminent services he had rendered for the emancipation of labour.

Meeting rose at 10.30. For the committee. The secretary *Lindegger*

From: Jacques Freymond, ed., *Etudes et documents sur la Première Internationale en Suisse*, Geneva: Droz, 1964, pp. 174-5. [On Morago see note 124. Robin later moved to London.]

9. Minutes of a General Assembly Meeting, Geneva Alliance for Socialist Democracy Section, 2 April 1870

Under the presidency of cit[izen] Grange, open at 9.00[pm].

Reading of the minutes of [the] preceding meeting. These were adopted.

Proposition of the committee to send a delegate to the Romande [Franco-Swiss] [IWA] congress, communicated by cit. *Grange*.

Cit. *Bakunin:* propounded the need for sending a delegate and read a draft mandate.

Cit. *Becker:* observed that the general assembly had decided not to enter the Romande Federation. We are, he said, a truly international section. We have members in many countries. Our work should have an international character; there is no necessity for us to join the Romande Federation. Also the cantonal [IWA] committee has twice refused us. Do we want to receive another rejection, and a kicking?

Cit. *Bakunin:* provided we always keep our flag aloft, we should have no fear of receiving a kicking. Reaction always rejects revolution, revolution must always demand its rights. The Federal Committee has refused entry into the federation of two propaganda sections, first of all of the Alliance, and of the section for socialist propaganda of La Chaux-de-Fonds. However these two sections have the same character as every central section. True, a federation should be composed of trades' bodies. In Belgium this might serve as a reason not to have propaganda sections, because revolutionaries are active in workers' sections, but the IWA would be destroyed here if there were no propaganda sections.

Cit. *Becker:* But always I would say that we should wait. Justice will have to be rendered to our principles and we will succeed; we should have patience until opinions are more enlightened. We are not in the federation, no harm there, because there nothing is to be done.

Cit. *Perron:* In principle an international federation should be an economic organisation, that is to say a federation of trades' bodies, a federation of productive workers. But that is the form of the future; in current conditions things cannot be so, and this is why there are propaganda sections in Lausanne, [Le] Locle, Neuchâtel, etc. Either central sections should not form a part of a federation, or all propaganda associations of the IWA should be admitted into the federation on the same basis. They should take part in the congress to present their ideas.

Cit. *Becker:* Central sections are another thing entirely; they are workers' associations from various trades, but of the same language.[346] These sort of sections might be called, one might say, mother sections. They form, make propaganda, and through their efforts trades' sections are formed.

Cit. *Bakunin:* The historic rights of central sections cannot be taken into consideration. Here in Geneva the central section is reactionary, revolutionary propaganda [needs] making. We should enter the federation because, outside it, we cannot make propaganda in trades' bodies' sections. We should not allow ourselves to be treated as rejected pariahs.

Cit. *Remy:* If we have been refused, that is no reason to retreat. We all know that lately in the Geneva IWA reaction has taken hold with terrible vitality. How many trades' bodies have not joined the IWA? Many – so we should have in the IWA many propaganda sections. We should join the Romande federation to have direct influence. To retreat, after having been twice refused is not reasonable. If we do not join the federation, we remain in the void. The central section will become ever more reactionary, already it would reject men of letters, workers of intelligence. Vis-à-vis this reaction socialist propaganda becomes ever more necessary and indispensable. We should insist.

Cit. *Perron:* Teachers, just as other productive workers, can set up a section.

Cit. *Remy:* That's impossible, there will never be a section of teachers in Geneva. Amongst teachers in Geneva you will not find even one who wants to join the IWA. That is why propaganda sections are needed, are indispensable, they are to be formed by workers of trades' bodies and by intellectual workers.

Cit. *Becker:* That's all true. But once again I repeat we should not provoke a kicking. We know that thirty of the Geneva sections are against us. So there will be war and scission which will always baneful for the IWA.

Cit. *Bakunin:* For the most part our section is formed of members of Romande sections. I see no reason why one would refuse to admit us into the federation.

Cit. *Remy:* proposes the following to the bureau: 'The delegate of the Alliance asks for his admission to the congress and to the Romande federation with the same rights as delegates of other sections.'

The president puts this to the vote. It is accepted by the majority.

Joukovsky is proposed as delegate – accepted by the majority.

Nomination of a member of the committee. Cit. *Remy* proposes Cit. *Bakunin*. Cit. *Grange* puts the proposition to the vote. Cit. *Bakunin* is unanimously named a member of the committee.

Cit. *Bak[unin]*: protests against the changes made in the [Alliance's] programme and regulations**, given that the procedure [that was used was] contrary to the regulations – that says that changes to regulations have to be advertised a month in advance to give all time for reflection as otherwise things may be done in haste.

After a short discussion it was agreed to advertise the changes proposed in earlier assemblies and to discuss them once more.

Cit *Grange:* proposed a collection to cover the costs of the printing to be arranged.

Cit. *Perron:* proposed to make a [collection] for the strikers at Le Creusot. That proposition is accepted unanimously. Four collectors are nominated.

The meeting closed at 11.

The secretary *N Joukovsky*

From: Jacques Freymond, ed., *Etudes et documents sur la Première Internationale en Suisse*, Geneva: Droz, 1964, pp. 188-190.

[** The changes in regulations and programme mentioned above included a change declaring that the Alliance should be *materialist* in its philosophy (rather than atheistic). This session took place two days before the opening of the congress of the Romande federation in la Chaux-de Fonds, at which the Romande federation split, with the minority – mostly Genevan delegates – withdrawing. It is notable that just two days before this confrontation the Alliance was still bringing together both Bakunin and Becker. They differed – not in seeing the majority of the IWA in Geneva as reactionary – but in tactics: as to how and when reaction was to be confronted. Utin, Marx's agent, attacked Bakunin for his atheism at the La Chaux-de-Fonds congress.]

10. Jura Federation: Polemic against the General Council, July 1872
On the General Council's revision of the preamble to the Statutes of the IWA.

The General Council pretended, before the Conference [of London, 1871] that the words 'as a means' had been cut out by the French translators, and that they should be reinserted in the French text [text as above, appendix of 1866]. Furthermore it was added that in the new edition of the Statutes, published in Paris in the spring of 1870, the words 'as a means' had already been added, a proof that the Parisian sections had properly recognised the *English* text, published in London by the general council in 1867, as the one original official text and that they had acknowledged the universally recognised French text as a bad translation.

Here, in the full light of day, can be seen the remarkable bad faith of Marx and his allies.

It is generally disregarded that the general statutes, approved by the Geneva general Congress of 1866, are in *French* and that there therefore exists a *French official text*, which is in no way a translation more or less accurate of an *English original*, but is the *true text* which was put to the vote and adopted by the congress. This *French official text*, may be found in the *Compte-Rendu* [Report of the Labour congress of the IWA held in Geneva, 3 - 8 September, 1866] forming a brochure of 30 pages, published in Geneva in 1866. And in this official text the third considering paragraph is set out as follows:

'That for this reason the economic emancipation of workers is therefore the great goal to which every political movement ought to be subordinated.'

The words 'as a means' are not to be found there. They are only found in the English edition (Rules of the IWA, London, 1867) published by the general council in 1867: *the following year*. So then, far from having supressed in a *French translation* words that existed in an *original, official, English text* it was the opposite that was the case; it was the general council that made the additions, in 1867, to a text that was *officially adopted in French* by the Geneva congress in 1866, of words that were not adopted by the Congress. And then, such is Mr Marx's shamelessness, that he speaks of 'errors of translation' of 'an insufficient knowledge of the English language by French translators!' when it is he who is the fraudster, deliberately falsifying Statutes adopted by a Congress!

From: *Mémoire présenté par la Fédération jurassienne de l'Association Internationale des Travailleurs à toutes les Fédérations de l'Internationale*, Sonvilier: Fédération jurassienne, 1873, pp. 206ff.

[August H. Nimtz has a contrasting perspective, he alleges that in 1866 the French contingent in Geneva, under the influence of the anarchist views of Proudhon, *conveniently* left out 'as a means' to rationalise its abstentionist political orientation. (August H. Nimtz, *Marx and Engels: Their Contribution to the Democratic Breakthrough*, State University of New York Press, 2000, p. 225). In fact socialist electoral political parties did not exist (they would be tiny bodies for many years to come). Proudhon had stood for election to the French national assembly. Those influenced by him largely defined themselves as mutualists. 'Anarchism' was as yet undefined and there was no abstentionist anarchist party. Few people knew of Marx in 1866 and he did not attend the Geneva congress to defend his perspectives. It was largely *after 1869* that Marx openly pressed the priority of electoral political party organisation as essential, everywhere. Before 1869 there was little or no discussion of electoral political party strategy. So some inadequacy and lack of appropriate *historical* justification is apparent in perspectives that hint at 'convenient' conspiracy in the text approved by congress. (It is true that Marx's draft (1864) had read: 'That the economic emancipation of the working classes is therefore the great end to which every political movement ought to be subordinate *as a means…*' Marx & Engels, *Collected Works*, Vol. 20, London: Lawrence & Wishart, 1987, p. 14). Given that the IWA had as yet not debated – *nor even considered* – what the relationship might be between forms of workplace-based unions and some imagined form of electoral-based or ideas-based parties and there was no reason why the IWA should have endorsed either abstentionism or electoral-party-politics; or prioritise one or the other above workplace labour organisation

The *Memoire* (p. 208) also sets out that statutory clauses allowing the General council to co-opt new members do not exist in the French official text of the statutes of 1867, and that the General Council had committed a fraud by adding such clauses. *Trans.*]

11. Resolutions of the Saint-Imier Congress of the International Workers' Association, 15-16 September 1872

First Resolution: *The position of federations meeting in Congress in Saint-Imier concerning the resolutions of the Congress of The Hague and of the General Council*

Considering that for workers' liberation the autonomy and independence of workers' sections and federations are primary requirements; that recognition of a congress's power to legislate or regulate would be a flagrant negation of this autonomy and freedom; as a principle, Congress denies the legislative power of any regional or general congresses, and recognises their role as being only to make manifest the needs, ideas and aspirations of the proletariat of the different places and countries, so that – as much as possible – they may be unified and harmonised; but never that a congress majority should [be empowered to] impose resolutions on a minority.

Considering also that the institution of a General Council in the International Workers' Association is, through its inherent lethal influence, a seedbed for ongoing violations of the freedom that should be the foundation of our great association; considering that the acts of the London General Council, now recently dissolved were, over the last three years, the living proof of the faults inherent in this institution; that, in order to increase its initially very limited power, it has resorted to the most despicable intrigues, lies, calumnies, in an attempt to sully those who dared to oppose it; that to obtain final realisation of its policies, it prepared the congress of The Hague well in advance with an artificially obtained majority. Obviously the sole aim of this congress was to ensure the triumph and domination of an authoritarian party within the International; and to achieve this goal it did not hesitate to trample on every vestige of justice and of decency. Such a congress cannot represent the proletariat of those countries represented there;

The congress of delegates of the American, French, Italian, Jura and Spanish federations meeting in Saint-Imier, declare their complete rejection of every resolution of the congress of The Hague, they in no way recognise the powers of the new General Council which it nominated; and, to defend their respective federations against the governmental pretensions of the General Council, and to save and fortify and promote the unity of the IWA, delegates have agreed the basis for a project of pact of solidarity between these federations.

Second Resolution: *Pact of mutual defence, solidarity and friendship, between the free Federations*

Considering that the greater unity of the International is based, not on the always pernicious or artificial organisation of some centralising power, but, on the one hand on the real commonality of aspirations and interests of the proletariat of all nations, and, on the other hand on the absolutely free and spontaneous federation of free sections and federations of every nation.

Considering that, within the International, there is a tendency, openly manifested by the authoritarian party of German communism at the congress of The Hague, to substitute its domination and the power of its leaders for the spontaneous and free organisation of the proletariat;

Considering that the majority at the congress of The Hague cynically abandoned every principle of the International adopting the ambitious perspectives of that party and of its leaders; and that the new General Council – named by that congress and being endowed with powers even greater than those that it arrogated to itself at the London Conference – threatens to destroy the unity of the International by attacks on that freedom;

The delegates of the American, French, Italian, Jura and Spanish sections and federations, meeting at this congress have agreed, in the name of these section and federations – and pending their definitive acceptance and confirmation – on the following pact for mutual defence, solidarity and friendship:

(1) Between the American, French, Italian, Jura and Spanish sections and federations and all others who would like to join in this pact, there

will be direct and regular correspondence and communication wholly independent of any governmental control of any sort.

(2) If the freedom of any one of these sections and federations should be attacked by a majority of a General Congress, or by a government or General Council created by that majority, all the other sections and federations will [come to its aid and] declare their absolute solidarity.

They loudly proclaim that this pact was concluded with its principal aim being to preserve the greater unity of the International endangered by the ambition of the authoritarian party.

Third Resolution: *The Nature of the Political Action of the Proletariat*
Considering:

That the desire to impose on the proletariat one uniform political programme or one line of conduct as the single path that might lead to its social emancipation is a presumptuous ambition, as reactionary as it is absurd;

That nobody has the right to deprive autonomous sections and federations of the incontrovertible right to decide for themselves and follow the line of political conduct that they deem best, and that any such attempt would inevitably lead to a most revolting dogmatism;

That the aspirations of the proletariat can have no purpose other than the creation of absolutely free economic organisations and federations, founded upon the labour and equality of all and absolutely independent of all political government, and that this organisation and this federation can only be the consequence of spontaneous action by the proletariat itself, of trades organisations and autonomous communes.

Considering that all political organisation could only constitute domination – to the benefit of one class and to the detriment of the masses – and that the proletariat, if it wished to take power, would itself become an exploiting and dominating class;

The congress assembled in Saint-Imier declares:

(1) That the destruction of all political power is the first duty of the proletariat;

(2) That the organisation of any and every so-called provisional or revolutionary political power, working for this destruction, can be only another deceit and it would be as dangerous for the proletariat as every existing government today;

(3) That rejecting all compromise to procure the achievement of social revolution, proletarians of every country should establish, beyond all forms of bourgeois politics, the solidarity of revolutionary activity.

Fourth Resolution: *Organisation of Labour Resistance – Statistics*

Freedom and labour are the basis of morality, strength, life and future wealth. But labour, if it is not freely organised, becomes unproductive and oppressive to the worker; and for this reason the organisation of labour is the essential precondition for the authentic, complete liberation of the worker.

However, labour cannot work in freedom without access to raw materials and the entire capital of society and cannot organise itself if the worker, free of economic and political tyranny, has not gained the right to complete development of all his faculties. Every State, which is to say, every top-down government or administration of the masses, being of necessity founded upon bureaucracy, upon armies, upon spying, upon the clergy, cannot ever bring about a society organised on the basis of justice and labour, since, by the very nature of its being, it is inevitably impelled to deny the former and oppress the latter.

As we see it, the worker will never be able to free himself from age-old oppression, unless that insatiable, demoralising body, is replaced by a Free Federation of all Producer Groups on the basis of solidarity and equality.

Already, in several places indeed, attempts have been made to organise labour to improve the conditions of the proletariat, but the slightest improvement has soon been taken back by the privileged class, which is forever trying, without restraint or limit, to exploit the working class. However, such are the advantages offered by these organisations [unions/workplace organisations] that, even as things now stand, one cannot do without them. Among the proletariat they increase the sense of fraternity and community of interests; they give some experience in collective living and prepare for the supreme struggle. Furthermore, privilege, authoritarianism and the political State are to be replaced by this free and spontaneous organisation of labour which, once in place, will offer an ongoing guarantee for the preservation of economic [labour] against political [bourgeois] organisation.

Consequently, leaving details of positive organisation to be worked out by the Social Revolution, our broad intent is to build solidarity and organisation. We regard strikes as a precious means of struggle, but we have no illusions about their economic results. We accept them as a consequence of the antagonism between labour and capital; they have as a necessary consequence that workers should become more and more alive to the abyss that exists between the proletariat and bourgeoisie and that workers' organisations should be strengthened, and, through ordinary economic struggles, the proletariat should be prepared for the great and final revolutionary struggle which will, destroying all privilege and all class distinctions, give workers the right to enjoy the full product of their labour within the community and thereby the means of developing their full intellectual, material and moral power.

The Commission suggests that congress should appoint a commission, and that it should be mandated to present to the next congress proposals for the universal organisation of resistance, with detailed labour statistical tables to throw light on this struggle. It recommends the Spanish organisation as the best of those now in existence.

Final Resolution
Congress proposes to send copies of the 'Pact of mutual defence, solidarity, and friendship', and of all its resolutions to all workers' federations throughout the world and to come to an understanding with them all concerning matters of general interest.

Congress invites all the federations which came together and concluded this pact for mutual defence, solidarity, and friendship to consult immediately with all sections or federations which may wish to accept this pact, to agree on the substance and timing of their international congress, hoping that it will be convened within the next six months at the latest.

From: James Guillaume, *L'Internationale*, 1909, part 5, chapter 1, pp. 6ff.

12. The Sixth Congress of the International, Geneva, 1-6 September 1873
Strikes and Trades Organisation – Congress discussion (extracts) and resolution.

Joukovsky, reporting for the Commission said: 'that the question of a general strike is subordinated to [the question of] how far the organisation of regional and international trades' has been completed; and to the statistical work that the International must carry out in view of such a strike. Also, a general strike being nothing other than a social revolution – because it would be enough to suspend work for ten days for the existing order to collapse – the Commission thinks that this question is not going to receive a solution from Congress, and all the more so because a discussion would put our enemies in the picture as to what means we might intend to use to [achieve] a social revolution.' ...

Alerini, commented on events in Alcoy. When strikers from particular trades were about to stop their action, 'the Spanish Federal Commission (based in Alcoy) proposed the launching of a general strike of all trades in the town, all committing themselves that no trade organisation would resume work until all had achieved satisfaction. This general strike lead to an armed struggle, in which local authorities were overturned, and prominent bourgeois were arrested as hostages; and, when General Velarde presented himself before Alcoy with the army, he was forced to negotiate; the hostages offered themselves up for mediation: the provincial government promised that there would be no reprisals taken against the insurgents; that the conditions that strikers demanded from their managers were to be accepted, and that a tax would be imposed on the bourgeoisie, the product of which was to be used to pay for the days lost during the strike. In consequence Alerini is a convinced partisan of the general strike as a revolutionary means.'

Guillaume commented that general strikes are the culmination of partial strikes. 'But is it necessary that it should break out everywhere at the same time, on a fixed date following some order? No, such a question should not be considered, nor should it be supposed that such things can be done so. Revolution has to be contagious. It should never be the case in a country when a spontaneous movement is breaking out, that one should want to defer an explosion using as a pretext that one should wait for other countries to be ready to follow.'

Not all the delegates wanted to pass a resolution on the General Strike. Hales – for the English federation – was opposed and later commented 'General Strike, General nonsense'; van den Abeele, said the Dutch federation was waiting to hear this congresses decisions, so he would abstain. Finally a resolution was passed unanimously:

'Congress, considers that in the current state of the organisation of the International no complete solution can be given to the question of a general strike, it urgently recommends workers to organise international unions of each trade, as well as active socialist propaganda.'[347]

Revised General Statutes of the International Workers' Association, 1873.
The IWA congress held in Geneva, 1-6 September 1873, reasserted the original 'Considering' paragraphs set out above – 1866. (See James Guillaume, *L'Internationale*, Book 1, pp. 11-21; 57-8; and Book 3, pp. 128-9.)

The Regional Federations represented at the International Congress meeting in Geneva on 1 September 1873, inspired by the above declaration of principles, have revised the general statutes of the International Workers' Association, and have adopted them in the following form:

[Articles]

1. The International Workers' Association has the goal of bringing about the unity of workers of all countries on the terrain of solidarity in the

struggle of Labour against Capital, a struggle that must achieve the complete emancipation of Labour.

2. Whoever adopts and defends the principles of the Association may become a member, subject to the responsibility of the section that admits them.

3. Sections and Federations forming the Association preserve their complete autonomy, that is to say their right to organise themselves as they see fit, to administer their own affairs, without any outside interference and to choose for themselves the path they intend to take, to achieve Labour's freedom.

4. A General Congress of the Association shall meet each year, on the first Monday in September.

5. Each section, whatever the number of its members, has the right to send a delegate to the General Congress.

6. The role of Congress is to be a meeting place for workers of various countries to present their aspirations, and through discussion to bring them into harmony. At the opening of congress each Regional Federation shall present a report on the development of the Association in the past year. Except for matters of administration, there will be no recourse to voting; questions of principle cannot be subject to a vote. General Congress decisions are mandatory only for those Federations that accept them.

7. Voting at a General Congress will be by Federation, each Regional Federation having one vote.

8. Each year Congress will give the responsibility for the organisation of the following year's Congress to a Regional Federation. The Federation so mandated will serve as the Federal Bureau of the Association. Any section of federation wishing matters to be placed on the agenda of Congress should address these to it three months in advance so that all Regional Federations are made aware of them. Moreover, the Federal Bureau may serve as an intermediary between federations for matters brought to its attention: general correspondence, statistics and strikes.

9. Congress will itself designate the city where the next congress is to be held. On the date appointed for Congress delegates will come together in regular fashion on the day and place appointed without there being a need for any special notification.

10. In the course of a year, at the initiative of a section or federation, a vote of Regional Federations may change the place and date of a General Congress or convene an Extraordinary Congress, in the light of events.

11. Whenever a new Regional Federation seeks to become a member of the Association, at least three months before the General Congress, it

should announce this intention to whatever Federation is acting as the Federal Bureau. The latter will make this known to all Regional Federations and these will have to decide whether or not to accept the new federation, and accordingly it will mandate its delegates to the General Congress, which in the last instance will decide.

13. Bakunin's last letter to Élisée Reclus, 15 February 1875
Lugano

Very dear friend,

Thank you so much for your good words. I have never doubted your friendship, this feeling has always been mutual, and I measure yours by mine. Yes you are right, for the moment revolution has gone back to bed. We are falling back into a time of evolution that is to say of revolutions that are invisible, subterranean and often even imperceptible. The changes that are happening today are very dangerous, if not for humanity at least for certain nations. It is the last incarnation of an exhausted class, playing its last card, protected by the military dictatorship of MacMahon-Bonapartism in France, or of Bismarck in the rest of Europe. I agree with you in saying that the hour of revolution has past, not because of terrible disasters that we have witnessed and the terrible defeats for which we have been the more or less culpable victims, but because, to my great despair I have observed – and continue to observe again day by day – that revolutionary passion, hope and thinking are not to be found at all amongst the masses, and when these are absent it is vain to complain, nothing can be done. I admire the patience and heroic perseverance of the Belgians and the Jurassians – these are the last Mohicans of the International – and despite every difficulty and every obstacle, in the midst of general indifference – they put up an obstinate front, they continue working calmly, as they did before catastrophe struck, when the general movement was on the rise, and when the least effort created a powerful effect. This work is all the more praiseworthy insofar as they may not see the benefit of it, but they can be sure that the effort will not be lost – nothing is lost in this world – and drops of water, though they may be invisible may go on to form an ocean. As for me, my dear, I was becoming too old, too infirm, too weary, and I should say to you too disappointed, to feel the desire and the strength enough to share in this work. I have very deliberately retired from the fray and I will spend the rest of my days in a contemplation that will not be idle but on the contrary very active intellectually and I hope that I will not fail to produce something of use. Immense curiosity is one of the passions which now dominates me. Once I had had to recognise that bad things had won out and that I was unable to prevent them, I put myself to work to study changes and developments with a quasi-scientific passion, and complete objectivity. What actors are at work, and what a scene! At the root of the entire situation in Europe are Emperor Wilhelm and Bismarck at the head of a great population of lackeys. Against them are the Pope with his Jesuits and the whole Roman Catholic Church with riches by the million, dominating a large part of the world through women, through the ignorance of the masses, through the incomparably skilled manoeuvring of their innumerable allies, and with their hands and eyes everywhere. The third actor, French civilisation, is incarnated by Mac-Mahon, Dupanloup and Broglie – tightening the screws on a great, but fallen people. Then, around them Spain, Italy, Austria, Russia, each one of them dressing themselves up for special events; further away Britain, unable to decide what it should become and further off the model republic of the USA cosying up to military dictatorship. Poor humanity! It is obvious that it will only escape this cesspit through an immense social revolution. But how will it make this revolution? Never has international reaction in Europe been so formidably armed against every popular movement. Repression has been made into a new science – one taught systematically to lieutenants in the military schools of every nation.

And what do we have, to attack these impregnable fortresses? Unorganised masses. But how should they be organised, when they lack even enough passion to save themselves, when they do not know what they should want, and when they do not want the only things that might save them. What remains is propaganda, such as is made by the Belgians and the Jurassians. That is no doubt something, but really not so much, a few drops of water in the ocean; and if there were no other means of salvation, humanity would have occasion to rot ten times before being saved. One other hope remains, universal war. These huge military states will surely destroy and devour each other sooner or later. But what a perspective! *[Manuscript ends.]*

14. Current demands, the Gotha Programme of the German Social-Democratic Party, May 1875

(1) the fullest possible extension of political rights and freedom in the sense of the aforementioned demands; (2) a single progressive income tax, for the commune and state and local, instead of all the existing taxes, especially the indirect ones, burdening the people; (3) unlimited right of association; (4) a working day norm corresponding with the needs of society, and the prohibition of work on Sunday; (5) prohibition of child labour and all forms of labour dangerous to women's health or morality; (6) legislation to protect workers' life and health, control to ensure healthy

housing for workers, inspection of mines, factories, workshops, and domestic workplaces by officials chosen by the workers themselves, and an effective system of enforcement of the same, sensible insurance; (7) regulation of prison labour. (8) complete self-administration of all Workers' social benefits.

[*Karl Marx commented that these demands contained nothing beyond the old democratic litany ... a mere echo of the bourgeois People's party, of the League of Peace and Freedom.*]

15. Resolutions of the Congresses of Verviers, 5 to 8 September 1877, and Ghent, 9 to 14 September 1877

On social revolution

Verviers, 8.9.1877. Considering that if social revolution is by its very nature international, and depends on being spread to all countries for its triumph, nevertheless there are certain countries which, because of their social and economic condition are more ready for a revolutionary movement. Congress declares: that it is the duty of every revolutionary to support morally and materially every country in revolution, as it is the duty to spread it, as only through these means is it possible to assure the triumph of the revolution in those countries where it breaks out. *Agreed by all federations except the Jura federation.*

The tendencies of modern production and property

Verviers, 8.9.1877. Considering that modern means of production tends, insofar as ownership is concerned, towards the accumulation of capital in the hands of a few and increases workers' exploitation; that this state of things – being the source of all social inequalities – needs to be changed; Congress considers that the achievement of collective property, that is to say the takeover by groups of workers of social capital, is a social necessity; congress also declares that a Socialist party truly worthy of being so-named should make plain the principle of collective property, not in some distant future but rather in its current programme and in its everyday activities.

This was the first matter discussed and voted on in Ghent on 11 September 1877. After many delegates had spoken two opposing resolutions were put:
 1.   Considering that as long as land and other instruments of production, which are the means for life, are owned and appropriated by individuals or groups, the economic subjugation of the mass of the people, and all the misery that results therefrom, will continue; Congress declares

that the State or the Commune, representing and encompassing all people should have possession of land and other instruments of labour. *(Sixteen delegates voted in favour – for the most part German, Flemish – including De Paepe, Greulich, and Liebknecht.)*

2. Considering that modern means of production tend, insofar as ownership is concerned, towards the concentration of social wealth in the hands of a few and thereafter all social inequalities. We believe that workers should take over social wealth and transform it into the collective property of federated producer groups. *(Eleven Verviers delegates voted in favour.)*

Politics and political parties

Verviers, 8.9.1877. Considering that the conquest of power is a natural tendency for all political parties and that this power has no other goal than the defence of economic privilege; Considering besides, that in reality current society is divided not into political parties but rather through economic situations – exploiters and exploited, workers and managements; wage-earners and capitalists; considering further that the antagonism that exists between the two categories cannot cease through the will of any power or government, but rather through the united efforts of all the exploited against their exploiters; for these reasons: Congress declares that there is no difference between *political* parties, whether they are called socialist or not, all these parties without distinction forming in its eyes one reactionary mass and it sees its duty as fighting all of them. It hopes that workers who still travel in the ranks of these various parties, instructed by lessons from experience and by revolutionary propaganda, will open their eyes and abandon the way of politics to adopt that of revolutionary socialism.

Ghent, 14.9.1877, the above resolution appeared in Ghent in amended form: Considering that the conquest of power is a natural tendency for all political parties and that this power will have consequences of nothing other than the creation of privileged positions; Considering also, that in reality current society is divided not into political parties but rather through economic situations – exploiters and exploited, workers and managements; wage-earners and capitalists; Considering further that the antagonism that exists between the two categories cannot cease through the will of any political power but rather through the united efforts of all the exploited against their exploiters; We declare it is our duty to combat all political parties, whether they are called socialist or not, hoping that workers who still travel in the ranks of these various parties, illuminated by experience will open their eyes and abandon the way of politics to adopt *anti-governmental* socialism. *(Eight Verviers delegates voted for this resolution – three others were absent;*

eighteen delegates – mostly Flemish and German – voted against.)

Ghent 14.9.1877. Considering that social emancipation is inseparable from political emancipation; Congress declares that the proletariat, organised as a distinct party opposed to all other parties formed by the wealthy classes, must employ all political means that promote the social emancipation of all its members. *(As with the voting on property and production the Flemish and German delegates who were present in greater numbers voted in favour of this text whilst eight of the Verviers delegates voted against it.)*

Ghent, 14.9.1877. Considering that current economic circumstances are the cause of all social injustices, considering that an object of all bourgeois political parties is the defence of this social order, considering furthermore that we have recognised that current order is preserved by force and can only be overturned by force, considering that the means that one should use should be fitting to the goal one wishes to achieve; Congress declares that workers should organise themselves on their own, against all bourgeois political parties. And to achieve social revolution, propaganda and activity should promote agitation for insurrection. *(Four delegates voted in favour: Chalain, De Paepe, Paulin, and Rodriguez, and two against; other delegates abstained.)*

[It was noted that a pact of solidarity could not be concluded between all the organisations attending these congresses, given that their principles and means of action differed on essential points. On the evening of 13 September a private meeting was held involving the Flemish, German and a few other delegates that resolved on the creation of a special pact between them, promoting mutual aid between parties whose programmes were analogous with that of the German socialists; it was to have a bureau hosted in Ghent. The delegates who had been in Verviers returned there on the 15th and reported back; a comment noted that labour in Verviers 'was energetically resolved to march beneath the banner of the International and will make every effort to propagate amongst Belgian workers the principles of revolutionary socialism in opposition to the tactics advanced by the socialists of the Flemish provinces.'][348]

On the organisation of trades' organisations

Verviers, 8.9.1877. Congress, while it recognises the importance of trades' organisations and recommends their formation on an international basis, declares that trades' organisations that have as their goal only the improvement of workers' situations, either through the reduction of working hours, or by the organisation of wage levels, will never accomplish the emancipation of the proletariat, and that trades' organisations should adopt as their principal goal the abolition of the proletariat, in other words the abolition of management and taking possession of the means of labour and the expropriation of their owners.

Ghent, 14.9.1877. Considering that in the struggle against the exploitation of man by man trades' organisations are one of the most powerful levers for the emancipation of labour; Congress suggests to all categories of workers as yet not organised, to create societies of resistance whilst recognising that the final goal of all labour organisations should be the complete abolition of waged-work. *(Agreed nem. con.)*

From: the *Bulletin de la Fédération Jurassienne*, 23 and 30 September, 1873.

16. 1877: The International falls apart. *(Trans.)*

In the spring and summer of 1877 some tension emerged between the majority of the Belgian federation, organising the Universal Socialist Congress in Ghent, and the rest of the IWA. At the request of the Belgian IWA the International's Federal Bureau had invited Social-Democrats to the Bern IWA Congress of 1876. These invitations prepared the way for the calling of a Socialist Congress open to all. What the outcome of such a Universal Socialist Congress might be was unclear. Was it to invite Social-Democrats into a wider IWA in which a variety of political strategies might be pursued? What were the best models for future action?

In May the Jurassians published a letter from an influential Belgian socialist Louis Bertrand[349] noting that a Paul Janson had been elected in Brussels beating a reactionary candidate by 3,000 votes. The Jurassians were not greatly impressed and noted that he had been elected as a liberal, and with the support of bourgeois voters.[350] A series of labour congresses held in Belgium in the first half of 1877 revealed profound disagreements as to how, where and for what ends the labour movement should organise.

On 20 and 21 May 1877, two socialist congresses met in Belgium, one a congress of the Belgian IWA federation in Jemappes, and the second at Mechelen, near Antwerp, a congress that founded a Social-Democratic party modelled on its German counterpart. At a subsequent congress, held in Brussels in June, Philip Coenen, the Antwerp-based secretary of the Belgian IWA federation declared that Flemish socialists 'have resolved to constitute a political party. As the French-speaking Walloons are partisans of an economic party, the formation of two separate federations is preferable, each of which will hold their congresses.'[351] So, a Flemish Social-Democratic party was formed. There was a dispute as to whether a francophone Labour Union should continue and whether it should involve itself in positive (Social-Democratic) politics or negative (abstentionist) politics. Some francophones went on to constitute a Brabant francophone Social-Democratic party. De Paepe declared that 'we wish to make use of all the rights and liberties accorded us by the constitution, as Belgian citizens, conquering with these rights and constitutional liberties all social, economic, political and civil rights'.

The call for the Ghent congress had invoked socialist co-operation and unity. The Jurassians did not have great hopes for it, but they spoke of it clearing away misunderstandings, and of it leading to a break with the sequence of insults that had featured in German-language press.[352] They were aware of some hostility in Germany. Liebknecht had already declared that it was important that the Bakuninist party should not dominate the upcoming congress in Ghent, and had said that if they did 'that congress would be harmful for the general labour movement'.[353]

The formation of Flemish and Francophone Social-Democratic parties in Belgium was indicative of future trends, showing that energies were being re-directed into these new bodies while all-inclusive labour organisations and the IWA were being side-lined.

In Switzerland too there had been attempts to set up a Social-Democratic party. A congress held in Neuchâtel, in May 1877, brought together members of socialist, workplace and *Grütli* associations.[354] It resolved that persons in constituent bodies who were also members of other bodies, the IWA for example, should not be allowed to retain membership of the new party, if they were members of bodies which disagreed with the tactics of the new party.[355] Of eighty delegates only one was a French-speaking Swiss. When meetings were opened to the public, speeches were translated from French to German, but not back from German to French, indicating that this new party might have been a largely a Germanic body.[356]

Whilst this was going on the International Federal Bureau of the IWA called for the annual IWA congress for 1877 to meet in Verviers. It proposed that it should be timed immediately before the Universal Socialist Congress in Ghent, so that delegates could decide in Verviers what policies they should promote later in Ghent. The Verviers IWA federation had a libertarian outlook and had resisted the project of forming a Social-Democratic party in Belgium. Coenen received the notice for the Verviers congress but did not pass on this notice to IWA sections. Neither he, nor De Paepe, nor any other representative of the Belgian regional IWA attended it. Subsequently the Jurassians' report on the Ghent congress noted De Paepe viewed the Universal congress as a *substitute* for the Verviers IWA's congress, and thus – in his view – the IWA 'had in advance abdicated things into the hands of the Universal Congress, from which something – as yet unknown – was to arise, something that could not be foreseen'.[357] This was not the perspective shared by other delegates to the IWA congresses of Bern and Verviers.

So, before delegates to the congress of Ghent assembled, much of the Belgian labour movement had already taken sides: instead of maintaining and developing links with other IWA regions, they were opting for a Germanic Social-Democratic model. Some were declaring that the anarchists were seeking to impose their politics on other socialists.[358] The Verviers congress adopted unrelenting anarchist positions[359] and presented these to the Ghent congress shortly afterwards. So the congress in Ghent, which had first been posed as a step towards greater unity, seemed fated not to achieve as much.

The Verviers Congress of 6-8 September 1877 resolved that the local IWA section should serve as the seat of the International Federal Bureau, subject to the approval of the absent Belgian regional IWA federation.[360] The Jura federation had been responsible for the running of that Bureau since 1874, and perhaps did not wish that responsibility to remain with them. A location in Verviers for the Bureau would have placed it within a federation with libertarian sympathies. However this was not to be. Some three months later the Belgian IWA federation, meeting in congress over Christmas decided that the International Federal Bureau of the IWA should be relocated to Brussels, placing it amongst persons who had not attended the Verviers IWA congress and who, in Ghent, had voted against the policies agreed there. Little was ever heard of it again.[361] The men in Brussels 'paralysed the very heart of the international'.[362] Nettlau wrote that De Paepe had become the 'gravedigger' of the IWA.[363]

The Ghent congress did set out some common ground amongst all delegates: it was agreed that working people had nothing to hope for from bourgeois parties and that [trade] unions should be promoted.

It was also plain that socialists with different politics could not work together. Differences should be explored but socialists of different persuasions agreed that they should not vilify each other.[364] Bertrand, Brismée, Coenen and De Paepe voted with Greulich, Hales and Liebknecht against the policies approved by the Verviers congress.[365]

The Ghent congress marked a realignment of socialist forces. IWA supporters were now firmly marked as anarchists competing with and critical of a growing Social-Democratic party-political movement.

The *Bulletin de la Fédération jurassienne* had articulated a critique of German Social-Democracy both before and after the Ghent congress. The *Bulletin* published a letter on the Gotha congress of May 1877 noting that German socialists' focused their hopes and activities on one unique goal: electoral agitation.[366] It expressed only guarded pleasure when a socialist was elected to represent Berlin's 6th constituency, because many of his 6,246 votes came from non-socialists.[367] Guillaume confronted Liebknecht in Ghent and caused an incident when he noted that in a recent election in Germany socialists had 'attenuated' their politics to make them more appealing to the electorate. He quoted the *Berliner Freie Presse* report of a Reichstag deputy, Johann Most,[368] saying that socialist colours were not to be found in their programme.

After the Ghent congress the *Bulletin* criticised the congress reports carried in *Vorwärts*. It noted that a resolution that had called for collective property had been subtly changed in translation. The French text had carried an amendment calling for property to be run in the future either by the state or through Communes – referring to the system of Communes as seen briefly in France in 1871. The German translation rendered communes as sub-divisions of the state, and not as a *different and alternative* political form.[369] The *Bulletin* also objected to reports implying that the *delegates of socialist organisations* had agreed various policies in Ghent; it noted that the voting there engaged only particular persons and organisations – the delegates of *some* socialist organisations – and that it was not the case that all socialists were in agreement.[370]

The *Bulletin* also criticised the Russophobia of the German Social-Democratic journal *Vorwärts*. In March 1877 the *Bulletin* carried a letter from Russian socialists criticising the editors of *Vorwärts*, arguing that *Vorwärts* should have refrained from insulting fellow socialists who had organised protests at the Kazan church in St. Petersburg in December 1876. *Vorwärts* had accused them of shockingly immature conduct. Where was revolutionary solidarity the *Bulletin* asked?[371] In the midst of the war between Russia and Turkey, in 1877-8, the *Bulletin* noted that *Vorwärts* took a one-sided line: it praised the Turks for being more civilised than their antagonists instead of looking for the liberation of all working people under the yoke of the Russian and Turkish empires.[372]

CHRONOLOGY
(International events and events in particular countries.)

1862: English and French and labour representatives meet at an International Exhibition in London.

1863: German General Workers' Association founded in Leipzig, led by Ferdinand Lassalle (Lassalle dies 1864).

1864: Founding of the International Working-Men's Association (IWA), St Martin's Hall Meeting, London. France – 'Manifesto of the Sixty', for labour rights; conditional legalisation of strikes. Schleswig war, Denmark defeated.

1865: French IWA leaders travel to London to insist that the General Council should not take on a leadership role: 'The General Council is only the heart of the IWA, congress will be its head.' IWA Conference in London. American civil war ends.

1866: Geneva: First IWA Congress, 66 delegates attend of which 33 are Swiss. Austrian Empire defeated in war with Prussia and Italy. First issue of *Der Vorbote* published in Geneva by J. Becker, it is distributed widely to German readers in Europe and North America, (ceases in 1871).

1867: Lausanne: Second IWA Congress 64 attend of which 32 Swiss. *Belgium* - Miners' strike defeated, soldiers kill three workers. *France* – many internationalists arrested. Riots in Lille.

1868: Brussels: Third IWA Congress 99 delegates of which seven Swiss – collective property ownership endorsed, workers called on to stop work in case of war. *Belgium* – March, army breaks up a 3,000 strong miners' occupation in Charleroi, six killed. *Cuba* – independence movement. *France* – IWA officials imprisoned. Government announces toleration of unions; membership mushrooms. *Spain* – military revolt, Queen Isabella deposed. *Switzerland* – Geneva, strike of some 2,500 building workers; IWA members. P. Coullery and J. Frey elected to local government. Founding of the Alliance for Socialist Democracy. First issue of *L'Egalité* published (it runs to 1872), it replaces P. Coullery's *La Voix de l'Avenir*. *UK* – beginnings of the TUC.

1869: September, Basel: Fourth IWA Congress 78 delegates, of which 25 Swiss; General Council motion on inheritance defeated; unions defined as foundation of a new labour-run society, discussion of electoral politics not prioritised. *Belgium* – violent strike conflicts in Seraing and in the Borinage. *France* – elections show decline in support for the government, army kills 14 miners, widespread strike wave. *Germany:* August, Eisenach, foundation of the Social-Democratic Workers' Party, it supersedes Becker's German language organisation. *Italy* – first IWA section organised. *Spain* – IWA, inspired by Fanelli, organises. *Switzerland* – January, Francophone-Swiss regional IWA federation created; strikes in Basel, Geneva and Lausanne; Swiss IWA membership peaks around 6,000.

1870: March, Marx sends an IWA *Confidential Communication* to German Social-Democrats vilifying Bakunin. July, Franco-Prussian War. September, Napoleon III defeated at Sedan, fall of the Third Empire, communes declared in Lyons and Marseilles. IWA Congress due to meet in Paris is relocated to Mainz and then cancelled; items for its agenda: industrial labour, rural organisation, public debt, relations between labour's social and political movements, property, banks, co-ops and mean of avoiding war. Engels moves to London. *Belgium* – demonstrations denounce army repression of strikers. *France* – January, strike at Le Creusot. *Spain* – June, first Spanish IWA congress in Barcelona, 90 delegates representing 40,000 workers. November, Amadeo of Savoy becomes King. *Switzerland* – April, La Chaux-de-Fonds, split in the Francophone-Swiss IWA regional federation leads to creation of rival federations, one based in the Jura, the other in Geneva. August, Geneva IWA expels Bakunin and his allies. Swiss Social-Democratic party founded (expires 1872), with *Tagwacht* as its journal.

1871: January, armistice suspends Franco-Prussian war. September – London IWA Conference, General Council majority endorses political parties and votes itself extended powers. *France* – February, elections, two IWA members elected. March, Paris Commune formed in revolt against republic based in Versailles; May, Commune vanquished: some 20,000 are shot, more deported; IWA banned; June, France invites other governments to supress the IWA: 'an association for hate and war.' Communard refugees spread radical influences. *Germany* – Bebel and Liebknecht imprisoned. *Italy* – Mazzini's antipathy to the Commune exposed by a tract prepared by Bakunin; IWA sections banned. *Spain* – short-lived constitutional monarchy; June, Spanish federation office moves to Lisbon to escape persecution. Strike wave, defeat in Cartagena. Valencia – IWA congress. *Switzerland* – November, Sonvilier Jura congress rejects London conference resolutions. *UK* – October, formation of British IWA Federation; Trade Union Act gives unions some protections, but picketing is made illegal.

1872: Fifth IWA congress, 2-7 September, in The Hague with some 61 delegates attending (of which 21 are members of the General Council). Bakunin and Guillaume are expelled and the General Council is relocated to New York. 15-16 September, Extraordinary Saint-Imier IWA congress, fifteen delegates (two Swiss) repudiate the decisions taken in The Hague. November, followers of Blanqui leave the IWA, declaring that it had failed to do its duty and had 'fled across the Atlantic'. *Belgium* – December, repudiation of decisions of The Hague by Belgian congress meeting in Brussels. *France* – March, new law bans organisations promoting strikes, prohibits affiliation to the IWA (repealed 1901). November, 22 out of 23 delegates at a French IWA meeting support electoral abstention. *Italy* – Cafiero, who had hitherto acted for Engels in Italy, announces his support for Anti-Authoritarians. August, Rimini IWA conference, Italian federation breaks with General Council (no delegates are sent to The Hague). November, policy to 'prevent disorder' announced in parliament. *Spain* – January, IWA banned; April, Carlists launch reactionary insurrection in the north; Saragossa, IWA congress, conflict between 'Anti-Authoritarians' and 'Marxists'; the latter, a minority, set up a new Madrid federation. December, congress of Cordoba, (44 delegates representing 20,000 to 45,000 workers) repudiates decisions of The Hague congress. *Switzerland* – wood workers win a strike in Zurich. *UK* – First Congress of the British IWA federation. *Uruguay* – IWA formed. *USA* – conflicts divides IWA (Spring Street & Tenth Ward); several strikes demand eight-hour day.

1873: January/February, New York General Council suspends Jura federation. The Spring Street USA federation and the Dutch federation repudiate the decisions taken at The Hague. British IWA federation breaks with General Council. May – New York General Council declares that all the IWA bodies that have rejected the resolutions of The Hague have 'placed themselves outside' the IWA. 1-6 September, Geneva, Sixth IWA Congress – attended by some 24 persons (of which four are Swiss) representatives from the Belgian, Dutch, English, Italian, Jura, and Spanish federations and others; 7-13 September, a pro-General-council-congress meets in Geneva. *France* – a list of IWA members is revealed to the police, two (of three) delegates of the General Council are exposed as turncoats; ongoing persecutions, labour organisation is banned. Anti-Authoritarians organize a congress in Lyons and publish *La solidarité révolutionnaire*. *Italy* – March, Bologna, second federal congress; planning for a rising disrupted by state repression. December – Italian Committee for Social Revolution founded to prepare insurrectionary movement. *Spain* – January, IWA congress in Cordoba; February – Amadeo resigns, republic proclaimed. June-July, cantonalist regional movements and risings; IWA prominent in Alcoy, Sanlúcar de Barrameda (Cadiz); general strike in Barcelona; repression; 300 shot in Seville. *Switzerland* – June, a labour congress in Olten creates the Labour Union (Arbeiterbund).

1874: March, Lugano conference – Italian federations' plans for insurrection not supported by other IWA bodies. Brussels, Seventh IWA congress (16 persons, of which 10 Belgians). *France* – April, Lyons, 26 labour activists imprisoned or deported in a mass trial, disrupting the IWA. Blanqui-ist manifesto issued. *Germany* – January, Socialists win 350,000 votes (6.8%) in national elections; *Italy* – attempted insurrection in Romagna, Castel del Monte; IWA banned. *Spain* – January, defeat of last rebel administration in Cartagena; June, (clandestine) 4th congress in Madrid; IWA banned.

1875: *Belgium* – foundation of a Labour Council (Chambre) in Brussels. *Germany* – September, congress in Gotha and formation of German Socialist Workers' Party. *Italy* – trials of IWA members – antipathy towards government secures acquittal. *Spain* – monarchy restored; annual IWA international congress unable to meet there; repression continues, federation still grows nevertheless and by 1882 it has 80,000 members. *Switzerland* – July, Saint Gotthard tunnel, militia opens fire on Italian strikers killing four of them, and wounding ten.

1876: July, Death of Bakunin; Dissolution of the 'Marxist' IWA. October, Bern, Eighth IWA congress, 28 delegates (18 Swiss based) plus invited guests. It agrees to call for a general socialist congress open to all socialists. *Belgium* – Regional congress agrees to campaign against child labour. *France* – state of siege lifted, Paris – labour congress. *Italy* – Florence, clandestine third congress of Italian IWA; insurrectionary deeds advocated as the most effective means of propaganda. *Russia* – December, demonstration in St Petersburg outside Our Lady of Kazan Cathedral. *USA* – Workingmen's Party formed.

1877: Russian-Turkish war (ends 1878). September, two congresses meet: the ninth and final international IWA Congress, in Verviers, with 20 persons present and in Ghent, a Universal Socialist Congress, attended by eleven from Verviers and 31 others (of 42 persons present, 27 are Belgians). *Belgium* – May, two congresses meet, an IWA congress and a second congress that results in the formation of the Flemish Socialist Workers' Party. June, a labour congress leaves open what 'politics' local bodies should adopt. December, last congress of the Belgian IWA Federation relocates the International's Federal Bureau from Verviers to Brussels where it ceases to function. *France* – August, IWA Federation formed, it holds a clandestine congress in La Chaux-de-Fonds, and publishes *L'Avant-Garde*. *Germany* – January, Socialists win 493,000 votes (9.1%) in national elections. Bebel and Liebknecht imprisoned. *Italy* – April, an unsuccessful 'propaganda by the deed' insurrection launched in Benevento. 'Legalist' libertarian congress in Milan. *Spain* – women protest against tax increases on foods and goods. *Switzerland* – March, confrontation between Jura federation supporters and police in Bern, 30 IWA members (inc. Brousse and Guillaume) fined and/or imprisoned (945 days in all), Bern IWA disorganised; referendum approves a maximum eleven hour day and a ban on child labour. *Uruguay* – IWA Federation formed. *USA* – Socialist(ic) Labor Party formed.

1878: No annual IWA international congress is convened. *Cuba* – independence movement defeated. *France* – labour congresses, state bans meetings and orders arrests; James Guillaume moves to Paris, *L'Avant-Garde*, organ of the French federation, ceases publication. The French government bans an international congress, scheduled to convene in Paris. *Germany* – assassination attempt on Kaiser, anti-socialist laws prohibit meetings and publications. Liebknecht writes 'We want to kill those [anti-socialist laws] with our lawfulness'. *Italy* – Cafiero, Costa et al. imprisoned; trial and acquittal of the Benevento insurgents; failed assassination attempt against Italian King Umberto; revival of IWA organisation, insurrection mooted, clandestine congress in Pisa. *Spain* – October – failed assassination attempt against King Alfonso; Mano Negra (Black Hand) organisation formed. *Switzerland* – *Bulletin* ceases publication. The Jura federation congress meets in Fribourg; it decides against working to organise a new international congresses. *USA* – rail workers' strike and shootings.

1879: *Belgium* – Formation of Belgian Socialist party. *France* – Marseilles labour congress, Federation of the Party of Socialist Workers of France created; Blanqui elected deputy. *Spain* – rural risings and riots. *Switzerland* – Brousse imprisoned for inciting anarchism. Kropotkin begins publication of *Le Révolté*. Jura congress meets in La Chaux-de-Fonds.

1880: *Belgium* – Mass demonstration in Brussels. Christmas, revolutionary/anarchist congress in Verviers calls for an international congress to meet in London. *France* – Amnesty for Communards. *Germany* – Radicals (Johann Most and Wilhelm Hasselmann) expelled from Socialist party. *Italy* – regional congresses held. *Switzerland* – August, La Chaux-de-Fonds, congress of the Jura federation attended by Kropotkin, Élisée Reclus and

Cafiero. Meeting of anarchists from northern Italy in Chiasso. Foundation of a national Swiss trades' union association.

1881: London – International anarchist congress. Chur (Switzerland) – international socialist congress. *France* – the funeral of Auguste Blanqui serves as a mass demonstration of Paris labour; labour congress in Paris, conflict between those for and against electoral priority. *Russia* – Tsar Alexander II assassinated. *Spain* – foundation congress of the Regional Workers' Federation (FRTE). Further congresses meet over the next seven years. Libertarians are polarised between 'syndicalism' and 'anarcho-communism'.

1882: *Spain* – congress in Seville, 254 delegates; *Switzerland* – Jura federation congresses in Lausanne and Geneva.

1883: *Italian* congress in Chiasso (Ticino, Switzerland). *Spain* – congress in Barcelona, 140 delegates; *Switzerland* – Jura federation congress in La Chaux-de-Fonds.

* * *

Notes on Sources:
Many texts on the IWA as well as its congress reports are available online. The best selection in print is Jacques Freymond's four volume series: *La première internationale*.

Many records are written and edited with partisan intentions. The General Council report of the Basel IWA Congress is an example. (The booklet has thirty pages long – but ten of these pages list congress delegates and advertisements for progressive books.) It takes a page to present the General Council's argument on inheritance, but does not inform readers that these views, and the motion it sponsored, were decisively rejected by the congress.

* * *

The International Working Men's Association, London: *Resolutions of the Congress of Geneva, 1866, and the Congress of Brussels, 1868.* http://archive.org/stream/resolutionsofcon00inte/resolutionsofcon00inte_djvu.txt; *Report of the Fourth Annual Congress of the International Working Men's Association, held at Basel, in Switzerland, from the 6th to the 11th September, 1869*; Published by the General Council, 1869; available via http://hdl.handle.net/10622/B6E656DD-15BA-4E47-A6F7-B7132F4544C3

AIT: *Compte-rendu du IVe Congrès tenu à Bâle en septembre 1869*, Brussels, Imprimerie Désirée Brismée, 1869. Available online: on http://books.google.co.uk/

AIT: *Compte-Rendu*, Congrès, Bern, 1876 http://gallica.bnf.fr/ark:/12148/bpt6k5544648f/f6.pleinepage.langFR

Bakunin, (Michel Bakounine), the most accessible selection is the six volume collection of his *Oeuvres*, edited by James Guillaume in French and published in Paris by P. V. Stock (Available online, e.g. http://fr.wikisource.org/wiki/Auteur:Michel_Bakounine). The *Ouevres complètes*, Amsterdam: IISG, 2000 on CD is most comprehensive.

Fédération Jurassien: *Bulletin*. Available online, see: http://www.la-presse-anarchiste.net; http://archivesautonomies.org/spip.php?article75

Federación Barcelonesa: *Federación*. Available online http://mdc2.cbuc.cat/cdm/search/collection/federacion/

Jacques Freymond, *La première internationale*, (four volumes), Geneva: Droz/ Institut universitaire de hautes études internationales, 1962-71.

James Guillaume, *L'Internationale: documents et souvenirs 1864-78*, (Four books, 1905, 1907, 1909 and 1910). Books 1 and 2 are available online in one volume (Paris, Société nouvelle de librairie et d'éditions, 1905); books 3 and 4 are available online in a second volume (Paris, Stock, 1909). The page numbering stops at the end of each book. References are given by volume publication date – 1905 for volume 1; 1909 for volume 2, with part numbers and chapter numbers. http://fr.wikisource.org/wiki/Auteur:James_Guillaume

Mathieu Léonard, *L'émancipation des travailleurs*, Paris: La Fabrique, 2011.

Franz Mehring, *Karl Marx – The Story of his Life*, London, Allen & Unwin, 1939. (Available online). The *Marxists* website (http://www.marxists.org/) has this and many other texts.

Mémoire présenté par la Fédération jurassienne de l'Association Internationale des Travailleurs à toutes les Fédérations de l'Internationale, Sonvilier: Fédération jurassienne, 1873.

Max Nettlau, *Der Anarchismus von Proudhon zu Kropotkin: Seine Historische Entwicklung in den Jahren 1859-1880*, Berlin: Fritz Kater, Verlag Der Syndikalist, 1927. (Available online).

NOTES

1. This translation largely follows this earlier text. The edition published in 2015 includes some revisions.
2. For example, Marcello Musto writes that with the exception of – Bakunin's unpublished and unfinished letter to *La Liberté* – Bakunin preferred the 'terrain of personal accusations and insults' to *reasoned* political responses. Marcello Musto, Ed, *Workers Unite!: The International 150 Years Later*, London: Bloomsbury, 2014, p. 51. See also Wolfgang Eckhardt, *The First Socialist Schism: Bakunin vs. Marx in the International Working Men's Association*, Oakland: PM Press, 2015; and *Political conflict in the International Workers' Association*, 1864-1877, http://monde-nouveau.net/spip.php?article559
3. Contemporary English language usage designated the IWA as the 'International Working Men's Association', *Trans*.
4. The author refers to a text in French, http://fr.wikipedia.org/wiki/Association_internationale_des_travailleurs#La_scission The equivalent text in English has a different nuances. (consulted 21.04.2014) *Trans*.
5. George Haupt, 'La confrontation de Marx et de Bakounine dans La première internationale: la phase initiale', in Jacques Catteau, Ed., *Bakounine – Combats et débats*, Paris, Institut d'études slaves, 1979.
6. The *Address* was not considered by the first IWA congress.
7. Proudhon is attributed with opposition to strikes. He says simply that strikes cannot fundamentally resolve social questions.
8. A reference to a manifesto of sixty workers, drawn up by Henri Tolain, on the occasion of partial elections in 1864, to denounce the inequity of French society, *Trans*.
9. James Guillaume: *Karl Marx, Pangermaniste*, Paris, A. Colin, 1915, p. 5. http://onlinebooks.library.upenn.edu/webbin/book/lookupid?key=ha001745501
10. Ibid.
11. In the French text 'de type syndical'. *Trans*
12. Marx took part in none of the congresses of the International, except for The Hague congress, constituted of delegates chosen carefully by himself.
13. Lewis L. Lorwin, *Labor and Internationalism*, New York: Macmillan, 1929.
14. 'Judging Mr Coullery' *L'Égalité* (Geneva), 31 July 1869. (http://kropot.free.fr/Bakounine-PolInter.htm) The considering clauses are reproduced in an appendix. *Trans*.
15. The abolition of inheritance had been a common demand amongst many socialists and featured in the *Communist Manifesto* of Marx and Engels, *Trans*.
16. Some congress members abstained and others were absent when it came to a vote. The votes of the representatives from the General Council were sufficient to prevent the majority of ordinary delegates obtaining a congress majority. *Trans*.
17. Extracts from the debate and resolution are quoted in an appendix. *Trans*.
18. *Mémoire de la Fédération jurassienne*, p. 82. See also: James Guillaume, *L'Internationale*, Book 1, Part 2, Chapter 11, 1905, p. 207.

19 At a later moment, at the congress of The Hague, when it came to rounding up people for mandates, it became clear that there was no German Federation.
20 'Fabrique' denoted professional worker citizens and voters active in skilled trades: jewellery, clock and watch makers, etc. *Trans.*
21 M. Nettlau, 'Les Origines de L'Internationale anti-autoritaire', *Le Réveil*, 16 September, 1922.
22 Franz Mehring, *Karl Marx*, op. cit, p. 471.
23 We consider as an ideological approach one that consists of taking an author's ideas literally, without critical examination. In such a fashion, *The Civil War in France* would be taken as a history book on the Commune, to be taken as such, containing the truth about this event, rather than a book presenting Marx's opinions on the matter, at given moment, and with particular reasons in mind.
24 While they saw possibilities of progress through parliamentary elections, the English Federation respected the right of each national Federation to elaborate its own tactics and policies, in the light of its own situation. *Trans.*
25 Liebknecht left Germany after the 1848 events and only returned in 1862; he was a democrat, and became a long serving Social-Democrat editor and leader. *Trans.*
26 Engels to Wilhelm Liebknecht, 22 May 1872; Marx & Engels, *Collected Works*, Vol. 44, p. 376. http://www.dearchiv.de/php/dok.php?archiv=mew&brett=MEW033&fn=465-468.33&menu=mewinh
27 The Geneva Alliance section was dissolved in August 1871, but a month later former members came together with exiled refugees from the Commune to found a 'Section de propagande et d'action révolutionnaire-socialiste' – (Section for propaganda and for socialist-revolutionary action.) James Guillaume, *L'Internationale*, Book 1, Third part, Chapter 10, 1905, p. 177ff. The London conference meeting shortly afterwards prohibited such sections.
28 Michel Bakounine, November - December 1872, 'De l'empire knouto-germanique', in Michel Bakounine, *Oeuvres*, Vol. 4, Paris: Stock, 1910, p. 424.
29 'Lettres à un français', in Bakounine, *Oeuvres*, Book 4, pp. 42-3.
30 Some 40% of the workforce. *Trans*
31 [Consider Mehring's comment]: And, when Marx wrote the General Council circular *The Fictitious Splits in the International*, indicting 'young Guillaume' for having denounced 'the factory workers' of Geneva as hateful 'bourgeois', that text did not pay the least attention to the fact that the 'Fabrique' in Geneva was a section of highly-paid workers in the luxury trades which had concluded more or less dubious electoral compromises with the bourgeois parties. Franz Mehring, *Karl Marx*, op. cit, p. 479.
32 In *The Communist Manifesto*, (Chapter II: Proletarians and Communists), Marx's list of measures reads: 1. Abolition of property in land and application of all rents of land to public purposes. 2. A heavy progressive or graduated income tax. 3. Abolition of all rights of inheritance. 4. Confiscation of the property of all emigrants and rebels. 5. Centralisation of credit in the hands of the state, by means of a national bank with state capital and an exclusive monopoly. 6. Centralisation of the means of communication and transport in the hands of the state. 7. Extension of factories and instruments of production owned by the state; the bringing into cultivation of waste-lands, and the improvement of the soil generally in accordance with a common plan. 8. Equal liability of all to work. Establishment of industrial armies, especially for agriculture. 9. Combination of agriculture with manufacturing industries; gradual abolition of all the distinction between town and country by a more equable distribution of the populace over the country. 10. Free education for all children in public schools. Abolition of children's factory labour in its present form. Combination of education with industrial production, etc, etc.

33 1891, introduction by Frederick Engels, 'On the 20th Anniversary of the Paris Commune', http://www.marxists.org/archive/marx/works/1871/civil-war-france/postscript.htm
34 Letter of 20 March 1869.
35 Letter of Marx to Engels, 20 July 1870 in Marx & Engels, *Collected Works*, Vol. 44, 1989, pp. 3-4. See also http://www.marxists.org/archive/marx/works/1870/letters/70_07_20.htm
36 Engels, letter to Bernstein, 12-13 June 1883, in Marx & Engels, *Collected Works*, Vol. 47, 1995, pp. 35-6.
37 See appendix. *Trans*
38 It had the function of an international political party. Its principles were atheism, federalism, socialism, anti-state-ism, anti-patriotism, solidarity between nations, equality of rights between the sexes, beginning with the right to education. The programme of this Fraternity stipulated that the supporter 'should be convinced that … women – different, but not inferior to men, should be like him, in intelligence, as free and industrious as him, and must be declared to be his equal in all social and political rights.' As for children, Bakunin says, their education should be paid for by society, 'and the latter – whilst it protects them against stupidity, negligence, or any ill will from parents – will have no need to take them away; children *belong* neither to society, nor to parents, but – freely – to themselves.' Gregory P. Maximoff (Maxsimov), *The Political Philosophy of Bakunin*, New York: The Free Press, 1953. p. 327.
39 Bakounine, *Oeuvres Complètes: Ecrit contre Marx*, Vol. 3, Paris: Champ Libre, 1972-83, p. 179; and *Oeuvres*, Vol. 4, Paris: Stock, 1910, p. 450.
40 James Guillaume, *L'Internationale*, Vol. 2, part 5 Chapter 2, p. 25.
41 Guillaume comments that the first IWA congress adopted the 'Considering' clauses unchanged, as drafted by Marx; but did not adopt his *Inaugural Address*. Bakounine, *Oeuvres*, Vol. 4, pp. 420-21. *Trans*.
42 'Fragment formant une suite de l'empire knouto-germanique' in Michel Bakounine, *Oeuvres*, Vol. 4, pp. 425-6. *Trans*
43 Ibid, p. 406.
44 Ibid, pp. 412-3.
45 Ibid, p. 418.
46 Ibid, p. 421.
47 Ibid, p. 433.
48 Ibid, pp. 433-4.
49 Ibid, p. 435.
50 Ibid, pp. 435-6.
51 Ibid, p. 427.
52 Michel Bakounine, 'Protestation de l'Alliance', *Oeuvres*, Vol. 6, p. 70
53 *Oeuvres*, Vol. 4, Paris: Stock, 1910, p. 436
54 Ibid.
55 Ibid, p. 438.
56 'Protestation de l'Alliance'. Michel Bakounine, *Oeuvres*, Vol. 6, p. 73.
57 This item was added to the agenda by the congress, after five other items set by the General Council and discussed by IWA sections in preparation for the congress. For lack of time it was not discussed. *Trans*.
58 The Basel congress of 1869 had resolved that addresses of IWA federations should be set out in the IWA press. Jacques Freymond, *La première internationale*, Vol. 2, p. 129.
59 Letter reproduced in James Guillaume, *L'Internationale*, Vol. 2, 1909, part 5 Chapter 2, p. 25.
60 Ibid.

61 Letter to the Brussels *La Liberté*, 1-8 October, 1872.
62 Franz Mehring, *Karl Marx*, op. cit, p. 482.
63 'La science et la question vitale de la révolution.' March 1870, Michel Bakounine, *Oeuvres*, Vol. 6, p. 280.
64 Ibid., p. 285.
65 Bakounine: 'Aux compagnons de la Fédération des sections internationales du Jura.' *Oeuvres Complètes: Ecrit contre Marx*, Vol. 3, Paris: Champ Libre, 1972-83, p. 74. See also http://icp.ge.ch/po/cliotexte/xviiie-et-xixe-siecle-revolution-industrielle-liberalisme-socialisme/revolution.industrielle.4.html
66 'La science et la question vitale de la révolution', March 1870.
67 Marx to Engels in Manchester; 13 January 1869. See http://www.marxists.org/archive/marx/works/1869/letters/69_01_13.htm
68 In the French, Bakunin describes the state as an 'institution anarchique'. At that time anarchism was not widely used to define a political doctrine. Bakunin defined himself as a 'collectivist' or a 'revolutionary socialist'. For this reason the word 'anarchism' may be placed in quotes. *Trans.*
69 James Guillaume, *L'Internationale*, Part 1, Chapter 11, p. 91.
70 Ibid, Part 2, Chapter 2, p. 109.
71 Bakunin writes in the third person in 'Rapport sur l'Alliance'.
72 These regulations – Règlements – are to be found on the web: anti.mythes.voila.net/syndicalisme/ait_aids.pdf
73 'Rapport sur l'Alliance', 1871, in Michel Bakounine, *Oeuvres*, Vol. 6, Paris: Stock, 1913, p. 157ff.
74 Letter to Anselmo Lorenzo, 7 May 1872. See: http://www.fondation-besnard.org/spip.php?article793 [p. 6.]
75 De Paepe would without doubt be the one who would give the clearest definition of a stateless society. See below: 'Proletariat and organisation'.
76 Open letter of the Central Bureau of the Fraternity, dated March 1869.
77 Bakunin refers to the mother section of the Geneva IWA meeting in the centre of the city. *Trans.*
78 'Rapport sur l'Alliance', 1871, in Michel Bakounine, *Oeuvres*, Vol. 6, Paris: Stock, 1913.
79 Ibid.
80 My emphasis.
81 It may be seen that Bakunin, in repeatedly naming the current he refers to, speaks of 'revolutionary socialism' but never of 'anarchism'
82 'Rapport sur l'Alliance', p. 181.
83 Romand refers to francophone Switzerland – la Suisse romande. *Trans.*
84 'Rapport sur l'Alliance', p. 202.
85 'Rapport sur l'Alliance', p. 227.
86 Ibid, pp. 229-230.
87 In his autobiography Kropotkin wrote that the Genevan IWA sections 'met in the vast Temple Unique, the hall of the Masonic Lodge. It could accommodate over a thousand people in its vast hall...' There workers could receive free instruction from a small number of middle class men. It was at one and the same time a popular university and a popular forum. Kropotkin had great doubts as to the sincerity of the agitation organised in this Temple Unique. Peter Kropotkin, *Memoirs of a Revolutionist*, Boston & New York, Houghton Mifflin, p. 177.
88 'Rapport sur l'Alliance', 1871, in Michel Bakounine, *Oeuvres*, Vol. 6, Paris: Stock, 1913, pp. 232-3.
89 The question of comprehensive education had been discussed at the Brussels congress of the IWA in September 1868. Bakunin's article 'L'Instruction intégrale' had been

published in the *L'Egalité* journal, on August 21, 1869.
90   Franz Mehring, *Karl Marx*, op. cit, p. 497.
91   Letter to *La Liberté* of Brussels, 1-8 October, 1872. Michel Bakounine, *Oeuvres*, Vol. 4, Paris: Stock, 1910, p. 349.
92   Michel Bakounine, *Oeuvres*, Vol. 4, Paris: Stock, 1910, p. 429.
93   Pëtr Kropotkin, *Memoirs*, op. cit, p. 178.
94   Bakunin, letter 'Aux compagnons de la Fédération des sections internationales du Jura', of February-March 1872, in *Oeuvres Complètes*, Vol. 3, Paris: Champ Libre, 1972-83, p. 74. See also *Oeuvres*, Vol. 4, Paris: Stock, 1910, pp. 196-7, 404-5.
95   In the French 'embourgeoiseé', *Trans.*
96   Letter to *La Liberté* of Brussels, 1-8 October, 1872. Michel Bakounine, *Oeuvres*, Vol. 4, Paris: Stock, 1910, p. 375
97   Letter to Theodore Cuno, 24 January 1872.
98   Anton Pannekoek, 'General Remarks on the Question of Organisation', 1938; http://www.marxists.org/archive/pannekoe/1938/general-remarks.htm
99   Bakounine, 'Aux Compagnons de la Fédération des Sections internationales de Jura', February-March, 1872, p. 53; see: http://www.fondation-besnard.org/spip.php?article2065
100 'Les institutions actuelles de L'Internationale au point de vue de leur avenir' Bakounine, *Oeuvres*, Ed. Lebovici, Vol. 3, Appendix 3, pp. 255-6. Cf. *Le Progrès* of Le Locle, #9; March 1, 1869; the article 'L'Internationale et ses institutions de l'avenir'.
101 'Sections de metièr'
102 'L'instruction intégrale'
103 See: David Shub, *Lenin*, Harmondsworth: Penguin, 1976, p. 219.
104 In France the commune is the smallest administrative area.
105 Preface by Jacques Duclos to the French Communist party document, *Au nouvel adherent*, p. 5.
106 *La vie du parti*, October 1966, p. 3.
107 Michel Bakounine, 'Protestation de l'Alliance', *Oeuvres*, Vol. 6, p. 56.
108 Ibid, p. 71.
109 Ibid, p. 72.
110 Ibid, p. 73.
111 Cf. René Berthier: 'La Révolution française comme archétype: 1848 ou le 1789 manqué de la bourgeoisie allemande' and 'La Révolution française dans la formation de la théorie révolutionnaire chez Bakounine', in *Les anarchistes et la Révolution française*, Paris: Editions du Monde libertaire, 1990.
112 Bakounine, *Oeuvres*, Vol. 4, Paris: Stock, 1910, p. 434
113 'de la nature de son but dépend essentiellement le mode et la nature même de son organisation.' See 'La question du programme', 'Aux compagnons de la Fédération des sections internationales du Jura' February-March 1872, *Oeuvres Complètes: Ecrit contre Marx*, Vol. 3, Paris: Champ Libre, 1972-83, p 74. See also http://icp.ge.ch/po/cliotexte/xviiie-et-xixe-siecle-revolution-industrielle-liberalisme-socialisme/revolution.industrielle.4.html
114 Ibid, pp. 75-6.
115 Ibid, p. 68.
116 Ibid, p. 69.
117 Bakunin does not formulate it explicitly so, but if there were only central sections in the IWA, it would be quite simply a political party.
118 'Protestation de l'Alliance', *Oeuvres*, Vol. 6, p. 70.
119 Ibid, p.76.
120 Ibid, p. 77.

121 This of course should not be confused with the eponymous movement which would appear in Russia.
122 'Protestation de l'Alliance', *Oeuvres*, Vol. 6, pp. 78-9.
123 'Frères de l'Alliance en Espagne', 12-13 June 1872.
124 Morago appears in (Guillaume, *L'Internationale*, 1909, part 4, chapter 3, p. 270-1.) as a [corresponding] member of the Geneva Alliance section. See appendix January, 1870.
125 The word 'direction' may be understood as having two meanings – 'forward path, and orientation' or 'directing group'. Both options are possible.
126 'l'explication dernière'.
127 This is what defines the Social-Democratic approach to the question of party-union division of labour, whatever means might be used – violent or non-violent.
128 Letter to Morago, 21 May, 1872. See http://search.socialhistory.org/Record/ARCH00018/ArchiveContentList; p. 13.
129 To be precise, if Marx wanted the IWA to adopt this principle, it was not the IWA that was to conquer political power, but rather Social-Democratic parties. It should be remembered that at the Congress of The Hague, Marx had had article 7a brusquely inserted into the IWA statutes, in an irregular manner. That article stipulated that 'the conquest of political power has become the chief duty of the proletariat'. It is these statutes alone that are considered as legitimate by the Marxist current.
130 In the French text 'syndicale' is used, i.e. forms of workplace organisation. *Trans.*
131 Letter to Morago, 21 May, 1872.
132 Ibid.
133 Bakunin's letter to *La Liberté* of Brussels, 1-8 October, 1872, notes that he never saw the details – the text – of this communication. Michel Bakounine, *Oeuvres*, Vol. 4, Paris: Stock, 1910, p. 367. *Trans*
134 Evident in this text of three or more pages are six outrageous misrepresentations and seven flagrant lies. On this subject Brupbacher, wrote: 'To every person on all the surface of the Earth, other than a handful of fanatics it will appear, from this communication, that the character of Marx is imprinted with ineradicable defilement.' Fritz Brupbacher, *Marx und Bakunin: Ein Beitrag zur Geschichte der Internationalen Arbeiterassoziation*, Berlin, Die Aktion, 1922. p. 98. https://archive.org/stream/2917094.0001.001.umich.edu
135 Michel Bakounine, 'De l'empire knouto-germanique', in *Oeuvres*, Vol. 4, Paris: Stock, 1910, p. 433.
136 Letter to *La Liberté* of Brussels, 1-8 October, 1872. Michel Bakounine, *Oeuvres*, Vol. 4, Paris: Stock, 1910, p. 388.
137 James Guillaume, *L'Internationale*, Part 3, Chapter 11, 1905, p. 194.
138 Mémoire présenté par la Fédération jurassienne, first part, p. 204. See also James Guillaume, part 3, Chapter 11, 1905, pp. 192ff.
139 Lewis L. Lorwin, *Labor and Internationalism*, New York: Macmillan, 1929, p. 44.
140 The Alliance section in Geneva was later dissolved. Former members set up new propaganda sections there and in the Jura with the support of exiles from the Paris Commune.
141 Marx and Engels would later declare that Robin, a Belgian who had resided for a short time in Geneva, represented the Jura Federation. Certainly Robin had some sympathy for the Jurassians, but sympathy was one thing and normal practice – the selection of a delegate after some discussion within an IWA body, such as had been normal practice hitherto before international meetings – was something else. In fact this meeting was termed a private conference and only parties trusted by the organisers were invited. Robin dismissed the proceedings as a scandal, and for his pains was told that he had resigned. He had in fact been expelled from the General Council. *Trans.*

142 James Guillaume, *L'Internationale,* 1909, part 4, chapter 3, p. 235.
143 The Sonvilier circular is available online: http://www.panarchy.org/jura/sonvillier.html
144 James Guillaume, 1909, part 4, chapter 1, p. 239.
145 Michel Bakounine, letter to *La Liberté* of Brussels, 1-8 October, 1872, in *Oeuvres,* Vol. 4, Paris: Stock, 1910, p. 388.
146 James Guillaume, *L'Internationale,* 1909, Part 4, chapter 6, p. 326.
147 Engels to Wilhelm Liebknecht, 22 May 1872.
148 [With the exception of the rump IWA federation based in Geneva] and the Germans who represented nothing.
149 James Guillaume, *L'Internationale,* Part 4, chapter 6, p. 338.
150 Bakunin's argument that solidarity was at the heart of the IWA is developed in his letter to *La Liberté* of Brussels, 1-8 October, 1872, in *Oeuvres,* Vol. 4, Paris: Stock, 1910, pp. 348-9. See also Bakounine, *Oeuvres Complètes,* Champ libre edition, Vol. 3, p. 411. Bakunin refers to arguments by Marx and Sorge, that to go into battle the IWA needed to have its strength centralised. *Trans.*
151 Franz Mehring, *Karl Marx,* op. cit, pp. 490-1.
152 'Rapport sur l'alliance'. Michel Bakounine, *Oeuvres,* Vol. 6, pp. 157ff.
153 See appendix for the full congress resolutions. *Trans.*
154 The recently formed American Federation split into two parts. One of them, the so-called Spring Street Federation, declared itself federalist on 19 January 1873.
155 Some remnants did support the decisions of the General Council: often organisations set up by persons close to Marx and Engels, bodies existing more on paper than in reality. *Trans.*
156 Things were more complicated – Marx knew that Sorge would never be elected to the General Council, even though people who might have elected him were on his side. Sorge was indeed detested by almost everybody. But Marx had a clause inserted in the new regulations that imposed on members of the General Council the inclusion of co-opted members – and this allowed Sorge in.
157 James Guillaume, *L'Internationale,* 1909, part 5, Chapter 3, p. 58
158 Ibid.
159 Bebel, *Volkstaat,* 16 March 1872.
160 The Jura and Romande Federations, and the German language sections.
161 From here on, when we refer to 'The International' or 'the IWA', what is being named is the legitimate organisation which rejected the decisions made in The Hague and which continued is normal life. When describing the debris which gathered around the former General Council, we will speak of the 'secessionist International' or the 'Marxified International'. The congress of The Hague was the fifth in the sequence of congresses. The 'continuity' International considering itself as legitimate, naturally continued the numbering from the Congress of The Hague; thus the Geneva Congress, held from 1-3 September, 1873, was the sixth. As we shall see German Social-Democrats contested the legitimacy of this sequence.
162 The General German Workers' Association (Allgemeiner Deutscher Arbeiterverein). Until his death in a duel in 1864 Ferdinand Lassalle was the leading figure in the quasi-socialist German left. *Trans*
163 Marx to Engels, 27 July, 1869; in Marx & Engels, *Collected Works,* Vol. 43, Moscow & London: Progress Publishers & Lawrence & Wishart, 1989, pp. 332-3.
164 Kautsky, who tried not to 'persist with the old-fashioned viewpoint of Marx' on the national question, would foresee in 1896, that 'the linguistic community constitutes a much more solid bond than the community of political struggle and action'. Cf. Claudie Weill, *International et l'autre, les relations inter-ethniques dans la IIe International,* Paris:

Arcantère éditions, 1987.
165 Marx & Engels, *Collected Works*, Vol. 44, pp. 367ff (371).
166 It should also be noted that in other countries, where the IWA was also prohibited, it still managed to develop.
167 Marx & Engels, *La Social-Democracie allemande*, Paris, 10/18, note 35, p. 352; (Annotated and with commentary by Roger Dangeville). Roger Dangeville (1925-2006) was a member of the French CP in 1956, which he left in 1966. Until 1977 he wrote for the review *Le Fil du temps*. He contributed to the discovery of unpublished texts of Marx. He was editor-in-chief of thematic compilations of Marx & Engels writings, with long introductions and impressive annotations, of exceptional utility. Notably: *Ecrits militaires*, L'Herne, 1970; Friedrich Engels & Karl Marx, *Le syndicalisme*, Paris, Maspero, 1972 (2 Vols.); Friedrich Engels & Karl Marx, *Le parti de classe*, Paris, Maspero, 1973 (4 Vols.); Karl Marx & Friedrich Engels, *La Russie*, Paris, U.G.E. 10/18, 1974; Karl Marx & Friedrich Engels, *La Social-Democracie allemande*, Paris, U.G.E. 10/18, 1975.
168 Franz Mehring, *Karl Marx*, op. cit, p. 482.
169 The regime of Napoléon III. *Trans*.
170 *L'Egalité*, No. 16, 8 May, 1869.
171 A section of Berthier's text on Marx and Engels and their reaction to events after 1848 is omitted from this translation. Berthier notes that Marx was excluded from the League of Communists, he was accused of promoting his personal interests. *Trans*
172 Note by Dangeville in: *Le Parti de classe, recueil de textes*, Paris: Maspero, II, p. 45.
173 See appendix for 1873, revised IWA statutes.
174 James Guillaume, *L'Internationale*, part 4, chapter 6, p. 341.
175 Letter, 3 May, 1873; Marx & Engels, *Collected Works*, Vol. 43, Moscow & London: Progress Publishers & Lawrence & Wishart, 1989, pp. 490ff; Engels lists those he wanted expelled. (p. 494).
176 Marx, letter to the New York General Council, 12 February 1872. Marx & Engels, *Collected Works* Vol. 23, p. 415
177 Letter, Marx to Friedrich Bolte, 12 February, 1873, Marx & Engels, *Collected Works*, Vol. 44, pp. 475-6.
178 Bakounine, *Oeuvres*, Vol. 4, Paris: Stock, 1910, pp. 345-6.
179 Marx pushed on with his manipulation to the point that Eccarius and Jung, [hitherto] his close allies, took issue with the way in which the congress of The Hague had been set up, with the decisions that were taken there and with the pretention that the General Council might impose one compulsory programme on IWA Federations. Jung criticised Marx and Engels for making of the congress of The Hague 'a sad hoax'. A congress of the English IWA Federation, held in London on 26 January, 1873, declared that the meeting in The Hague had been out of order and that its resolutions had no validity.
180 Cited by Arthur Lehning, Bakounine, *Oeuvres Complètes*, Champ libre, Vol. 3, p. 466.
181 Ibid.
182 *Oeuvres*, Vol. 4, Paris: Stock, 1910, p. 352.
183 Cited by Arthur Lehning.
184 The congress president, Josseron, was later appointed a local police commissioner, with responsibility for morality. *Trans*.
185 My emphasis. Georg [Iuri] Stieklow [Steklov], *Die Bakunistische International nach dem Haager Kongress: Ein Beitrag zur Geschichte der Internationalen Arbeiterassoziation*, supplement to *Neue Zeit*, April 1914. (http://archive.org/stream/diebakunistische00stek#page/n1/mode/2up) ‚Abgesehen von den Vereinigten Staaten, in denen zu der Zeit die Bewegung noch sehr schwach war und sich hauptsächlich auf

die deutschen Emigranten beschränkte, die dabei im Streite miteinander lagen, stand eigentlich keine Nationalföderation hinter dem Generalrat.' (Outside the United States – where at the time the movement was still very weak and limited essentially to German émigrés, who quarrelled one with another, there were no national federations behind the General Council.)

186 He turned out badly, joining the anti-Semite Christian social movement.
187 Becker used the term 'Delegiertenmacherei' for his fabrication of credentials and delegates, and noted that they were created out of nothing 'gleichsam aus der Erde gestampften.'
188 James Guillaume, *L'Internationale*, 1909, Part 5, chapter 5, p. 138.
189 Cited by Guillaume, ibid, p. 137.
190 Letter to Sorge, 27 September 1873, in *Collected Works*, 1989, Vol. 44, p. 534.
191 Ibid, p, 535.
192 Engels to Marx, 21 September 1874, *Collected Works*, 1989, Vol. 45, p. 51
193 Letter to Sorge, 27 September 1873, in *Collected Works*, 1989, Vol. 44, p. 535.
194 James Guillaume, *L'Internationale*, 1909, Part 5, chapter 5, pp. 145-6.
195 Ibid, p. 147.
196 From the perspective of 1914 such words might seem prescient – but neither Marx (in respect of the behaviour of the majority of German Social-Democrats), nor Bakunin (in respect of the CGT Labour Confederation) can be credited or blamed for the decisions taken by tendencies some forty years on. Nevertheless the sympathies of Marx and Engels for German national unity and for the influence of what Engels would call 'German communism' were thrown in their face by those – like James Guillaume - who continued to see Germany as a force for reaction. Any amalgam – of nationalism and socialism, or nationalism and reaction – might be used for reactionary purposes. *Trans*
197 James Guillaume, *L'Internationale*, Vol. 2, Book 1, p. 11.
198 The 'loi Dufaure', passed on 14 March 1872, set up severe punishments for each individual member of the International.
199 The paragraphs beginning 'The bureaucratic manoeuvres of Marx and his entourage ... up to this note are translated from Berthier's revised text : '*La fin de la première internationale*, p. 267-9.
200 Cf. G. Steklov, *Die Bakunistiche International*, p. 17.
201 Bakunin: 'Letter to the comrades of the Jura Federation', October 1873; Guillaume, *L'Internationale,*, 1909, part 5, chapter 5, pp. 145-6.
202 Peter Kropotkin, *Memoirs of a Revolutionist*, Houghton Mifflin Company, Boston and New York: Houghton Mifflin Company, 1899, p. 245.
203 Bakounine, *Oeuvres*, Vol. 4, Paris: Stock, 1910, p. 418.
204 See below on the congress of Olten.
205 James Guillaume, *L'Internationale*, 1909, part 5, chapter 10, pp. 253-4.
206 *Solidarité*, 28 May 1870.
207 James Guillaume, 1905, part 3, chapter 2, p. 43.
208 These texts are from a letter addressed to the English Federal Council of November 1872, the letter quotes an article first published in the Jura Federation's press, in June 1870. *Trans*.
209 James Guillaume, 1909, part 3, chapter 2, p. 43.
210 James Guillaume, 1909, part 5, chapter 3, p. 75.
211 *Bulletin de la Federation jurassienne*, cited by James Guillaume.
212 Quoted in an appendix. *Trans*.
213 This formula, 'the fraction that is called anarchist' is clearly intended to make it understood that the author is putting himself at some distance from the term

'anarchist', that he does not subscribe to it, and that that term appears to be used by others to designate the federalist current of the International.
214 James Guillaume, 1909, part 6, chapter 7, pp. 77-8.
215 Annexed to the German Empire after the Franco-Prussian war.
216 James Guillaume, ibid, pp. 81-2
217 In 1870, in Zurich, Hermann Greulich brought together a few IWA sections around his journal, *Tagwacht*. It would lay the foundations of the Swiss Social-Democratic party. In 1873 he would be a participant in the creation of the Swiss Labour Union (Union ouvrière Suisse, Arbeiterbund), a composite network bringing together Grütli and IWA sections, unions, German labour education groups, etc. *Tagwacht* was its journal.
218 A reference to the pamphlet of Engels.
219 James Guillaume, 1909, part 6, chapter 7, p. 87.
220 Ibid.
221 Ibid, pp. 89-90.
222 Ibid, p. 89.
223 Note 302 has further extracts from this speech.
224 The latter, under the name of Muslim Bosnians, would become the victims of the Serbs, in 1991
225 James Guillaume, 1909, part 6, chapter 8, p. 99.
226 And curiously this connects with at least the spirit of the motion that would be voted at the Stuttgart congress of the German Social-Democratic party in 1907, prohibiting any common action with the bourgeoisie.
227 James Guillaume, ibid, p. 100.
228 'La situation politique en France' (Letter to Palix) Lyons, 29 September - early October 1870. Bakounine, *Oeuvres*, Vol. 4, p. 195.
229 Revolutionary catechism, (1866).
230 The cantonalist insurrection of 1873 was launched by radical bourgeois elements wholly discontented with the new constitution, seeing it as overly centralist. Although badly organised, they ordered the closure of churches, the confiscation of church assets, taxes on the rich, the armament of the people, and the distribution of lands to day labourers. Libertarians supported the movement and attempted to give it a socialist direction.
231 Letter to Celsio Cerretti, 13-27 March 1872.
232 Bakounine, *Oeuvres*, Vols. 2 and 4.
233 http://kropot.free.fr/Bakounine-Instrucintegr.htm 'All-Round Education', in Mikhail Bakunin, *From Out of the Dustbin: Bakunin's Basic Writings 1869-1871*, [Ed. Robert M. Cutler], Ardis Publishers, Ann Arbor, 1985, p. 111ff.
234 http://gallica.bnf.fr/ark:/12148/bpt6k7516r
235 P. Ansart, *Marx et l'anarchisme*, Paris, Presses universitaires de France, 1969, p. 319.
236 Ibid.
237 Paul Brousse (1844-1912), a French socialist, spent some years in exile after the Commune and worked for the *Bulletin de la Fédération Jurassienne*, and subsequently supported French socialist parties.
238 Jean-Louis Pindy (1840-1917), fled France after the Commune, and died in the Swiss Jura.
239 James Guillaume, *L'Internationale, documents et souvenirs*, 1909, part 6, chapter 8, pp. 101-2.
240 Germans only joined the IWA as individuals.
241 Dühring was not gentle with Marx. He declared in *Kritische Geschichte der Nationalökonomie* that the Paris Commune was hurt more by Marx and by Marxists than by reactionaries.
242 James Guillaume, 1909, part 6, chapter 8, p. 102.

243 James Guillaume, ibid, p. 105.
244 One would have to wait until the Dresden congress of 1903 for German Social-Democrats to adopt a motion condemning any participation in a coalition with bourgeois political bourgeois parties. They arranged the adoption of a text almost identical to one from the Amsterdam International congress of 1904: 'Congress condemns most energetically revisionist attempts seeking to replace glorious and proven tactics based on class struggle with political concessions to the established order – which would end up changing a revolutionary party desiring transformation ... of bourgeois society into a socialist society ... into a party content to reform bourgeois society.
245 James Guillaume, *L'Internationale, documents et souvenirs*, 1909, part 6, chapter 7, pp. 61-2.
246 James Guillaume, ibid, p. 72.
247 The international congress of 1875 was postponed at the request of the Italians and Spanish members because, facing repression, their participation was impossible. The situation in France was much the same.
248 In reality, such attempts had begun well before the death of Bakunin. See above ... *attempted reconciliation*
249 James Guillaume, ibid, p 72.
250 James Guillaume, ibid, p 70.
251 See appendix. *Trans.*
252 Marx to Sorge, 27 September 1877.
253 James Guillaume noted that this sentence perhaps means 'duty demanded that each person should try to spread the revolution into their own homeland'.
254 James Guillaume, *L'Internationale, documents et souvenirs*, part 6, chapter 14, p. 261.
255 Facing the reverses of the Commune and of the revolutionary actions in which he participated Bakunin had come to the conclusion that 'the revolutionary moment has passed by'. So, he recommended 'propaganda by the deed' having in mind direct actions that might serve as examples. But stupidity and demagogy were the law in the anarchist movement, and the formula was interpreted as a recommendation for acts of individuals which had nothing to do with the thought of the great activist. (Gaston Leval, *La crise permanente de l'anarchisme.*)
256 *Révolté*, December 25, 1880, cited by Jean Maitron. It should be recalled that *Révolté* was edited by Kropotkin and that it is not very probable that the opinion set out here contradicted Bakunin's ideas.
257 *Le mouvement anarchiste en France*, Vol. I, Paris, Gallimard, 1992, p. 118.
258 The falling membership of the Jura Federation at the time of the Verviers congress suggests its decline. Marianne Enckell indicates that in 1870, which was the best year for Jura sections, there were 726 members. In 1873, the Jura Federation had barely 400 members. (Marianne Enckell, *La Federation jurassienne, les origines de l'anarchisme en Suisse*, L'Âge d'Homme, 1971, p. 65.)
259 Marc Vuilleumier, in *Cahiers Vilfredo Pareto*, No. 7-8, Droz, Geneva, 1965, p. 64.
260 Chancellor Bismarck used these two [failed] assassination attempts to enact an Anti-Socialist law, in October 1878.
261 See: Christian Beuvain, Stéphane Moulain, Ami-Jacques Rapin, Jean-Baptiste Thomas, *Révolution, lutte armée et terrorisme*, Vol. 1, Paris: L'Harmattan, (Dissidences), 2006.
262 E. Bernstein, *My Years or Exile*, Chapter 2, 1922. http://www.marxists.org/reference/archive/bernstein/works/1915/exile/ch02.htm
263 James Guillaume, *L'Internationale, documents et souvenirs*, 1909, part 6, chapter 7, pp. 69-70.
264 Ibid, p. 107.

265 The latter was not a member of the International but he had taken part in the creation of an 'Independent Club for Socialists' and had sent a message to the *Bulletin* of the Jura Federation to announce itself: 'Comrades, we have the pleasure of informing you of the creation in Geneva of an Independent Club for Socialists. The study of differences dividing various socialist fractions; bringing every sort of Socialist closer: that is the mission that Club members have taken on. There is reason to hope that the club – composed of Socialists belonging to any group – will play its part in action for the revolutionary cause...' Three years earlier Gutsmann had been president at the congress of Olten, and then of the central committee of the *Arbeiterbund*. He was nominated as a delegate to the Bern congress. Congress gave Gutsmann the right to take part in its deliberations as it did Vahlteich, the German Social-Democrat representative.

266 A body of culturally patriotic workers and artisans. Non-Swiss were not allowed membership.

267 The *Bulletin* of the Jura Federation of January 7, 1878, revealed that 'following the passing of the factory law making managements responsible for any of their workers' accidents, a Zurich textile business 'intended to dispense with all less able workers, persons kept on out of humanity. It would appear that such a class of workers is present in every factory in smaller or greater numbers, and this contingent provides the greatest number of accidents.' To avoid such measure, village communes from which such workers are drawn have taken on the commitment to take on responsibility for accidents in the place of employers. The *Bulletin* stressed that management took on 'less able workers' 'as a means of saving money, and not at all out of humanity'. There, stresses the *Bulletin*, is one of the means used by managements to subvert progress. *Tagwacht*, which published so much propaganda in favour of a factory law 'now begins to see that management will be cunning enough to search out means to evade legal conditions that they might find awkward.'

268 James Guillaume, 1909, part 6, chapter 4, pp. 42-3.

269 'There was Bazin, a Frenchman living in Brussels and representing a French group in London; Zanardelli, an Italian representing some groups from Milan, Palermo and Mantua, or, to be more precise the editors of two well known journals: *Povero* and *Plebe*; Bert (a pseudonym), the delegate of a group from Puteaux near Paris; Paulin (pseudonym) a delegate of a group in Lyons; lastly Robin (pseudonym), a delegate from a group in Paris. Ibid, Part 6, Chapter 14, pp. 266-7.

270 See appendix. *Trans*.

271 James Guillaume, ibid, p. 271,

272 Of the three persons named Jules Montels (1843-1916) was the only one not to go back on his convictions. This internationalist Communard had a lifelong antipathy for Marx, because the latter had insulted Communards.

273 Although this did not prevent them, shortly afterwards joining the parliamentary current which they had [earlier] criticised.

274 James Guillaume, ibid, p. 275.

275 Michael Maltman Barry (1842-1909), was a curious person. His closeness to Marx demonstrates the extent to which the latter might surround himself with men whose lives were ambiguous. After meeting and becoming a friend of Marx, Maltman Barry declared that he was a Marxist, but stood – unsuccessfully – as a candidate in several elections as a conservative. He was, temporarily, president of the IWA but was quickly forced to resign from the organisation having been accused of being a spy; this did not prevent his further activity in radical circles. What helped him come close to Marx was indubitably his anti-Russian and pro-Turk positions. In the elections of 1880, Maltman Barry was a defeated candidate of the Conservative Party in Dundee.

276 *James Guillaume comments*: re this remark: „Der Genter Kongress, so viel er sonst zu

wünschen übrig lässt, hatte wenigstens das Gute, dass Guillaume et Ko. total von ihren alten Bundesgenossen verlassen wurden. Mit mühe wurden die flämischen Arbeiter abgehalten, den grossen Guillaume durchzuprügeln.' I need only say that this attitude, that Flemish workers were alleged to have adopted, existed only in the deceitful reporting of Maltman Barry, or in Marx's malicious desire. Always the working people of Ghent treated us all with the greatest of cordiality; we saw how far Ghent workers were readily helpful when we called for help from some of them in order to guarantee the safety of Kropotkin.' Guillaume's account of the congress in Ghent is in 1909, part 6, chapter 14, pp. 265ff.

277   James Guillaume comments: Re: 'Them' meaning 'Guillaume and Co.' This is totally false, throughout the length of the Ghent congress I had the most cordial relations with De Paepe and with all the other Flemish, except for Coenen.
278   James Guillaume comments: 'Brismée, whilst he voted against us, never ceased to treat me with the same friendship as he had done previously.'
279   James Guillaume comments: 'The attitude of Hales was extremely 'correcte' i.e. polite.
280   James Guillaume comments: 'Marx was not unaware that Maltman Barry was the delegate of the London *Kommunistischer Arbeiterverein* [Communist Workers' Union], since he himself says that he had had the latter go to the Ghent congress; but he was perhaps somewhat reluctant to admit this to Sorge.'
281   James Guillaume comments: 'In chapter 15, page 301, [of my book] one can see a letter written to me by Jung on 2 December 1877. One can judge as to whether, as Marx believed, he had separated himself from us.'
282   Marx & Engels, *Collected Works*, Vol. 45, p. 277.
283   G. M. Stekloff, *History of the First International*, London. Martin Lawrence, 1928. Available online: http://www.marxists.org/archive/steklov/history-first-international/
284   For the history of the Jura Federation, see the indispensable work: Marianne Enckell, *La Federation jurassienne, les origines de l'anarchisme en Suisse*, L'Âge d'Homme, 1971. (New edition: Genève: Éditions Entremonde, 2012.)
285   One can see from time to time a tendency among certain anarchists to refer to the notion of 'party'. In the *Communist Manifesto*, a party is simply a movement that brings together people in agreement on certain points – communism in this case. Malatesta uses the word in the same meaning when he says: 'We consider as an anarchist party all of those who desire to contribute to the achievement of anarchy, and in consequence have a need to define an objective to be achieved and a path to taken.' (*Organizzazione*, 1897, 'Organizzatori e antiorganizzatori' in *L'agitazione*, Ancona, 4 June, 1897.) Later, with the development of Social-Democracy, the party became an organisation bringing together people on an inter-class basis, and looking to take power, either peacefully, or through violence. The fascination of certain anarchists with the notion of party is some kind of collateral effect of their fascination with Marxism, the latter being in turn linked directly to the gaps in their knowledge of anarchist theory. To be coherent, and for obvious reasons, one cannot use the same word to designate two completely antagonistic organisational forms: one that looks to seize power, the other that looks to destroy it.
286   Auguste Spichiger (1842-1919), was a jewellery worker; he was an activist in the Jura Federation and became its president.
287   Rodolphe Kahn, worker engraver, was a French refugee and Communard. He was a delegate of the Lausanne German language section for study and propaganda. In February 1876 he helped re-found the Lausanne section of the Jura Federation. 'Its foundation was particularly due to the initiative of a French refugee, Rodolphe Kahn.' (J. Guillaume, *L'Internationale, documents et souvenirs*, Book 4, p. 31.)
288   *L'Avant-Garde*, Year 2, No. 33, 26 August 1878. Cited by Charles Thomann, *Le*

Mouvement anarchiste, op. cit, p. 128. [Available online].
289 Cf. Marianne Enckell, 'Agitazione comunale o municipalismo libertario?' in *A rivista anarchica*, Year 30, No. 266, October 2000. In the lines that follow I summarise very briefly Marianne Enckell's article.
290 Cited by M. Enckell, 'Agitazione', op. cit.
291 1878 was a year particularly rich in assassinations: 24 January an attack by Vera Zassoulitch on General Trepov, police chief of Saint-Petersburg; 16 August, in Russia, the assassination of General Nikolay Mezentsev, chief of political police, by Kravtchinski; 21 October in Germany: Bismarck seized the pretext of attempts on the life of the Kaiser to establish a Reichstag emergency law (a so-called 'little state of siege') against socialists; 17 November in Naples, a failed assassination of King Umberto I of Italy by a young anarchist, Giovanni Passannante. This attempt would provide the pretext for repressive action against internationalist activists.
292 Peter Kropotkin, *Memoirs of a Revolutionist*, op. cit, p. 263.
293 *L'Avant-Garde*, 2nd year, No. 34, 9 September 1878, cited by Charles Thomann, op. cit.
294 Many of these activists did not work and if we were cynical we might say that the introduction, by communist-anarchists, of the notion of 'to each according to their needs' without it being linked in any way to an obligation to work, perhaps reflected concerns about their own situation.
295 Revolutionary Catechism, in *Bakunin on Anarchy*, translated and edited by Sam Dolgoff, 1971. online: https://www.marxists.org/reference/archive/bakunin/works/1866/catechism.htm
296 Edouard Dolleans, *Histoire du movement worker*, Vol. II, Paris, Librairie Armand Colin, 1948, p. 11. Available online - http://classiques.uqac.ca/classiques/dolleans_edouard/hist_mouv_ouvrier_2/hist_mouv_ouvr_2.html
297 Frederick Engels, 'On Authority', 1872; published: 1874 in the *Almanacco Republicano*; https://www.marxists.org/archive/marx/works/1872/10/authority.htm
298 Gaston Leval said to partisans of 'base-ism' at all costs, that wherever there is a 'base' or a 'circumference' there is also forcibly a 'top' or a 'centre': the true question was one of knowing what sort of relation existed between the one and the other.
299 'To vote, is to abdicate: revolutionary anarchist abstention'. Paris [France]: Fédération anarchiste, 1986. Textes de Thyde Rosell, Maurice Joyeux, Roland Bosdeveix, Sebastien Basson, Jean-Marc Raynaud, Gaetano Manfredonia.
300 Malatesta, *L'Agitazione*, Ancona, 4 July 1897, in: Errico Malatesta, *Articles politiques*, Paris: 10/18, 1979, pp. 92-4.
301 Marianne Enckell, 'Fédéralisme et autonomie chez les anarchistes', *Réfractions*, No. 8, 2002, p. 8.
302 Cf. Amédée Dunois: 'Anarchism is not individualist; it is federalist, "organised" in the main. One might define it as thorough federalism'. *Anarchisme et syndicalisme, Le Congress anarchiste international d'Amsterdam*, (1907). Introduced by Ariane Miéville and Maurizio Antonioli, Paris: Nautilus – Editions du Monde libertaire, 1997, p. 157. Note that Amédée Dunois, like César De Paepe, would end up leaving the anarchist movement.
303 'For them the group was simply a school of education; there was to be no office, no treasury, each person was independent. Members were busy being themselves, and then sought development, and education; discussion was there to discover what was good or bad, each person was to act according to their temperament and ability. No one was told do this, or do that ... As a school of education, the group was also a place for camaraderie, for free meetings and discussions with recognised friends, or passing comrades (no one would seek to make them reveal their identities), a place where nobody was concerned with making or collecting dues.' (*Les Anars des origines à*

hier soir, Paris: Editions du Monde libertaire-Editions Alternatives libertaires, 2001. 4. 'Des attentats au syndicalisme révolutionnaires'.)

304 Peter Kropotkin, in *Modern Science and Anarchism*, defines anarchism as follows: 'In the struggle between the individual and the state, anarchism, like its predecessors in the eighteenth century, is on the side of the individual against the state, of society against the oppressive authority.' http://www.anarchy.no/kropot1.html

305 '[T]he congresses of an anarchist organisation, whilst they suffer, as representative bodies from all the imperfections I have mentioned are free from any authoritarianism because they do not make law and do not impose their deliberations on others. They serve to maintain and extend personal contacts among the most active comrades, to summarize and provoke the study of programmes of activity and its ways and means, to make everybody aware of what activity is most urgent and the situation in various regions, to elaborate diverse opinions current amongst various streams of anarchist opinion and to prepare some kind of sounding amongst them. Their decisions are not binding, but simply proposals, advice and suggestions to be put to all concerned. They become obligations to be implemented only for those who accept them, insofar as they accept them. The administrative organs they nominate – correspondence commissions, etc. – have no managerial powers, they take initiatives only on behalf of those who specifically solicit and approve of their initiatives. They have no authority to impose their own views, or present them as the official views of the organization but as with any group of comrades they can certainly defend and propagate them. They publish congresses resolutions and any proposals and opinions communicated to them by individuals and groups; and they serve those who want to make use of them, to facilitate relations between groups, and cooperation between those who are in agreement on various initiatives; but all are free to correspond directly with whoever they like, or make use of the other committees nominated by specific groupings. Any opinions and tactics may be expressed and used by individual members of an anarchist organization so long as these do not contradict accepted principles and do not hinder the activities of others. In any case a particular organization endures as long as its unity has a stronger basis than the grounds for its dissolution; otherwise it disbands and makes way for other, more homogenous groupings. Certainly the permanence and long life of an organisation depends on how successful it has been in the long struggle we must wage, and it is natural that any institution instinctively seeks to last indefinitely. But the duration of a libertarian organisation must be the consequence of the spiritual affinity of its members and of the adaptability of its constitution to the continual changes of circumstances. When it is no longer able to accomplish a useful mission, it is better that it should die.' *Il Risveglio*, Geneva, 15 October, 1927.

306 Stirner's writings would begin to have a greater impact towards the end of the century. His book, *The Ego and His Own* became available in English, in 1907.

307 Gaston Leval, *La crise permanente de l'anarchisme*. (http://monde- nouveau.net/spip.php?article259)

308 Concerning the man of theory, Bakunin wrote on *Capital*: 'This is a work that should have been translated into French long ago, because nothing, that I know of, contains an analysis so profound, so luminous, so scientific, so decisive, and if I may express it so, so merciless in its unmasking of the formation of bourgeois capital, and the systematic and cruel exploitation that capital continues to exercise over proletarian labour. The only defect of this wholly positive work (let *La Liberté* of Brussels be not displeased), it is positive in the sense that it is based on a profound study of economic works, without admitting any logic other than the logic of facts – the only defect, I would say – is that it has been written, in part, but only in part, in an excessively metaphysical and abstract style, and this has induced erroneous words from the Brussels *La Liberté*, and

this makes it difficult to read and more or less unappetising for most workers. And it is principally workers who must read it nevertheless. The bourgeoisie will never read it, or if they read it, they will never want to comprehend it, and if they comprehend it they will never discuss it; this work being nothing other than a sentence of death, scientifically motivated and irrevocably pronounced, not against them as individuals, but against their class. Bakounine, *Oeuvres*, Book 3, Paris: Stock, 1908, pp. 209

309 'Protestation de l'alliance' in Michel Bakounine, *Oeuvres*, Vol. 6, Paris: Stock, 1913, pp. 62-3.

310 Cf. Roger Morgan, *The German Social Democrats*, op. cit.

311 Bakunin: 'Letter to the comrades of the Jura Federation', October 1873, Guillaume, 1909, part 5, chapter 5, pp. 145ff.

312 *Ibid.*

313 René Berthier, 'Sur le terrorisme anarchiste', http://www.monde-nouveau.net/spip.php?article315

314 I place the term 'anarchist' in quotes because to me it does not seem appropriate to describe thus the so called 'Anti-Authoritarian' International. It may be used for some activists of the International, but not for all. Anarchism cannot be identified with the IWA – rather it was some sort of consequential development.

315 *Le Temps*, 12 August 1893.

316 See the work of Guillaume Davranche, 'Pelloutier, Pouget, Hamon, Lazare et le retour de l'anarchisme au socialisme (1893-1900)', *Cahiers d'histoire. Revue d'histoire critique*, 110, 2009.

317 René Berthier, 'Marxisme et anarchisme: Rapprochement, synthèse ou séparation?' http://www.monde-nouveau.net/spip.php?article325

318 René Berthier, 'Pouvoir, classe ouvrière et dictature du prolétariat', http://www.monde-nouveau.net/spip.php?article166

319 René Berthier, 'Bakunin, "disciple" de Marx?' http://www.monde-nouveau.net/spip.php?article327

320 René Berthier, 'L'anarchisme dans le miroir de Maxmilien Rubel' http://www.monde-nouveau.net/spip.php?article260

321 Cf. Éric Vilain, *Lire Stirner*, http://monde-nouveau.net/IMG/pdf/LIRE_STIRNER_-_12-07-2011_-_Word.pdf

322 Errico Malatesta, looking back on this period, would say that although Bakunin was an inspiration he himself was no longer a 'Bakuninist'. *Trans*

323 Cf. Gaston Leval, *Bakunin, fondateur du syndicalisme révolutionnaire.*

324 See appendix. *Trans*.

325 Élisée Reclus, *Évolution et Révolution dans l'idéal anarchiste.* Marie Fleming, *The Anarchist Way to Socialism: Elisée Reclus and 19th Century European Anarchism*, London: Croom Helm, 1979.

326 See the section above on The Question of the Conquest of Power; quoted from: Marx to Engels, 20 July 1870, *Collected Works*, 1989, Vol. 44, p. 3.

327 The latter would soon go over to Social-Democracy.

328 *Collected Works*, 1989, Vol. 44, p. 220, emphasis added. See also: R.P. Morgan, *The German Social Democrats and the First International*, Cambridge University Press, 1965, p 183.

329 Hermann Jung was a watch maker in Clerkenwell and was a delegate for the general council. He acted for many years as secretary for Switzerland on the IWA general council. He collaborated with Marx for many years but broke with him in the run up to the congress in The Hague.

330 Bruhin was a publicist, and procurer-general of the Basel city-state, delegate for the Basel sections.

331 Brismée, a printer, delegate for a Brussels section.
332 Robert, professor, a delegate for sections in La Chaux-de-Fonds.
333 Goegg, edited *Das Felleisen*, delegate for German workers in Switzerland, from Geneva.
334 Bürkli, was a delegate for a consumer society in Zurich.
335 Swiss women only acquired the right to vote in national elections in the 1960s.
336 Bakunin was a delegate for sections in Lyons and Naples.
337 Rittinghausen, a publicist (editor?) a delegate for sections in Cologne.
338 Murat, a delegate for mechanics' sections in Paris.
339 Hins, a professor, a delegate for the Belgian General Council.
340 Liebknecht, a delegate for the Eisenach party congress and the *Demokratisches Wochenblatt*.
341 Dereure, a delegate for shoemakers' sections in Paris.
342 Starke, a cleaner, a delegate for shoemakers' sections in Basel
343 Langlois, publicist, a delegate for metal workers' sections in Paris.
344 Adapted from Jacques Freymond, *La première internationale*, Vol. 2, op. cit., 1962; and from Association internationale des travailleurs: *Compte-rendu du IVe Congrès tenu à Bale en septembre 1869*, Brussels, Imprimerie Désirée Brismée, 1869. Available online: on http://books.google.co.uk/
345 Pindy, a delegate for carpenters' sections in Paris.
346 Becker had organised a German language focused structure from Geneva with its journal circuiting in many countries and as far away as North America.
347 James Guillaume, *L'Internationale,* 1909, part 5, chapter 5, pp. 116-18, 121.
348 *Bulletin,* 30.9.1877, p. 10.
349 Socialist politician. (1856-1943). His work: *Le parti ouvrier et son programme*, Brussels, (2nd edition) 1886, was written as a political ABC, available online. http://gallica.bnf.fr/ark:/12148/bpt6k68319c
350 *Bulletin de la Federation jurassienne,* 13.5.1877.
351 Police report: 'Congrès ouvrier tenu à Bruxelles les 3 et 4 juin 1877.'
352 *Bulletin,* 1.7.1877
353 *Bulletin,* 17.6.1877.
354 A public meeting revealed that many of the Grütli's members usually voted for conservatives.
355 The Jurassians pointed out how odd it was that Greulich's project should support a Universal all-encompassing congress of socialists, while seeking to exclude critics from a Swiss Labour Union,.
356 *Bulletin,* 27.5.1877. This congress was convened by Greulich's Arbeiterbund; Grütli associations were invited to attend whilst the Jura Federation was not. *Bulletin*, (29.4.1877). Subsequently the Grütli congress decided against supporting this party and the project foundered.
357 *Bulletin,* 23.9.1877, p.4.
358 Police report: 'Congrès socialiste préparatoire tenu à Bruxelles, les 19 août 1877.'
359 See appendix above. *Trans.*
360 The congress was attended by delegates from French, Italian, Jura and Spanish regional federations and from sections or groups in Belgium, Egypt, Germany, Greece and Russia.
361 The Jura federation's *Bulletin* editions of 23 and 30 September 1877 report on the Verviers and Ghent congresses. The edition of 4 February 1878 reported on the Belgian Regional congress of 25-26 December, 1877.
362 Charles Thomann, *Le Mouvement anarchiste,* op. cit., p. 117.
363 Max Nettlau, *Der Anarchismus von Proudhon zu Kropotkin: Seine Historische Entwicklung in den Jahren 1859-1880*, Berlin: Fritz Kater, Verlag Der Syndikalist, 1927, p. 268n.

364 Such non-aggression was poorly observed even in this congress; one IWA delegate, Costa took issue with the word 'conspirator' [intrigant] being applied by another delegate, Zanardelli, towards those involved in the Benevento events. *Bulletin*, 30.9.1877, p. 7.
365 These policies are set out in an appendix. *Trans.*
366 *Bulletin*, 3.6.1877.
367 *Bulletin*, 24.6.1877.
368 Johann Most (1846-1906) was a journalist and German Reichstag deputy (1874-80). He was imprisoned for his radical politics, turned to anarchism and in 1880 was expelled from the Social-Democratic party. Forced into exile, he relocated to the USA where he suffered further spells of imprisonment.
369 *Bulletin*, 30.9. and 20.10.1877.
370 *Bulletin*, 28.10.1877.
371 *Bulletin*, 25.3.1877.
372 *Bulletin*, 28.10.1877. An earlier bulletin (12.8.77) had reminded readers that Marx had accused Bakunin of being a Russian spy, and reproved editors who continued such thinking, exciting the German *people* to hate the Russian *people*.

INDEX

Abeele, Henri van den, 184
Abstentionism, see *Electoral politics*
Acollas, Emile, 32
Alerini, Carlo, 183
Alliance for Socialist Democracy, 9, 17, 18, 31-48, 60, 64, 69, 73, 75-7, 139, 166-7, 174-7
Amberny, Jean-Antoine, 24, 48-9
American (USA) Labour and IWA, 17, 77, 94, 96
Anarchism, 10, 14, 27, 59, 62, 93, 101, 116-7, 136, 140, 145, 147, 150, 152-7, 160-3, 205
Anarcho-Syndicalism, 1, 28, 50, 64, 117; see also Syndicalism
Anseele, Edouard, 142
authority, 155-7, 181
L'Avant Garde, 134, 150

Bakunin, Michael, vii, 6, 9-13, 17-28, 31-3, 47-9, 54-65, 66, 73, 88, 92, 93, 94, 99, 102-3, 109, 119-23, 142, 153, 154, 158-60, 163-4, 170, 175-7, 186-7
Bakununism, viii, 163
Bakuninists, 7, 8, 14, 15, 18-9, 56, 110, 112
Barry, Maltman, 142, 144, 213n
Bebel, August, 13, 82, 87, 124, 125, 128-9
Becker, Johann Philip, 5, 10, 35, 37, 85-7, 96-8, 112-3, 158, 174, 175-6
Belgian Labour and IWA, 1, 8, 13, 26, 37-8, 75, 88, 100, 102, 115-8, 127, 131, 134, 136, 145, 164, 175, 186, 191-3
Bernstein, Eduard, 124, 135
Bertani, Agostino, 121
Bertrand, Louis, 191, 193
Bignami, Enrico, 97
Bismarck, Otto von, 32, 88, 100, 121
Blanc, Louis, 37
Blanquists, 7, 93-4
Brismée, Désiré, 142, 144, 169, 193, 217n
Brosset, François, 43, 44, 45

Brousse, Paul, 123, 132-5, 141, 142, 143, 146, 147, 148, 150
Bruhin, Caspar, 169,
Bulletin de la Fédération Jurassienne, 109, 114-15, 129, 133, 139, 149, 193, 194
Bürkli, Karl, 169, 217n

Cafiero, Carlo, 66, 116, 132, 135, 150
Cambassedes, 46
Chalain, Louis, 1, 90
Coenen, Philip, 191, 193
Cohn, James, 68
Costa, Andrea, 132-5, 142, 143, 146
Cornellisen, Christiaan, 164
Coullery, Pierre, 5, 7, 69, 70, 168
Covelli, Emilio, 132
Croisier, Pierre, 88
Cuno, Theodor, 49, 87

Dangerville, Roger, 87-90
David, Edward, 94
Dereure, S, 171, 218n
Desjacques, Maurice, 174
Dolleans, Edourd, 153
Dühring, Eugen, 125
Dumartheray, 150
Duplieux, Jean-Baptiste, 5
Dutch Labour and IWA, 17, 75, 137, 184
Duval, Theodor, 37, 76

Eberhardt, Ali, 128
Eccarius, Johann G, 5, 36, 68, 144
L'Egalité, 43, 51, 68, 69, 84, 88, 168, 173
Egyptian Labour and IWA, 131
electoral politics 13-5, 18, 27, 79, 88, 91, 104-7, 110, 119-23, 178-9, 181, 193-4
Enckell, Marianne, 148
English (British) Labour and IWA, 4, 5, 10, 17-18, 28, 29, 75, 91, 93
Engels, Friedrich, 7, 9, 14, 16, 17, 29, 46, 47, 64, 67, 74, 81, 87, 89, 92, 93, 102, 103, 125-6, 163, 203n

INDEX   221

Fabrique, 9, 11, 39, 40, 42, 45
Fanelli, Giuseppe, 18, 34, 38, 42, 45
Favre, Jules, 32
Federalism, 16, 55, 58, 79-80, 108, 154-5
Ferré, H, 128
Fink, Wilhelm, 10
Franz, Jakob, 138-9
French Communist Party, 12, 53
French Labour and IWA, viii, 4, 8, 24, 26, 42, 73-5, 88, 94, 101, 123, 135, 161; see also *Paris Commune*
Fribourg Congress (Jura), 100, 146
Friscia, Saverio, 42
Fritzsche, Friedrich, 124

Gambuzzi, Carlo, 42, 121
Garibaldi, Giuseppe, 4, 32
General Council of the IWA, 2, 5, 8, 9, 17, 28-30, 35-6, 39, 63, 66, 72-3, 81, 88, 94-9, 101-3, 114, 115, 129, 173
Geneva Labour and IWA, 11, 13, 24, 26, 39-45, 76, 84, 97; see also *Fabrique*
German Labour Movement, 16-16, 74, 85-8, 102, 110, 111, 124-9, 159; see also Social Democrats (German)
Ghent Congress – see *Universal Socialist Congress*
Goegg, Amand, 169, 217n
Grange, Charles, 174, 175, 177
Greek Labour and IWA, 131
Greulich, Hermann, 112, 138, 139, 141, 142, 189, 193
Grütli, 138, 192
Guesde, Jules, 153
Guétat, L, 37, 76
Guillaume, James, vii, 2, 5, 6, 11, 34, 48, 66, 67, 72, 73, 77, 90, 106-11, 118-9, 129, 132-7 *passim*, 140-4 *passim*, 149, 160, 184, 194
Guilmeaux, 174
Gutsmann, Bruno, 138

Hales, John, vii, 18, 29, 30, 68, 104, 142, 144, 193
Haupt, George, 3
Hegel, Georg W, 23
Heng, Fritz, 46
Herzen, Alexander, 32, 66
Herzig, Georg, 150
Hins, Eugène, 88, 171, 217n
Hödel, Emil H, 134
Hugo, Victor, 32

International Workers' Association (IWA), see *regions*: Belgian, English, French, Italian, etc; General Council; IWA Congresses and Conferences
IWA Congresses and Conferences:
    1865, (London Conference), 5
    1866, (Geneva Congress), 5, 6, 19-20, 39, 165-6, 177-9
    1867, (Lausanne Congress), 6-7
    1868, (Brussels Congress), 7
    1869, (Basel Congress), 7-9, 26-7, 66, 72, 169-73
    1871, (London Conference), 11, 67ff
    1872, (The Hague Congress), vii, 1-2, 10-11, 17, 73-6, 94, 95
    1872, (St. Imier Congress), 1-2, 77-80, 84, 179-183
    1873, (Geneva Congresses), Federalist 90, 99, 113, 183-6; Marxist 95-103
    1874, (Brussels Congress), 104-5
    1876, (Bern Congress), 105-6, 116, 129, 136, 139
    1877, (Verviers Congress), 131-5, 140, 188-91
Italian Labour and IWA, 13, 43, 75, 77, 116-7, 121, 132, 133, 139, 147

Janson, Paul, 191
Johannard, Jules Paul, 93
Joukovsky, Nikolai, 137, 177, 183
Jung, Hermann, 5, 93, 94, 169, 217n
Jura IWA Federation, 1-2, 8, 18, 68, 69, 70, 81, 83-5, 92, 105-6, 110, 118-9, 127-8, 132, 133, 137, 146, 149-53 *passim*, 164, 177-9, 186

Kahn, Rodolphe, 128, 147, 149, 214n
Kropotkin, Pierre, 49, 103, 146-153 *passim*, 156, 164
Kugelmann, Ludwig, 66
Kulisscioff, Anna, 135

Lafargue, Paul, 46, 59, 66, 76, 92
Landauer, Gustav 161, 162
Langlois, Amédée-Jérôme, 171, 218n
Lassalle, Ferdinand, 4, 85, 124-5, 129, 208n
League for Peace & Liberty, 32-3, 35, 56
Lemonnier, Charles, 32
Lenin, Vladimir I, 12, 15, 52, 64
Leval, Gaston, 157
La Liberté, 100

Liebknecht, Wilhelm, 10, 13, 66, 74, 85, 87, 126, 129, 140, 170, 189, 192, 193, 194, 217n
Limousin, Antoine, 4
Lindegger, Antoinne, 174
Lorenzo, Anselmo, 29, 60
Lorwin, Lewis L, 5
Luxemburg, Rosa, 161

MacMahon, Patrice de, 164, 187
Maitron, Jean, 133
Malatesta, Errico, 116-7, 132, 135, 138, 139, 147, 155, 157, 215-6n
Marx, Karl, vii, 1, 3, 5, 6, 7, 9, 12-14, 16, 19, 23, 33, 46, 47, 56, 59, 6, 64, 66, 67, 75, 81, 85, 89, 93, 95, 98, 101, 102, 113, 131, 144, 158, 159, 163, 178, 188
Marxism, 10, 12, 14-16, 30, 63-4, 79, 112, 124, 160, 162
Marxists, 2, 7, 8, 13, 48, 56, 90, 103, 160
Marzotti, Filippo, 135
Mazzini, Giuseppe, 47, 121
Mehring, Franz, 9-10, 16, 30, 47, 76, 88
Mill, John Stuart, 32
Monatte, Pierre, 53, 101
Montagne, 168
Montels, Jules, 142, 143, 146
Mora, 60
Morago, Tómas González, 60-62, 174, 206n
Most, Johann, 161, 194, 218n
Murat, A, 170, 171, 217n

Napoleon III, 4, 32
National Suisse, 111
Netherlands – see *Dutch Labour*
Neue Zeit, 66
Neuer Sozial-Demokrat, 129
Nieuwenhuis, Domela, 161, 162
Nobiling, Karl Eduard, 134

Oberwinder, Heinrich, 99
Odger, George, 5
Olten, Congress of, 107-8, 138

Paepe, César de, 5, 7, 38, 50-52, 113, 115, 116, 136-8, 140, 141, 144, 145, 189, 190, 192, 193
Pannekoek, Antonie, 50
Paris Commune, 1, 15, 27, 62, 100-1, 163
Paulin, Auguste, 190
Pelloutier, Fernand, 101
Perrachon, Josephe-Etienne, 4
Perret, Henri, 37, 98

Perron, Charles, 36, 137, 175, 177
Pindy, Jean-Louis, 107, 108, 123, 134, 146, 172, 204n
Portuguese Labour and IWA, 29, 137
Le Progrès, 43, 105, 168
propaganda by the deed, 133, 135, 147
Proudhon, Pierre-Joseph, 4, 6, 17, 23, 28, 79, 122-3, 154, 178
Proudhonists (Mutualists), 7, 8, 27, 47, 79, 102

Quinet, Edgar, 32

Radicals & Radical Party, 11, 12, 30, 32, 38, 40-49, 119, 121
Ralli-Arbore, Zamfirij Konstantinovitch, 93
Reclus, Elié, 32, 38
Reclus, Elisée, 32, 147, 150, 163, 186
Remy, Théodor, 176-7
Révolté, 133, 134, 150
Rey, Aristide, 38
Rinke, Ernst O, 146
Rittinghausen, Moritz, 170, 217n
Robert, Fritz, 169, 171, 217n
Robin, Paul, 45, 148, 169, 171, 173-5
Rochat, Charles, 68
Rodriguez, 190
Romande Federation, 43-4, 68-9, 83-4, 95, 106
Rossetti, Blaise, 83-4
Russia, 131, 194
Russian Revolution, 12

Schindler, Samuel, 174
Schweitzer, Johann Baptist von, 85
Schwitzguébel, Adhémar, 2, 6, 69, 73, 77, 84, 146, 147, 148, 151, 170, 171
Second International, 53, 64, 102, 111, 136-7, 161
Sémard, Pierre, 53
Sentiñon, Gaspard, 45
Serno-Solovievitch, Alexander, 33
Serraillier, Auguste, 97
Slav lands and peoples, 47, 63, 92, 117-8
Social Democrats (German), vii, 8-13, 19, 28, 30, *passim*, 48-50, 66, 74, 86-8, 123-4, 140, 145, 159, 161, 168-9, 187-8; *see also* German labour movement
Social-Democracy, 60-61, 64, 116, 118, 131, 133, 135-7, 143, 145; *see also* Second International
Solidarité, 106, 110
solidarity, 19, 25-6, 31, 143

Sonvilier (Jura Congress), 69-72
Sorge, Friedrich, vii, 81, 91, 94, 96, 97-99, 102, 144
Spanish Labour and IWA, 8, 13, 18, 28, 34, 66, 75, 76, 81, 100-1, 117, 121, 137, 183-4
Speyer, Karl, 102
Spichger, Auguste, 146, 147, 214n
Stalinism, 66
Starke, Rudolf, 171, 218n
Steklov, Yuri, 96, 145
strikes, 23-4, 80, 183-4
Swarm (pseudonym), 74
Swiss Labour and IWA, 8, 13, 30, 107-8, 118, 137-9, 167-8, 192; see also *Geneva, Grütli, Jura, Olten, Romande*
Syndicalism, 116, 133, 151, 161, 163; *see also* Anarcho-Syndicalism

Tagwacht, 105, 106, 110-3, 138
Tolain, Henri-Louis, 4
Le Travail, 134
Turkey, 194

Universal Socialist Congress (Ghent, 1877), 130, 131, 135-7, 140, 188-91
Utin, Nicholai, 24, 49

Vahlteich, Julius, 124-6, 138
Vaillant, Edouard, 90
Varlin, Eugène, 5, 7
Velarde, Enrique, 184
Voges, 128
Volksstaat, 74, 93, 110, 129
Vorbote, 86
Vorwärts, 113, 114, 194

Walter (pseudonym), 74
Ward, Osborn, 95
Werner, Emil-August, 146
Wroblewski, Walery, 92

Zabicki, Anton, 68